Canada and the Battle of the Atlantic

ROGER SARTY

Canada and the Battle of the Atlantic

ART GLOBAL

Canadian Cataloguing in Publication Data

    Sarty, Roger Flynn, 1952-
    Canada and the Battle of the Atlantic
    ISBN 2-920718-65-7

1. World War, 1939-1945 - Naval operations, Canadian. 2. World War,
1939-1945 - Campaigns - Atlantic Ocean. 3. Canada - Armed Forces - History
- World War, 1939-1945. I. Title.

D779.C2S26 1998   940.54'5971   C97-941634-5

Project coordinator: Serge Bernier

Publisher: Ara Kermoyan

Editing: Jane Broderick

Jacket illustration: Canso plane, National Aviation Museum, 28934
                Frigate: HMCS *Waskesiu*, PMR 83-637
                U-Boat: illustration by Gilles Archambault

Endpaper:
Leonard Brooks, 1911-1965
Atlantic Convoy
Water Colour, Ink, Pencil and Charcoal on Paper, 47.6 cm x 75.8 cm
Canadian War Museum # 10078

Art Global
384 Laurier Avenue West
Montreal, Quebec H2V 2K7 Canada
ISBN 2-920718-65-7

Cet ouvrage a été publié simultanément en français sous le titre de : *Le Canada et la Bataille
de l'Atlantique*
ISBN 2-920718-64-9

Art Global acknowledges the financial support of the Government of Canada, through the Book
Publishing Industry Development Program, for its publishing activities.

All possible efforts have been made to identify the copyright holders and we apologize for any
involuntary omissions.

TABLE OF CONTENTS

ABOUT THE AUTHOR

Roger Sarty, Senior Historian at the Directorate of
History and Heritage, National Defence Headquarters, Ottawa,
is one of the foremost authorities on the maritime dimensions
of the Canadian military experience.
A graduate of Duke University and the University of Toronto,
Dr. Sarty has published widely on the history of land, air and naval forces,
most recently The Maritime Defence of Canada
(Canadian Institute of Strategic Studies, 1996).
He contributed to the official history of the Royal Canadian Air Force
and is co-author of the forthcoming official history
of the Royal Canadian Navy.

ACKNOWLEDGEMENTS

*This volume, and the series of which it forms a part, owes it existence
to the unstinting support of the Minister of National Defence, the Deputy Minister
and the Chief of the Defence Staff. Serge Bernier, Director of History and Heritage,
led the project with patience and wisdom. Members of this newly organized directorate
cooperated like a long-established team.*

Canada and the Battle of the Atlantic *could not have been written without the
published studies and manuscript reports prepared by present and past members of the
naval history team. Initially an ad hoc group, the team became fully established in
1990. These scholars are: W. A. B. (Alec) Douglas, former Director General History
and founder of the naval team, Catherine Allan, Pamela Brunt, Shawn Cafferky,
Robert Caldwell, Jan Drent, Robert Fisher, William Glover, Donald Graves,
Michael Hennessy, William Johnston, Kenneth Mackenzie, Douglas McLean,
Michael McNorgan, Marc Milner, William Rawling, Jane Samson, Michael Whitby
and David Wiens. Several of these people have worked far beyond the expected limits
of short-term appointments, or contributed on a voluntary basis out of personal
commitment to Canadian maritime history.*

*Alec Douglas and Richard Gimblett worked through the entire manuscript;
John Armstrong, Rob Fisher and Doug McLean corrected particular chapters.
Gabrielle Nishiguchi looked after the naval illustrations, assisted with research
and helped coordinate the project. William Constable produced the maps, and
Carl Vincent selected the air force photographs. Brenda Donaldson untangled the prose
of the early drafts and filled gaps in research. Jane Broderick edited the volume.*

*At the Directorate of History and Heritage, Isabel Campbell and Donna Porter
carry on the department's tradition of excellence in archives services. Similarly the
Canadian Forces Photographic Unit and the Mapping and Charting Establishment
efficiently met considerable demands despite competing pressures. Laura Brandon and
Margot Weiss at the Canadian War Museum researched and made available the war
art that is such an important feature of this series. At the National Archives,
Paul Marsden has fully maintained the splendid service previously provided by
Barbara Wilson and Glenn Wright. Also generous have been the staffs of the
Operational Archives at the US Naval Historical Center, the US National Archives
and Records Administration, the Naval Historical Branch of the UK Ministry of
Defence and the UK Public Records Office.*

In this publication, veterans often speak through the medium of transcribed interviews. The late Hal Lawrence, himself a decorated veteran of the Battle of the Atlantic and a noted author, interviewed over a hundred former members of the Royal Canadian Navy on behalf of the Department of National Defence. At this same time, in the 1980s, the Ottawa Branch of the Naval Officers' Association of Canada established the Salty Dips committee. This group, under the leadership of the late J. A. M. Lynch (a veteran of the Royal Canadian Navy who also served in the Royal Canadian Air Force and with the Royal Navy), conducted and transcribed interviews as a voluntary contribution to the department's history programme. Other veterans have willingly responded to questions and come forward with photographs and papers. The very existence of the department's maritime forces history programme owes much to veterans themselves.

Any strengths of this book reflect the skills and commitment of the people who have contributed. Slips in the compilation and interpretation of the rich materials they have provided are my responsibility.

PREFACE

This book commemorates one of the remarkable achievements of the Second World War. Canada, which in 1939 had only a tiny nucleus of maritime industries and armed forces, soon became a major participant in the Battle of the Atlantic. It was the longest and most important sea campaign of the war: Great Britain's survival and the liberation of Europe depended upon merchant-ship cargoes that had to be delivered in the face of a powerful enemy submarine blockade. Over 100,000 Canadian men and women kept open the sea routes. They operated hundreds of warships, merchant ships and aircraft, most of them manufactured in Canada by more than 125,000 workers in plants and building yards that seemingly sprang into existence.

For the first time in over a hundred years, Canada's shores were the scene of sustained combat. Merchant-ship convoys sailed from Canadian ports and enemy submarines hunted them within sight of east-coast cities and deep within the St Lawrence River. Canadian homes were shaken by the roar of torpedo and depth-charge explosions. The citizens of quiet seaside towns had to rush to pull dazed survivors from the paralysing cold of the Atlantic and the St Lawrence.

Perhaps more than any other campaign of the war, the Battle of the Atlantic became Canada's own. This was a tribute to the sheer determination of the large numbers of people who served with distinction in every corner of the ocean from North American waters to the shores of Iceland, Britain, France and North Africa. In the early years of the conflict, young, half-trained personnel struggled against a skilful enemy, and a cruelly unforgiving environment, in poorly equipped vessels and aircraft. The people were cold and wet — and not a few of them sick — much of the time. Nevertheless, they made the grade, quickly, convincingly, even brilliantly. Their persistence and talent is inspiring. I salute them, and the many Canadians who supported their efforts, often selflessly, and, when moments of crisis demanded it, courageously.

The people who produced this book were inspired by the veterans with whom they talked for many hours. One of the goals of the team was to capture that experience by reproducing the words of those who served, and publishing their personal snapshots. The result is something of a family album, one that I hope will be a keepsake for all who were directly touched by the Battle of the Atlantic, and those who want to learn more about a profound experience in the story of our country.

The Honourable Art Eggleton
Minister of National Defence

PROLOGUE

1940 AND 1918

On Nov 6th [1940] beat up to 34 knots[1] and went to aid of "Melrose Abby" being shelled by submarine. Came upon it shelling ship and opened fire at extreme range. Sub dived just a shooting, was really good. In company with Harvester. Searched for sub all that day and night. Let go in all 88 depth charges. Wow what a night! Next morning (7th) we found large oil patch (2 acres) [nearly a hectare] and a wine bottle floating on surface. Believe we must have sunk it. Sure hope we did. The poor devils must have had a very rough time though. Believe it was an Italian as she was very large and had a gun forward and aft. It was a bit of all right while it lasted but I'm certainly grateful that I was on top and not below.

William R. Acheson, signalman in HMCS *Ottawa*[2]

This drama unfolded in the broad eastern Atlantic, about 650 kilometres off Ireland in the western approaches to the British Isles. Canadian warships had been operating in British waters since the end of May 1940. The breakthrough of the German armies to the Channel coast of France that month had directly threatened Britain with massive attack and Canada had sent four destroyers to help the mother country. These were all the warships in the tiny Royal Canadian Navy (RCN) that were immediately available for extended service. HMCS *Ottawa* had sailed across from Halifax in early September to replace one of the original four that had gone home for a much-needed refit.

When *Ottawa* and her consort, the British destroyer HMS *Harvester*, sighted the surfaced Italian

submarine, they were at the tail-end of a frustrating five-day mission, typical for the over-extended destroyer force. The conquest of France not only deprived the Commonwealth of its strongest naval ally, but gave the German navy Atlantic ports right on Britain's doorstep. The German submarine fleet promptly launched an offensive, from their new French bases, against the transatlantic shipping that was Britain's lifeblood. The Royal Navy (RN), always Britain's first line of defence against invasion, now found itself stretched paper-thin in order to provide additional forces for the defence of shipping as well. By shifting traffic to northern British ports, forming as many ships as possible into protected convoys and pressing air patrols to the limits of the mostly short-ranged aircraft then available, the British had pushed the U-boats out into the ocean where the breadth of the seas allowed evasive routeing and made it much more difficult for the enemy to find shipping. Unfortunately, destroyers and other warships suited for anti-submarine escort were so few in number that they could accompany convoys no further than about the first 650 kilometres. At that point, they had to break off and join an incoming convoy as it entered the zone of greatest danger.

German submarines, reinforced by their Italian allies, began to hunt at the outer limits of the escort zone. They kept in regular radio contact with their headquarters, commander-in-chief U-boats (Befehls-haber der Unterseeboote, or BdU), which could thus direct submarines to reinforce any one of their number that located a convoy. British — and Canadian — shore stations listened intently for these signals. They were as yet in unbreakable machine-generated 'enigma' cipher, but radio direction-finding triangulations gave rough approximations of the positions from which U-boats were signalling. These intercepts, and the fleeting, often incomplete messages from ships under attack, were the only information available for the British Western Approaches command in its efforts to rush the few anti-submarine warships to where they were most needed. The situation of the escorts might be compared to that of a small-town fire brigade hurled into a large city under siege by pyromaniacs, from its business centre to its outermost suburbs.

In the early hours of 2 November, *Ottawa* and *Harvester* had sailed from Scotland's River Clyde with a fast troop convoy. They broke off on the morning of the 4th to head north to meet a merchant ship convoy inbound from Canada. Hours later, before the destroyers had reached the eastbound convoy, Western Approaches ordered them to backtrack south

at speed to help a Gibraltar-bound merchant-ship convoy, whose escort had departed, that seemed to have been located by a submarine. The destroyers rushed to the position, only to find that the unprotected Gibraltar convoy had already scattered in hopes of throwing the submarine off the scent. *Ottawa* and *Harvester* searched in vain through the night for the merchant ships. Next morning, Western Approaches ordered the destroyers to support another outbound convoy, but almost immediately countermanded with instructions to reverse course once again to the position of a ship reporting itself under attack. Nothing turned up, and fuel was running low because of the high speeds at which the warships had been dashing to and fro. On their way home they were to help two ships of the Gibraltar convoy that had collided when that convoy dispersed. During the morning of 6 November the destroyers were searching at the last reported position of the damaged ships when a signal arrived that one of them, *Melrose Abbey*, was being chased by a submarine 170 kilometres to the northeast. The warships were now so low on fuel they could only proceed at economical speed, 24 knots, for three long hours. Then luck changed. *Melrose Abbey* managed to get out a signal that it was being shelled by the submarine at a position only 55 kilometres from the destroyers. The warships increased to their maximum speed of 34 knots and arrived in the nick of time, in the scene young William Acheson found so thrilling.

In reality, the hunt had not gone as smoothly as Acheson described. *Ottawa* had opened fire too soon, at a range of nine kilometres, when there was no chance of a hit on the small profile of the surfaced submarine. The Canadian destroyer had then been too slow to reduce speed and unwittingly had overrun the submerged boat. The limitations of asdic, as sonar was known in the Commonwealth navies, allowed little room for error. It took the destroyers over five hours to make a solid contact. *Ottawa* made that contact, and this was no small achievement. However, it was the more experienced British ship which had initially suggested the search track that had led to the contact. Commander E. R. Mainguy, RCN, commanding officer of *Ottawa*, was senior to *Harvester's* captain and had thus led the chase and directed the hunt and depth-charge attacks that continued for 15 hours after the first asdic contact. Professional to the core, Mainguy made no attempt to cover up his mistakes:

It is considered that the first major error was made in opening fire, as it is not believed that the submarine was aware of our presence until our shells started to fall

HMCS *Ottawa* in September 1940 and in September 1942, days before its destruction by German torpedoes. (Courtesy of Ken Macpherson)

around him. As some justification for this and all subsequent errors it may be mentioned that this was "OTTAWA's" first sight of an enemy vessel, so perhaps I was over-keen. It seemed an absolute certainty, also "OTTAWA" has never exercised with one of our submarines … However, I do not wish to make excuses. "HARVESTER" naturally feels very upset about the whole operation. I should like to emphasise that as far as I know he made no mistakes, and he was most helpful and restrained.[3]

Initially it did not seem to matter. The commander-in-chief himself was convinced that the submarine had been destroyed. He commended both the Canadian and the British destroyer and particularly congratulated the asdic and depth-charge crews. He was right to do so, for the underwater weapons systems demanded much of personnel, in both technical proficiency and precision teamwork. The sonic 'pings' of the asdic were projected in a narrow, searchlight-like beam fixed at an angle of about 45 degrees downward from the keel of the warship. The effective range was some 1200 metres or less. Thus it took excellent ship manoeuvring and inspired estimation of the underwater course the submarine might be following to make any sort of contact. The echo from the target could easily be missed unless the ears of the asdic operator were sharply attuned. In turn, the asdic control officer had to interpret accurately the data presented by the asdic range and bearing recorder. This device, although at the leading edge of technology at the time, was primitive. Echoes triggered a pointer that marked a line, giving approximate range and showing the change of bearing, on chemically treated paper that rolled across the instrument at a constant rate. It fell entirely to the sharp senses and trained instinct of the asdic team to distinguish a submarine from the similar echoes and recorder data produced by schools of fish, flotsam or anomalies in the water. The depth charge — a 180-kilogram barrel containing 136 kilograms of high explosive and fitted with a fuse activated by water pressure — was little changed from the first models developed during the First World War. It had to explode within less than five metres of the hull of a submarine to ensure serious or lethal damage to the tough hull, a level of precision that was all but impossible with asdic. The answer was to saturate the estimated location of the submarine. *Ottawa* was fitted with two depth-charge rails at the stern and a single depth-charge thrower on each side. The thrower was essentially a mortar, onto which the crew had to hoist a depth charge strapped to a heavy steel cradle whose base seated into the mouth of the barrel. A propellent

charge in the mortar blew the cradle and depth charge clear of the side of the ship. In an attack, *Ottawa* launched five depth charges — one from one rail, two from the other side and one from each thrower — to create a box-like pattern. Because asdic allowed only very rough approximations of the submarine's depth, the charges were set at two or three different depths. Properly executed attacks required split-second coordination between the asdic personnel on the bridge forward and the depth-charge crews at the three widely separated stations in the after part of the ship. *Harvester* packed a larger punch, for it had already been fitted with a second pair of depth-charge throwers so that it could fire a 10-charge pattern. (Canadian warships lagged behind their British counterparts in fittings of new equipment, and that would soon become an important issue.)

The only sure method of attack was for the destroyer to race directly over the enemy and drop the charges slightly ahead of the submarine to allow for its movement forward as the charges sank. One of the shortcomings of the asdics then available was that the attacking ship lost contact as it neared and passed over the submarine. The depth charges had to be fired by estimate based on the submarine's last known position, which left great potential for error, even if the enemy captain did not suddenly turn as the warship approached. One method of solving this problem was to have a ship hold the contact with its asdic and guide in the second ship for the attack. It was this tactic that *Ottawa* and *Harvester* patiently executed.

The glow of a near-certain victory was quickly extinguished. The records of every anti-submarine attack were scrutinized by highly experienced officers, at the British Admiralty, known as the U-boat Assessment Committee. They were professional sceptics in the league of the coldest magistrate. They had to be. Britain's survival depended upon the effectiveness of the anti-submarine forces, and anti-submarine actions, unlike those of traditional surface warfare, rarely ended with a clear view of a shattered hulk and with survivors and dead alike bobbing in the oil-scummed water. Experience in the First World War and since September 1939 had shown how much punishment both Allied and enemy submarines could absorb. Evidence counted for everything, and frustrated ships' crews, who scoured the positions of attacks for bits of wreckage, grumbled that the Assessment Committee were ghouls unsatisfied unless one was able to skim the shattered internal organs of the victims from the surface and present them in glass jars. The Assessment Committee did indeed

The answer was to saturate the estimated location of the submarine: depth-charge explosions.
(Directorate of History and Heritage, 0-8521)

welcome such definitive evidence, and its intentionally conservative conclusions were almost always spot-on throughout the war. In the case of *Ottawa* and *Harvester*'s attack, a rising gale and shortage of fuel had precluded a thorough search for wreckage, and the committee downgraded the result of the action to 'probably damaged.' Not until 1983 would work by British and Italian researchers, using sources not available to the Assessment Committee, establish that *Ottawa* and *Harvester* had in fact destroyed *Faa di Bruno*. Commander Mainguy, who after the war rose to the rank of vice-admiral and became Canada's chief of the naval staff, went to his grave in 1979 regretting that he had never achieved a confirmed 'kill' in the Battle of the Atlantic; but his son, who also became an admiral in the Canadian navy, was able to raise a glass for his father when word arrived of the revised assessment.

Whether *Ottawa* had shared in the destruction of the Italian warship or only helped to inflict damage did not much matter from the perspective of the RCN in 1940. This was only the second time since the founding of the service in 1910 that a Canadian warship had been in a position to strike back at the enemy. *Ottawa* had, despite its recent arrival in the fighting theatre and its jitters at the opening of the action, performed at the high standard of the RN, arguably the most professional and unquestionably the most combat-experienced in the world. Commander Mainguy's error at the beginning of the attack, moreover, was to have been too aggressive, to have struck immediately with everything he had. That is nothing less than vindication, for the Canadian navy's previous face-to-face encounter with the enemy, on 25 August 1918, had been a humiliation.

The circumstances had been strikingly similar to those of *Ottawa*'s attack over 22 years later, although the location had been close in to Canada's own east coast. The armed yacht HMCS *Hochelaga*, while on patrol south of Newfoundland, not far from the islands of St Pierre and Miquelon, sighted the large, long-range U-boat *U-156* on the surface. The German sailors were completing the destruction of several fishing schooners. Instead of charging to the attack, *Hochelaga*'s captain turned away to get help from three other small patrol ships that were cruising a few kilometres away. By the time the little warships returned there was no trace of the submarine.

That may well have been the best outcome for the crews and their families, for the Canadian vessels of 1918 were warships in name only. *Hochelaga*, one of the better ships, was a luxury yacht that had been purchased in the United States and armed with a pair of 12-pounder guns (which fired a five-kilogram shell) that would have been utterly out-ranged and ineffective in the face of the 45-kilogram shells from the two 15-centimetre guns mounted on the deck of *U-156*. The Canadian vessel's underwater armament consisted of a handful of depth charges and a hydrophone, an underwater microphone with almost no ability to determine the position of a target that had been only recently installed and in whose use the crew had little training.

Although the senior officers of the court martial convened against the commanding officer of *Hochelaga* were shocked at the evidence of the lack of proper organization and discipline in the ship, they should not have been. The officer had come out for duty as a recruit at the beginning of the war and learned on the job in small, converted civilian ships that carried out duties more akin to peacetime anti-smuggling and coast guard duties than preparation for combat. Since the outbreak of war, the British surface fleet had been able to bottle up the German fleet in the North Sea. This had given rise to the conviction in the British Admiralty that the Canadian navy needed only to keep watch in coastal waters for mines that might be surreptitiously dropped by fast German merchant vessels, or for signs that German agents were trying to set up refuelling caches in isolated inlets. Although German submarines were very good at evading Allied warships and attacking merchant shipping, British authorities believed there was little possibility that U-boats would attempt to cross the ocean.

Late in 1916 a submarine did just that, sinking five Allied ships off the coast of the then-neutral United States. The vestigial Canadian navy then had less than 18 months to build up an anti-submarine combat capability, virtually from scratch, before the U-boats made a concerted attack on the North American coast in the spring and summer of 1918. Although senior officers privately worried that the small, ill-crewed vessels would be *'practically at the mercy'*[4] of one of the big submarines, which *'at any time … may sink a whole division'*[5] of the patrol craft, the court martial found that *'the "HOCHELAGA" should have been steered at full speed towards the enemy vessel … and all means of offence available made use of in [an] effort to inflict damage or destroy the enemy.'*[6] The commanding officer was dismissed from the service.

To make the sting of *Hochelaga*'s flight worse, *U-156* had been especially bold — even dashing — during its six-week mission on the North American coast. After laying mines off New York that sank a

… warships in name only: the First World War armed yacht HMCS *Hochelaga*. (DHH, CN-3400)

major US warship, the cruiser *San Diego*, the submarine had chased a tugboat so close to a popular Cape Cod beach that the U-boat's heavy shells had ricocheted over the heads of bathers. The submarine, after eluding American patrols, had then suddenly appeared off Halifax, sinking a tanker within 50 kilometres of the entrance to the harbour.

The submarine had subsequently popped up again off Canso, Nova Scotia, and captured the Canadian steam fishing trawler *Triumph*, which the German sailors armed and then used to sink fishing schooners. In the case of the unarmed fishing vessels, the Germans were scrupulous in ensuring that the crews had time to stow sufficient provisions in their boats and get clear on a correct course for shore. When a gunfire attack on a small Newfoundland steamer that the Germans had mistakenly taken to be armed destroyed the steamer's lifeboats, the submariners took the crew on board and found a schooner to which they transferred the Newfoundlanders. Some reports in the North American press began to show a grudging admiration for the humane buccaneers.

There was no such consideration for the Canadian navy. Hundreds of fishermen who streamed ashore demanded to know where the navy had been when they were under attack. It was one more in a series of controversies that had haunted the service from its founding.

CHAPTER I

THE LONG STRUGGLE FOR CANADIAN MARITIME FORCES

The Royal Canadian Navy (RCN) was not established until 1910, and its founding had more to do with party politics than defence. Canadians had been content to rely upon the security provided by Britain's Royal Navy (RN) — foremost in the world — until Germany's massive naval expansion in the years prior to the First World War had polarized opinion over whether, and how, Canada should help the mother country. It was an intensely emotional debate that bared fundamental disagreements about the very nature of Canada. Those who saw their nation as a flowering of British civilization nurtured by British protection pressed for the offer of a generous cash gift to bolster the RN's warship construction programme. Others condemned a naval initiative of any kind. These Canadians saw their country as a New World nation that owed nothing to the violence-prone Old World across the Atlantic. Meddling in the arms races of Europe, they insisted, would inevitably result in the country's youth being butchered in remote imperialistic wars that were of no concern to Canada.

Prime Minister Wilfrid Laurier's compromise was to create a Canadian navy intended primarily for the defence of Canadian waters. In times of international crisis or war, the government could assign Canadian warships to serve under RN command. However, Parliament would have to confirm the decision within 15 days. Laurier's policy satisfied few and contributed to the defeat of the Liberals by Robert Borden's Conservative party in the general election of 1911. Borden's policy fared no better. His legislation granting $35 million for British battleship construction triggered a bitter Liberal backlash in Parliament that killed the bill in May 1913. The Conservatives meanwhile let the nucleus organization created by the Liberals moulder. The two cruisers, HMCS *Niobe* and HMCS *Rainbow*, purchased by the Laurier administration from the RN as training ships, mostly lay at dockside. *Niobe*, in a foreshadowing of the new service's fate, had run aground on the southern Nova Scotia coast on an early voyage and required major repairs that dragged on month after month.

On the outbreak of war in August 1914, the clock seemed to roll back to the 18th or early 19th century. RN cruisers returned to Halifax to protect the vast shipping traffic from North America upon which the Allied war effort became increasingly dependent. Although *Niobe* and, on the west coast, *Rainbow* got to sea, it was only with the help of key personnel lent by the RN. As the Laurier legislation allowed, the ships operated as part of the newly arrived British squadrons. Similarly, although the important Halifax base remained nominally Canadian, officers for key positions had to be borrowed from the RN, and they responded to the needs of the British cruiser commanders while all but ignoring the distant Canadian Naval Service Headquarters (NSHQ) in Ottawa. The only operations by Canadian ships under Canadian control were patrols in harbour approaches carried out by chartered tugs and a handful of small steamers taken over from such civil departments as Marine and Fisheries. In most cases the civilian crews were simply offered entry into the Canadian navy as hostilities-only volunteers. Their sole training in naval duties came from brief courses and from what they learned from the few experienced naval personnel who were assigned to each ship.

Sir Robert Borden, for his part, was glad to comply with British advice that Canada's war effort should focus on the provision of troops to fight on the western front. He did not want to stir up the politically contentious naval question. British leaders, moreover, promised that, should enemy warships reach Canadian waters, the RN would immediately send any additional forces needed to deal with the problem.

When Canada faced U-boat attacks late in the war the British were in no position to fulfil this promise. The RN cruisers on station at Halifax — over 120 metres in length, displacing 5000 tonnes or more, with a heavy-gun armament and crews of 500 seamen each — were designed to counter the traditional threat of enemy surface warships. Their slowness and lack of manoeuvrability made them sitting ducks for submarines, a new technology that the Germans had unexpectedly exploited to counter the mastery of the British surface fleet. The best anti-submarine ships proved to be destroyers. These were fast, 900-tonne warships, with at least twice the speed and with a much heavier armament than the biggest, fastest armed steamers available in Canada. All of Britain's destroyers, however, were needed in European waters to counter the main submarine assault. The United States had joined the war against Germany in April 1917, but all of the American navy's destroyers were also needed on the other side of the Atlantic.

Canada was on its own. Thus during the last 18 months of the war, while the Canadian Corps was winning hard-earned battle honours in France and Belgium, on the home front the navy and the infant shipbuilding industry were scrambling. The navy's tiny east-coast flotilla had to be expanded immediately from only a dozen vessels to over a hundred. By now, opposition politicians and the press were well used to mocking the amateurish, obviously improvised efforts of the navy. At Halifax, shortly after 9 am on 6 December 1917, these criticisms found devastating confirmation. The inbound freighter *Mont Blanc*, laden with a lethal cargo of explosives, detonated off the north end of the Halifax waterfront after colliding with the outbound steamer *Imo* in the narrow approaches to Bedford Basin. It was the largest man-made explosion before the age of the atomic bomb. A quarter of the city was flattened, killing 2500 and injuring 9000 others. The navy was responsible for traffic control in the port during wartime, and in the minds of outraged Haligonians therefore bore a share of blame for the tragedy. Although such conclusions were not entirely fair, the consequences were shattering to the reputation and morale of the navy. The harsh words of the Ottawa *Evening Journal* were echoed in many quarters:

Yet upon this simple policeman's job the Canadian Naval Service, with all its frills and feathers, its admirals and commanders, captains and lieutenants, fine uniforms and gold lace, fell down. Result ... innocent men, women and children killed, thousands injured and several hundred blinded for life ... The horror is too appalling, the measure of official neglect too ghastly.[1]

People were prepared to believe the worst about the navy when, eight months later, U-boats began to run amok off Nova Scotia in the face of what appeared to be no effective opposition. In the words of one opposition MP, while ships were being sunk offshore, 'naval officials at Halifax were trifling at pink teas and playing bridge whist.'[2]

The truth was quite different. The main targets of the U-boats were in fact the ocean-going merchant ships that carried supplies to Britain. Yet the German submarines succeeded in destroying a total of only three of these large vessels in Canadian waters in 1918. The U-boats could not find any other major ships because these were being sailed under naval control in convoys protected by warships, and that was the main job of the little Canadian fleet.

Convoy was an ancient method of trade protection and, until 1917, senior naval and merchant-shipping authorities in Britain believed it to be obsolete in the age of steam. Modern shipping seemed too

A quarter of the city was flattened: Halifax dockyard after the explosion of 6 December 1917. (DHH, CN-3317)

vast, too dependent upon speed for efficiency and too intricately tied to fuelling facilities and other technical port services to permit group sailings. Any effort to re-orchestrate this mammoth, worldwide enterprise, it appeared, would bring the system into disarray more effectively than the enemy could ever hope to. During the spring of 1917, when disaster loomed as U-boats in the western approaches to Britain destroyed as many as one in four ships on the transatlantic run, the Admiralty finally tried convoy. It was an instant success. Naysayers, it turned out, had overstated the administrative problem, failing to understand that much of the voluminous trade from British ports was local traffic. The big transatlantic ships that carried over 50 percent of British imports numbered in the hundreds, not thousands, and thus could be managed. Equally important, it quickly became clear that U-boats could not find convoys. Where previously the independent sailing of 30 ships had given the submariners 30 chances to search them out over a period of days or weeks, now there was only one fleeting chance. Thirty ships sailing together at sea, moreover, are not visible from much further away than a single ship. With group sailings, the naval control authorities could readily route shipping clear of areas where U-boats were known to be hunting. As one expert put it, *the ocean suddenly seemed to the U-boats to be devoid of shipping.*[3]

The Canadian navy made a modest but indispensable contribution to the success of the convoy system in 1917–18. Halifax and Sydney, with support from Saint John, New Brunswick, Quebec City and Montreal, had quickly become principal ports for the assembly and dispatch of vessels to Britain. The RN sent a handful of senior officers to organize the convoys, but the system was dependent upon RCN personnel, and the transportation experts and facilities of such companies as Canadian Pacific Railways.

Not least important was the flotilla of patrol craft that Canadian industry and the navy managed to build and get to sea within a few short months. Merchant shipping was most vulnerable in waters close to the coast, where the vessels could be most readily located by submarines. Indeed, submarines moving freely and quickly along the coast, hunting down ship after ship, posed the greatest danger. To prevent this, large numbers of small, armed craft were needed for three roles: to screen merchant ships as they lumbered out of Halifax and Sydney and formed up into the large transatlantic convoys; to escort smaller groups of merchantmen between Canadian ports; and to maintain a general watch along the coast. Far from home and any possibility

of repair, the U-boats did not dare risk even the minor damage that one of the small patrol vessels might inflict (which may account for the quick disappearance of *U-156* when HMCS *Hochelaga* came into view). Another deterrent was the fact that the radio-equipped patrol vessels could call for help.

The Canadian flotilla faithfully carried out the coast-watch and shipping-escort roles. They did better than should have been expected given the haste with which the ships had been built and the crews recruited. This achievement was appreciated only dimly, if at all. The failures had been so spectacularly obvious, while success, measured in ocean-going merchant ships *not sunk*, was exceedingly subtle. To the extent that Canada had a naval tradition — most of the population lived in the continental interior, far from the sea — it was overwhelmingly British, with a pantheon of blood-spattered, victorious heroes. The defining figure was Admiral Horatio Nelson, who favoured intense close-in fights and was shot dead at the moment of triumph at Trafalgar in 1805. More locally there was Captain Philip Broke, pioneer of brutally concentrated naval cannon fire, whose frigate HMS *Shannon* smashed the larger USS *Chesapeake* in 1813 and then ceremoniously led the blood-drenched hulk of the American ship into Halifax harbour. The influence of such heroes was especially strong in the Canadian navy itself, whose officers had either transferred from the RN or been trained in the British service. Nothing of the Canadian naval record during the First World War seemed to offer inspiration or hope for a better future.

Yet in the bitter disappointments of 1918 lay the seeds that would produce the first-class fighting unit HMCS *Ottawa* proved itself to be 22 years later. The path was by no means direct. It twisted through political thickets and swamps. This was nothing new for the navy, but for once there would be hands to help pull it clear of the mud and the barbs.

Strikingly, given the RN background of all the senior RCN officers, they were the first to grasp clearly that the course of the war at sea in 1914–18 threatened Canadian interests more important and enduring than a score of fishing schooners. The price of naval dependence on larger allies was that decisions about defence and merchant shipping in Canadian waters and at Canadian ports were made in London and Washington. Paradoxically, at this very time Canadian boys were being killed and maimed by the tens of thousands on the battlefields of Europe to establish Canada's place among nations. When U-boats were hovering off Prime Minister Robert

... the navy and the infant shipbuilding industry were scrambling: newly completed anti-submarine drifters at Montreal, 1917. (DHH, CN-3201)

Borden's home province of Nova Scotia in 1918, he finally got the message.

One sign of Borden's eleventh-hour conversion was the aggressive manner in which he brought about immediate organization of a new and costly branch of the navy, the Royal Canadian Naval Air Service (RCNAS), in September 1918. The main assistance the US Navy (USN) had been able to give was two flying-boat units that arrived at Halifax and Sydney late in August. Experience in European waters had demonstrated the effectiveness of air patrols in anti-submarine defence. U-boats, which had to run at speed on the surface to find shipping, cleared out of areas regularly visited by aircraft, and never attacked convoys under air escort. Although the American units barely had time to start flying during the fall of 1918, there was no question aircraft would be an essential element in the protection of the Canadian coast if the war continued into 1919, as was universally expected. With their ability to cover large areas quickly, aircraft were a natural means for protecting Canada's vast coastal frontiers. Borden hurried the RCNAS into existence so that it could take over the role as quickly as possible: *'At present we are dependent upon the United States for our air protection; we cannot very well be content with this position permanently.'[4]* This was the genesis of Canada's substantial maritime air force of the Second World War. Like the naval forces of 1939–45, these air formations emerged late, after a complicated chain of largely political developments.

Convinced as Borden was about the need to put Canada's maritime defences on a more solid footing, after the armistice on 11 November 1918 he had little support, even among his closest cabinet colleagues. Quite aside from the contempt in which many held the navy, new military initiatives were all but impossible to justify in the wake of 'the war to end all wars.' Catching this strong sentiment in 'public opinion,' the government quickly disbanded the RCNAS early in December 1918.[5] The USN made a gift to Canada of the 12 flying boats they had operated in Nova Scotia, and these became the charge of a new Air Board, created in 1919. This board was to look after all aspects of federal aviation policy and operations, both military and civilian. It had a rich pool of talent from which to draw among the thousands of young Canadians who had served in the British flying services during the war. The emphasis, however, was on civil aviation, not least because the officials who advised the government pointed out that the efforts to create a purely military naval service had never garnered public support.

Indeed the naval question was causing fresh controversy even as the Air Board set to work. Admiral-of-the-Fleet Earl Jellicoe, late commander-in-chief of the RN's Grand Fleet, visited Canada in 1919 and advised that a minimally adequate coast-defence naval force would cost no less than $5 million a year. So reluctant were the members of the cabinet that they insisted C. C. Ballantyne, minister for the Naval Service, would have to convince the government caucus MPs. According to Sir George Foster (who was acting for the vacationing prime minister):

Ballantyne went in [on 20 March 1920] ... sure of success, and gave a good explanation & sat down beaming for results. Well, the Caucus knocked it sky-high — only two or three favourable & these moderately so. The agreement was that he should present it, argue for it, & Ministers should say nothing — let the Caucus have its head. So the Caucus had its head & made a thorough job. But two or three of our Ministers broke faith, and told members he [sic] did not want it & Sir Henry [Drayton, Minister of Finance] even clapped applause when some Member hit it hard ... Poor 'B' came out wilted & discouraged & mad ...[6]

Ballantyne was so angry that he embarrassed his colleagues by sending out orders and letters of dismissal that virtually shut down the service. That forced a quick, face-saving compromise: the minister could have an annual budget of $2.5 million.

The navy not only had been saved, it apparently had a bright future. Britain provided free of charge, from its stock of now surplus wartime ships, two submarines, the destroyers *Patrician* and *Patriot* and the cruiser *Aurora*. Most important was the cruiser. This type of ship was the building block of a sea-going navy. These formidable warships were the smallest that could operate fully independently, virtually anywhere at any time. They had the armament to fight any but the very largest surface warships, the size to remain at sea for weeks in all weathers and the endurance to steam thousands of miles without refuelling. Unlike *Niobe* and *Rainbow*, which had been outdated when Canada acquired them, *Aurora* was fast and thoroughly modern. Although one of the smallest cruiser classes — some 3200 tonnes — the vessel was over 120 metres in length and could accommodate more than 300 personnel. This, together with the ship's sea-going endurance, would make it a good training ship.

It was too good to be true. The Liberals, under William Lyon Mackenzie King, returned to power in the general election of December 1921. Among the new government's early moves were further cuts in defence spending, including a reduction of the navy's

annual budget to only $1.5 million. The logic seemed inescapable. At that very moment, at the Washington naval conference of 1921–22, the great powers agreed to scrap many of their existing capital ships and build no more for 10 years.

Fortunately, the professional head of the navy was a tough-minded, politically skilled optimist, Commodore Walter Hose. His predecessor, Vice-Admiral Sir Charles Kingsmill, a Canadian who had served much of his life in the RN, had been in his mid-50s when he came back to launch the new service as a retirement career. Well as Kingsmill had done to navigate the navy through its intensely troubled first decade, he had never been comfortable with the political intrigue and bureaucratic one-upmanship of Ottawa. It was a different world from the orderly environment he had known as a sea-going officer in the British service. Hose, British by birth, had transferred from the RN to the RCN in 1912, when he was in his late-30s, precisely because he felt stifled by the structured routines of a big, well-established navy. He wanted to make a difference, and officials and politicians recognized him as someone with whom they could do business.

Hose was no mere seeker of influence. His experience all through the war as the front-line commander of the improvised Canadian sea forces gave him a solid grasp of what truly was essential. 'Heartsick,' he gave up the cruiser and the submarines, and reorganized the navy as primarily a reserve force. In fact two reserve forces came into being in 1923. The Royal Canadian Naval Reserve (RCNR), with a strength of some 200, was for *officers and men who have followed a sea-faring life.'[7]* They received a course of naval training every year or two at Halifax or Esquimalt. The Royal Canadian Naval Volunteer Reserve (RCNVR), for those without professional maritime experience, comprised units located mostly at inland cities, the concentration of the Canadian population. These volunteers — students, businessmen, clerks and factory workers — attended training sessions at local drill halls one or two nights per week through the year, and in the summer went to Halifax or Esquimalt for two weeks' full-time training. The RCNVR soon had nearly 1000 members. Although both reserve forces were modelled on British organization, there was a crucial difference. The British reserves provided a modest augmentation to the large professional service; the situation in Canada was reversed. The tiny permanent force, now limited to 400 personnel, existed mainly to train the reserves.

Hose understood from his wartime service on the coasts that the immediate protection of the ports and sea frontiers in a future conflict would depend upon reservists manning armed civilian ships and such small, basic patrol vessels as could be hurriedly built. Major warships, whether Canadian or Allied, would never be numerous enough to keep the close watch on the country's huge coastlines that experience in 1914–18 had shown to be essential for both security and sovereignty. Modest vessels — armed fishing craft, yachts and customs steamers — were perfectly adequate for most purposes, so long as they were manned by competent crews. That had been the problem, and Hose's nightmare, in the previous war. Because the naval reserves had not been properly organized as a result of the political controversies over naval policy, Hose had to rely on raw recruits who had not been able to get the best value out of the craft that were available.

Hose's quick shift of focus in 1922–23 to the most mundane basics of national defence delighted the Liberal government. They were interested only in the basics. The Commodore's scheme was all the more appealing because it echoed Canadian traditions of the land forces — a militia with only a small number of regular troops to serve as instructors. (The Canadian Corps of the First World War, which through over three years of continuous hard service became a very professional army, was to Canadian politicians an aberration best forgotten.)

Yet Hose did not abandon the dream of a sea-going service, or the professional interests of the regular force. The big cut had left only the two destroyers, one of which went to each coast, together with a couple of the trawler-type anti-submarine and mine-sweeping vessels built in the emergency programme of 1917–18. According to received naval thinking, the destroyers did not provide much basis for a fleet. They were a highly specialized type that had evolved, only a few decades before, from the first modern torpedo boats. These had been developed by Britain's naval competitors in the late 19th century in the hope that small, fast craft, using powerful new torpedo weapons, could defeat the RN's heavy ships. The British counter had been somewhat larger fast craft known as 'torpedo-boat destroyers' that had a heavier gun armament than torpedo boats and carried torpedoes as well. The original role of the torpedo-boat destroyer — a designation that was soon shortened to simply 'destroyer' — was to accompany the fleet to ward off enemy torpedo boats and then turn the trick by launching torpedo strikes against the enemy's major warships. First World War destroyers, like *Patrician* and *Patriot*, had been designed to dash out into the North Sea for a few days with the

Grand Fleet, or make quick sweeps against German torpedo craft that made independent patrols in the English Channel. They still looked more like torpedo boats than sea-going warships. The long hull was knife-like and the upper deck almost barren of superstructure, crowded with torpedo equipment and guns. The crew, only some 80 seamen, had to be squeezed into accommodation spaces fitted around the compartments for the powerful steam-turbine engines.

Cramped and uncomfortable, destroyers were a hardship posting. They offered nothing of the accommodation and orderly routine needed to carry out well-rounded training. The British suggested that Canada might obtain slower and less heavily armed but more spacious and cheaper general-purpose patrol vessels ('sloops') as a stepping-stone to the day when the government might see its way clear to acquire cruisers.

Hose stood firmly by destroyers. He wanted at least six of them, as the nucleus of the fleet. This was the barest minimum that could provide essential support to small, local patrol vessels on one coast only. It was just such a force that the British had recommended, and been unable to provide, to counter the U-boat offensive against Nova Scotia in 1918. As Hose knew from that experience, destroyers were the smallest true fighting ships that would give the Canadian service independent striking power should a future war bring further surprises. He also knew that the service was fated to operate on a shoestring and appreciated the depth of the political resistance to cruisers. The two attempts to procure them in 1910 and 1920 had ended in disaster. These big, high-seas ships raised the spectre of distant entanglements in the military affairs of the Empire that were anathema, especially to Mackenzie King's Liberals. As it was, the politicians and officials were delighted to have a professional sailor who did not toe the Admiralty line. The idea of a destroyer force committed directly to the defence of Canadian waters to uphold Canadian interests fitted nicely with the Liberals' nationalist foreign policy.

The government followed through, although at a glacial pace. In the late 1920s the worn-out *Patriot* and *Patrician* were replaced by two similar surplus British destroyers that had lain virtually unused since their completion shortly after the First World War. They were commissioned in the RCN as HMCS *Vancouver* and HMCS *Champlain*. At the same time, King's government ordered the construction in Britain of two destroyers of the latest type then coming into service in the RN. On their completion in 1931,

HMCS *Skeena* and HMCS *Saguenay* were assigned to Esquimalt and Halifax, respectively, for a total of two destroyers on each coast. The new vessels were impressive. At 1200 tonnes displacement, they were nearly a third larger than the First World War types and carried more than twice the weight of armament. The complement of each was nearly 150 seamen, which resulted in a near doubling of the strength of the RCN to 700 regular personnel.

The King government belatedly undertook this programme to guard against clear dangers to sovereignty, much the reason for Borden's changed views in 1918. Recurring tensions between the United States and Japan during the 1920s raised the danger of war between these powers, in which case Canada's position would be exceedingly difficult. Britain did not have the naval resources to establish a strong presence in the eastern Pacific. The defence of British Columbia would be dependent upon the Americans, who would have every reason to occupy the coastal parts of the province if Canada was not in a position to guarantee the security of the area. British Columbia's coastal waters were the most practical route for the reinforcement of Alaska, and, by the same token, the logical staging point for Japanese attacks on US west-coast ports.

Appropriately, the new Canadian destroyers arrived just at the time of the Japanese invasion of Manchuria in the fall of 1931, the first of the crises that signalled the shakiness of the international order. It was also a time of deepening economic depression. The Canadian government slashed defence funding even as the forces begged for the resources to carry out basic precautions on the west coast. By 1934, Major-General A. G. L. McNaughton, head of the army and air force, was so worried that he recommended scrapping the navy so that the funds could be used to buy additional aircraft. Given the years required to build warships and train their crews, this seemed the only hope for quickly providing comprehensive surveillance of British Columbia's waters should the escalating tensions in the Far East explode. The Royal Canadian Air Force (RCAF), born from the Air Board's early ventures into aviation policy, had become a fully established armed service with regular units in 1924. These units, however, had been almost entirely committed to civilian operations such as air photography for mapping and anti-smuggling and forest protection patrols. McNaughton was confident that with sufficient money the organization could quickly be re-equipped. In the end, however, Hose won the argument for the very survival of his service by observing that intruders into Canadian

HMCS *Niobe*, one of two cruisers purchased from Britain in 1910 to launch the Royal Canadian Navy. (DHH, DB-4171)

Britain provided free of charge ... the destroyers *Patrician and Patriot: Patriot* on the slipway for repairs at Esquimalt, BC, 1921. (DHH)

waters would most likely come at night or in foul weather, when aircraft would be blind or grounded.

The Liberals had the good luck to be out of office in 1930–35, the worst years of the Depression. The election of October 1935 that brought King back to power occurred against the backdrop of Fascist Italy's invasion of Ethiopia, the beginning of the accelerating disintegration of stability in Europe. War on both the Atlantic and the Pacific now seemed an early possibility. King, in the face of strained finances and widespread isolationist sentiment, launched a partial rearmament programme. He sought to avoid political pitfalls by promising to concentrate on the immediate defence of Canada. He would not in any way commit the country or make preparations for the dispatch of an army overseas, as had been done at such a ghastly cost in 1914–18. Even within these limits, the armed forces got scarcely half the funds they requested. That meant the defence of one coast only. In view of the strong British naval support available in the Atlantic, and evidence of growing US concern about the security of British Columbia's coast, the choice had to be for the Pacific. An interesting feature of the debates in public and within government about rearmament was that the navy had ceased to be controversial. Indeed, the prime minister's key argument against isolationism was a reminder about the menace of maritime attack:

Canada is more vulnerable to-day than it ever was. It is becoming more vulnerable every day because of the advances being made in modern science, particularly military science. We are vulnerable to attack on three fronts, the Atlantic, the Pacific and the north ... I know of no reason — I have given the matter some little thought although I have no expert knowledge — why in war-time an enemy ship that might have escaped from the control of the British navy, or the United States navy, if you like, could not come up the St. Lawrence river as far as the city of Quebec, bomb that city, bomb other cities in the neighbourhood, send out aeroplanes from its deck and attack Montreal and cities as far west as Toronto.[8]

The rearmament programme gave priority to the air force and the navy, the services most directly concerned with coast defence, over the land forces. The bulk of the new funds went to the air force. In part this reflected the cost of re-equipping the RCAF for military operations and developing airfields and other facilities that were virtually non-existent in coastal areas. It also reflected advice the government continued to receive, both from its own military and from American and British leaders, that air power would be the critical dimension in all phases of a future war.

Another consideration may have been the direct links the government saw between aviation and national economic development — a tribute to the wisdom of the air force staff in wholeheartedly focusing on civilian tasks since the service had been founded. Aviation was already proving to be an essential means of transportation and for carrying out other services in Canada's enormous, thinly populated territory. By contrast, Canada was not a significant player in the intensely competitive international business of ocean shipping, a fact that explains the faint support enjoyed by the navy. (Canadian businessmen, however, were masters of taking advantage of the cut-throat market to get cheap shipping services, which is why they played an important part in helping to organize the convoy system in both world wars.)

In theory, General McNaughton's jeremiad about the length of time it took to build naval forces was correct, but the service made much faster progress than anyone could have expected, and at a much lower cost. Encouraged by Canadian rearmament, the Admiralty made available from its active fleet four modern destroyers, near sisters of *Saguenay* and *Skeena*, at a fraction of the cost of new construction and with early delivery. The government seized the opportunity. The vessels came into the RCN as HMCS *St Laurent* and HMCS *Fraser* in early 1937 and HMCS *Ottawa* and HMCS *Restigouche* in the fall of 1938. *Vancouver* and *Champlain* were retired, giving the RCN a flotilla of six modern destroyers. Four of these warships were stationed on the west coast, in deference to the worries about British Columbia's security that US President Franklin D. Roosevelt was now personally communicating to King.

* * *

After nearly 30 years of failed and incomplete experiments, Canada finally had an effective, if small, sea-going squadron, one that reflected Canadian ideas and needs and was fully manned by qualified Canadian personnel. The paradox was that the long quest for a 'national' organization had created such instability that the service survived only by means of the RN's support, both material and spiritual. Because of the political uncertainties and severely constrained resources, young Canadian officers of the 1910s to 1930s spent the formative parts of their careers in the British service, and luckily so for them. One of the foundations of the Canadian service, when it was established in 1910, was the Royal Naval College of Canada. Boys of 15 entered for a three-year course of academic and naval subjects, weighted

towards the applied science needed for navigation, gunnery and ship engineering. Those successful were then to undergo a four-year apprenticeship, much of it at sea in major warships with suitable accommodation and instructional staff, to advance from cadet to midshipman and finally sub-lieutenant, the most junior serving rank. Although the college continued to take in annual classes until the big cut of 1922 forced its closure, the virtual demise of the Canadian fleet after 1911 left no alternative but to send successive classes of graduates to British cruisers and battleships. Since the improvised Canadian coastal flotilla of the First World War offered no suitable employment and policy remained in a state of flux in the early postwar years, most of the young officers remained with the British service until 1922–23. Those from the earlier classes had the unparalleled professional opportunity of receiving highly responsible appointments in the whole range of warships of the expanded wartime fleet in the most active combat theatres. They then completed their qualifications as lieutenants, the working-level rank, while having the chance to cruise about the globe from the Baltic to China and India as the RN re-established its peacetime routine as policeman of the oceans.

The organization to which the young officers returned was too small to be self-sustaining. '*I shall always remember,*' wrote F. L. Houghton of his return to Halifax in 1923 after eight years with the RN, '*the farewell party given to my predecessor, Lt Cuthbert Robert Holland Taylor which lasted into the early hours, at which time he was carried off the ship on a mattress, partly as a mark of respect to a popular officer … I can still hear in my mind the last words he managed to articulate before he quietly and appropriately passed out: "I've seen a Navy die, boys; I've seen a Navy die!"*'[9] Taylor was right in the sense that there were billets for only 26 of the RCN's 59 officers, few of which offered the range of responsibilities needed for professional growth.

There were, however, no releases of these valuable personnel, who constituted the RCN's only hope for the future. Neither did stagnation set in through limited and repetitive work. Hose appealed for help, and the Admiralty responded by agreeing regularly to give Canadian officers appointments in the RN, virtually as if they were members of that service. Thus, after an officer did four years' duty with the RCN, usually half of it in a staff or instructional position ashore and half in one of the destroyers, he could look forward to two years with the British fleet. These tours often included courses in one of the RN's many speciality schools, which were also research centres for the development of new equipment and techniques. The new groups of officer cadets entered in the late 1920s and again in the late 1930s, to man the new destroyers, came from the now tri-service Royal Military College of Canada, or joined the navy after graduation from a collegiate-level civilian school. Immediately on joining the RCN they went to the RN for three or four years, for the sub-lieutenant's qualification. Petty officers and senior ratings also spent long periods with the RN, meeting standards for specialization and promotion that were common to the two Royal navies.

Aside from first-class training, the Canadian personnel were indoctrinated into a tradition-steeped, ritualized way of life. Houghton recalled some of the sacrosanct customs of the Gunroom, the name for the accommodation compartment reserved for midshipmen, in HMS *Cumberland* in 1915–16:

Then there are the Gunroom traditions that go back well before the days of Nelson. One of these is 'Breadcrumbs.' If the Sub [sub-lieutenant in charge of the midshipmen] and the senior snotties [midshipmen] happen to be discussing some matter which is not considered fit for the ears of juniors, the Sub gives the order 'Breadcrumbs!' Whereupon all warts — as they are usually known — hurriedly jam their fingers in their ears. Sometimes the Sub will address some unsuspecting wart in his normal voice, and if the chap so much as twitches, indicating that he had unstopped an ear, he was for it.

Sometimes the Sub reaches a point where he feels he is thoroughly sick of the sight of all warts, in which case he picks up a fork and lays it on a beam or ledge above his head — in the days of wooden ships it would have been jabbed into a beam. This is 'Fork in the Beam.' Immediately all juniors make a concerted dash for the door … There is inevitably a mass of struggling bodies endeavouring to get through the door and the last one out receives the professionally aimed assistance of a senior's boot.[10]

The impact of the British model is particularly clear in the memoirs of K. F. Adams. He was completing his final year at the Royal Naval College of Canada in the spring of 1922 when a visibly upset Commodore Hose had come personally to inform the boys that the college was closing and there was no possibility of a permanent naval career for any of them in the reduced force. Only in the expansion of the late 1920s did a space open for him in the RCN. Adams was thus older and more reflective than the usual junior officer when he was first appointed to a British warship, the cruiser *Calypso* in the large Mediterranean Fleet. It is not too much to say that the

very meaning of 'navy' and his chosen career suddenly came into focus:

It all made sense. The organization of the Fleet as a whole and that of each individual ship was excellent. Every one including the most junior seaman knew what he was doing and why he was doing it. Discipline was strict but always just and fair. Morale was high because of the respect held by juniors for the seniors.[11]

Service with the RN could also reinforce Canadian identity. C. E. Richardson, who joined the RCN as a rating in 1924 when he was 15 years old, recalled that Canadians were usually referred to as 'Yank' because of their North American accents. In the 'Roaring 20s', that let Richardson in for a lot of teasing on the many occasions he served with the RN: *'I got blamed every time Al Capone shot somebody. Or Legs Diamond killed somebody: 'They done it again Yank, old Al Capone done it again ...''[12]* Richardson's Ontario accent showed the influence of Canadian life, for he had been born in England, the son of a British soldier who had transferred to the Canadian regular army. Even with that background, prior to joining the RCN Richardson had been unaware that there was such as thing as a Canadian navy; he was informed of that fact and talked out of his plan to join the USN by a family friend.

W. H. Willson, who joined as an officer cadet at the end of 1936, quickly learned about the distinctiveness of Calgary's culture when he and his friend, W. S. T. McCully, arrived at Gieves, the elegant London tailor that outfitted officers from the RN and all Commonwealth navies.

Bill McCully ... was wearing a big plaid black-and-white jacket with large checks, about four inches across. The Gieves man took it away from him and Bill said, 'Where are you going with my jacket?' and he said, 'I don't think you'll need this sir.' I had a leather tie, chrome leather ties were the 'in' thing in Calgary when I left ... he took my leather tie away and I saw a man drop it in a waste basket ... I just knuckled under: but Bill was very brash and he blew [his] top ... The Gieves man said, 'I don't think you can wear it sir. I don't think you'd be allowed to take it aboard.'[13]

F. C. Frewer, who also joined in the late 1930s, and immediately departed for training in the RN, vividly recalls his return to the Canadian service early in the Second World War.

I always remember the very first trip with Saguenay being terribly impressed by Gus [Lieutenant-Commander G. R.] Miles ... [H]e was seeing his defaulters the first day at sea and I think there was some leading seaman who had to write up the ship's log and had been derelict in his duty ... He stood in front of Gus Miles,

my first taste of a senior Canadian Naval officer ... and gave him a long song and dance about the reason why he hadn't been able to write up the log properly. And Gus just looked him right in the eye and said, 'Bullshit.' Having been reared in the RN I thought, 'Hey, we're back in the Canadian Navy.'

Frewer also remembers that there could be a darker side to the mixing of the two national styles:

I was always over-awed by the RN. I'll tell you one time as a junior officer of the St. Laurent up in Hval Fjördur [Iceland] I think it was, I was told to go over to [a British battleship] by the Captain to pick up a ... 'By Hand of Officer' Top Secret message. So I got in my best uniform, called away the ship's boat. Off I went feeling terribly important, alongside the [battleship HMS] Nelson or the Rodney, I forget which one, went on up to the quarterdeck ... the Officer of the Watch was a very beautifully turned out RN Lieutenant with his telescope under his arm looking rather like Commander Whitehead, peering at the horizon. I doubled smartly up to him on the quarterdeck of the Flagship, came to a grinding halt, snappy salute and announced, 'I am Sublieutenant Frewer, Sir, from the Canadian destroyer St. Laurent.' He just looked me up and down and said, 'How thrilling!' That just killed me, I could have throttled that guy there but this is the effect RN officers had on the RCN, we all felt like country bumpkins.[14]

Canadian seamen did not have to cross the Atlantic to be in the bosom of the imperial naval family. The whole of the RCN functioned as a division of the America and West Indies station. Aside from the close link provided by a seconded RN intelligence officer in Ottawa (whose role will be described below), the commander-in-chief himself regularly visited both coasts and the capital to offer advice and keep in close touch with all developments. He had to, for if war were to break out in the Pacific, his main base would be Esquimalt, and if the conflict was in Europe, Halifax would again become the focus of most operations. Although the King government made much of the fact that Canada was not obliged to participate in another British war, the prime minister never questioned the right of British warships to use the Canadian bases. Nor did he interfere with what amounted to joint planning for everything from fuel stocks to the earmarking of civilian vessels on the coasts suitable for naval service in an emergency.

In terms of warships, the America and West Indies station and the Canadian service were two halves of a whole. The British cruiser squadron was the main deterrent to attacks in Canadian waters, but, given the small number of these warships and the

The modern destroyer HMCS *Saguenay* at Montreal with the older destroyer HMCS *Champlain* in 1932. (DHH, Dillon Collection)

At Halifax, the cramped dockyard was still little changed from when the RN had vacated it in 1904. (Courtesy of Ken Macpherson)

enormous scope of the station — two continents, the RCN destroyers were an invaluable reinforcement. The ability of the Canadian vessels to establish an armed presence in the northern part of the station, or rapidly to come south, if that was needed, gave the tiny fleet an importance that belied its meagre strength.

Although Canada jealously guarded its authority over the RCN fleet, the British and Canadian warships worked closely together. The climax of each year for the Canadian ships was a three-month winter cruise to Bermuda and the Caribbean for joint exercises with the British squadron. These manoeuvres were a quantum leap from the limited single-ship or two-ship programmes that were all that could be carried out within the Canadian service and, of course, they gave the RCN crews a regular opportunity to test themselves against warships that were as well run as any in the world. The exercises of 1934 were especially challenging, for the Home Fleet, including four battleships and an aircraft carrier, had come to the Caribbean that year. F. L. Houghton, then the newly appointed commanding officer of HMCS *Vancouver*, recalled the strain of the manoeuvres:

I shall not easily forget one pitch-dark moonless night in heavy seas, out in the wide Atlantic east of Barbados when the Canadian Flotilla was ordered to carry out a dummy torpedo attack on the 'enemy' Fleet led by the Commander-in-Chief himself. It was to be made under full wartime conditions — no navigation lights and strict wireless silence.

From a position well ahead of the Fleet our four destroyers crashed through the waves at thirty knots, ships pitching madly, mast-high spray flying over their bridges. It was impossible to see more than a few yards ahead of us.

Vancouver was the last ship of the line, but we were disposed quarterly to port on a line of bearing, so that the other three Canadians were somewhere off my starboard bow and of course completely invisible. I felt very much alone.

Suddenly a searchlight was switched on dead ahead of Vancouver, *the sharply defined, bluish beam aimed directly at our bridge. This clearly meant we were under fire from NELSON's secondary armament. Luckily for us, the Flagship, leading the 'enemy' line, had spotted us; we were obviously much nearer our target than we had calculated. In fact,* Vancouver *was actually on a collision course with the huge battleship … 'Hard-a-Starboard! Stand by to fire torpedoes!' As we swung round, we 'fired' four fish, indicating the moment of firing by shooting off a green Very's light. Whether or not, in the*

circumstances, our torpedoes would have struck home or indeed if we were still afloat must forever remain a matter for conjecture. I can only remember feeling at the time that I had had quite enough excitement for one night.[15]

In January 1939 Houghton, now commanding *Saguenay*, participated in less grand exercises, which more closely reflected the type of operations that would likely occur in the western Atlantic. The Canadian destroyers, spread out at maximum visibility distance from each other, pounded back and forth through the Caribbean searching for the big British cruisers HMS *Exeter* and HMS *York*, which were playing the part of enemy surface raiders trying to avoid the destroyers and attack merchant shipping. The Canadians ultimately succeeded, making contact at night after Houghton, a signals (i.e., communications) specialist, detected a radio transmission from the cruisers. He captured the frustration of the long searches in verse inspired by the illumination shells periodically fired from the destroyers' guns when hunting in darkness:

Twinkle, twinkle little starshell —
How I wish that when you fall,
You'd show up that blasted cruiser —
I can't see a thing at all![16]

Paradoxically, in view of the Canadian navy's primarily anti-submarine role during the coming conflict, anti-submarine training was perfunctory during the 1920s and 1930s — little more than dropping a few depth charges. It was an area of expertise that the Canadian service wanted to develop, but, with the loss of the submarines in the budget cut of 1922, useful training became impossible. Nor could it be given priority in the straitened circumstances. The most likely enemy was Japan, whose navy was centred on large surface warships. Asked by the government to economize in the equipment of *Saguenay* and *Skeena*, the Canadian naval staff elected not to include the expensive asdic outfits. That said, the training the Canadian ships received in formation sailing, searches and night operations was just as useful for anti-submarine as anti-cruiser warfare.

The danger that war might begin in the Atlantic before the Pacific became apparent only with Germany's aggression against Austria and Czechoslovakia in 1938. Although the focus of German naval construction continued to be battleships and cruisers, at the end of 1938 Hitler announced he was expanding U-boat construction to parity with Britain's fleet of about 60 vessels. There was now reason to anticipate a substantial submarine offensive. Accordingly, the British Admiralty stepped up preparations for anti-

submarine warfare during the last months of peace. These included intensified joint planning with the Canadian service to organize shipping from North America into convoys at Halifax should the Germans again attack merchant vessels.

The preparations were greatly facilitated by the fact that an organization already existed, albeit in skeleton form, to keep track of British Commonwealth shipping around the world, and Canada had always participated in that organization. Immediately after the First World War, the Canadian navy was determined to reform the system of merchant-shipping control, including convoy organization, so that in a future conflict RN officers would not again take charge of these operations at Canadian ports and leave NSHQ ignorant about developments in the country's own waters. As a result of the Canadian pressure, the British Admiralty agreed that Ottawa was the logical place from which to run and coordinate shipping control not just at Canadian ports, but at US ports as well. The Canadian government, for its part, agreed to accept the appointment of an RN officer at NSHQ as director of naval intelligence. This arrangement safeguarded British interests and gave the Canadian navy expertise it did not possess. All through the 1920s and 1930s, the British officers who served tours in the Ottawa intelligence billet played a central role in Canadian naval planning, and also kept close touch with British consular officials at American ports who would be responsible for control of shipping in wartime.

Fortunately, Commander E. S. Brand, RN, who arrived to take over as director of naval intelligence in July 1939, was fresh from duty in Scotland as a mobilization planning expert. He was also a man with inexhaustible energy, and he swept like a whirl-wind into the tiny, rather quiet world of NSHQ, then housed in a couple of floors over a delicatessen in an Ottawa office building. Brand vividly described the long-suffering reaction of the Canadian officers to his descent upon them in the midst of the heavy, sticky Ottawa summer in those days before the general installation of air conditioning:

I said now we must get on with some plans and fast as there is a war coming soon. Frankie [Houghton, then staff officer, plans and signals] said 'That's all very well but we have no money here for that kind of thing.' I said 'You make paper in this Country don't you?' He said, 'Oh yes.' So I said 'Well let's get some of that and at least make some plans.' So we settled down to it. Having had the experience of Rosyth [in Scotland] I had no difficulty in sketching out similar plans for 'Commanding Officers Atlantic and Pacific Coasts' [at Halifax and Esquimalt]

and 'Naval Officers in Charge' at Quebec, Sydney, St John [New Brunswick], Vancouver and Prince Rupert [responsible for both control of merchant shipping and command of naval activities at these ports]. Cutting their staff to the bone ... still produced a need for a lot more officers than were available to the RCN...

I went to Cdr Cuth Taylor the Director of Personnel and showed [the plans for the ports staffs] to him. He merely grunted 'Where the hell do you expect to get this lot from?' I replied 'Well you have got to find them from somewhere but though I have only been in this country three weeks I have a hunch that if war breaks out quite a lot of Canadians will want to join the Navy.' He replied 'Well if these are the sort of plans you are making I hope you are bloody well right.' — I was ...[17]

Vital as such administrative arrangements were for the protection of British Commonwealth shipping, little could be done to provide the hundreds of additional armed craft that would be needed for anti-submarine duty in British and Canadian waters and elsewhere. British shipyards were already working to capacity to overcome the effects of peacetime budget restrictions and the naval disarmament regime on the fleet.

In Canada the situation was a great deal worse. The naval staff now estimated the RCN's minimum requirements at nine destroyers on each coast for defence against both surface and submarine raiders, and much larger numbers of smaller patrol vessels, many more than could be found among civilian craft suitable for conversion. Commodore P. W. Nelles, Hose's successor and one of the first officer cadets to have joined the RCN, pleaded with the government to begin procurement of these ships. Almost all of them would have to be built in Canada, he warned, because of the strain on British resources. The government, already worried about the political repercussions of escalating rearmament costs, was unwilling to face the recurring multi-million-dollar expenditures that would be needed to revive the moribund Canadian shipbuilding industry. Always small, in the 1930s it had to eke out an existence mostly with repair work. Nelles had to be content with $1 million, to buy the last destroyer the RN was willing to release from its fleet. This vessel would be commissioned in the RCN as HMCS *Assiniboine* in the fall of 1939.

The RCAF was in a similar situation, but for different reasons. The government, because of its strong commitment to aviation, had placed orders for military aircraft to stimulate Canadian industry. Deliveries, however, would not begin until well into 1940 at the earliest. British industry could not help, and the

air staff urged purchases of aircraft in the United States, the solution both Britain and France were adopting as needs outran their manufacturing capacity. Discussions between King and Roosevelt about the west-coast defence problem, and secret meetings between the Canadian and American staffs, had meanwhile begun to build mutual confidence, while underscoring Canada's need to get its coast defences in order. When in the fall of 1938 the German occupation of Czechoslovakia's Sudetenland threatened war, the US Army quickly offered maritime patrol aircraft from its own supply. It was a generous gesture at a time when worldwide rearmament had stripped markets bare of 'off the shelf' military aircraft. The Canadian government approved the $6 million purchase, but then quickly cancelled it when the crisis passed. The cabinet would not run the political risk of spending large amounts of taxpayers' money in the United States unless war actually broke out.

As it was, the RCAF had only a single squadron on the east coast, No 5 at Dartmouth. It had been formed in 1934 by bringing together small flying-boat detachments that supported the Royal Canadian Mounted Police in the interdiction of 'rum running' vessels off the coast. The new unit had abandoned that role in late 1936 and begun full-time maritime patrol training. Links between the RCAF and the RAF were not anything like the close ties between the RCN and the RN, but 5 Squadron's work was based on British manuals and information gained by officers who visited the United Kingdom.

The Canadian service did not act on one critically important piece of advice. Problems in coordinating air and naval operations during exercises had resulted in the British forces creating regional air and navy Area Combined Headquarters to control operations in the waters around the United Kingdom. On the sound principle that the navy had ultimate responsibility for the defence of shipping and the protection of the coast against sustained attack, the regional naval commander laid down tasks for both sea and air forces. Working side by side with the naval commander in the Area Combined Headquarters, the air commander could fully grasp exactly what was required, and instantly translate it into action according to the most suitable aircraft available and specific air force operating procedures. One of the great benefits of the combined headquarters was that information from air, naval and all other sources could be rapidly assembled and integrated onto a single common plot from which both commanders worked. Everyone was always singing from the same song sheet.

Neither the RCN nor the RCAF had the least interest in forming a combined headquarters, partly because the two services were so completely absorbed by the demands of creating basic operating capabilities. It also reflected the sensitivity in both services — the smallest and most junior ones in Canada — about their status. Both had felt the effects of the army's dominance of the Canadian military establishment. They politely agreed to maintain their separate headquarters and operations rooms in Halifax.

Eastern Air Command, a regional headquarters for the control of air force activities in the eastern provinces, was not established until late 1938, the direct result of the Czechoslovakian war scare. Although the aircraft supply problem did not allow the creation of additional flying units, work had begun on a large programme of airfield construction on the east coast. This early start in creating an infrastructure would prove to be a priceless asset.

CHAPTER II

WAR, 1939–1940

We were in Bar Harbor, Maine, with USS San Francisco and that was a very significant evening, we were at a debutante ball with the officers of San Francisco and suddenly, before midnight I think, the Admiral between dances said, 'Will all officers please muster in the room off the dance floor.' We all went in there and he said, 'Gentlemen,' it was very dramatic now that I recall, 'Gentlemen, will you please get back to the ship right away because a state of war is about to exist with Germany and we are sailing as soon as we all get back on board.' We said good-bye to our American counterparts, and the nice girls that we were having fun with, and I well recall the officers of the San Francisco saying, 'Stick in there, we are right behind you, we'll be in the war in no time whatsoever.'

F. C. Frewer, one of three Royal Canadian Navy (RCN) midshipmen in the cruiser HMS *Berwick*, August 1939[1]

25th August 1939 … I decided, in view of the political situation, to sail in H.M.S. BERWICK from Bar Harbour [sic] … in order to be more readily able to carry out offensive action against enemy shipping …

26th August 1939. The BERWICK groped her way out of Bar Harbour in thick fog at 1130. The U.S.S. SAN FRANCISCO could only faintly have seen H.M.S. BERWICK'S masthead as she left but played The National Anthem as the ship sailed.

Vice-Admiral Sir Sidney Meyrick, Commander-in-Chief, America and West Indies Station[2]

War was in fact more than a week away. Germany invaded Poland on 1 September. Britain and France, respecting their joint guarantee to Poland, declared war on Germany on 3 September. Canada did not formally enter until 10 September. Prime Minister William Lyon Mackenzie King had always promised that 'Parliament will decide' whether Canada would be at Britain's side in another major war. It was a keystone of his nationalist policies. He had won much political capital by running against the memory of the Borden government's tragically costly participation in the land war in Europe in 1914–18. Honouring his pledge, the prime minister recalled Parliament from summer recess. The government put forward a resolution for entry into the war, and it passed in the Commons with only four Members opposed.

Meanwhile Britain scrupulously respected Canadian autonomy. The America and West Indies station war plan had the words 'if available' inscribed beside the list of Canadian ships that would be needed. On 25 August Admiral Meyrick asked the Canadian government's permission for his cruisers to use Halifax, even though British ships had every right to do so under an agreement Canada had never challenged (Meyrick instantly received a warm, positive response). Frewer recalled similar care aboard *Berwick*, as the cruiser continued to prowl the sea lanes off Nova Scotia and the northeastern United States, when Britain declared war on 3 September:

It was pretty exciting because Scruffy O'Brien, Johnny Charles and I under these very dramatic circumstances, were asked whether we wanted to stay in the battle, you must remember that Canada was not in the war at that stage of the game … and so for a week, having been

asked by the Captain did we want to be landed or stay in the Navy and fight the battle with the Royal Navy, we decided we would stay with the RN and signed this document so ostensibly we were serving with the Royal Navy for the first week of the war before Canada entered it.[3]

The delayed declaration of war was a largely symbolic display of Canada's growing status as a nation in its own right. In 1914 the British declaration of war had automatically bound Canada and the rest of the Empire. Now Canada was making its own decision. At least as early as the time of the Czechoslovakian crisis of September 1938, however, Mackenzie King had been utterly convinced that it was Canada's 'self-evident national duty' to back Britain up in the defence of democracy. When Admiral Meyrick visited Ottawa in June 1939 the prime minister assured him that Canada would do its part.

King was as good as his word. From the moment word first reached Ottawa from London on 21–22 August, about the danger of impending war, the government authorized the Canadian forces to prepare in lock step with the British. Partial mobilization began late on 25 August, full mobilization on 1 September. On that date Naval Service Headquarters (NSHQ) signalled the ship and coastal commanders to *'Ship warheads and be in all respects ready for action. Do not start an engagement until ordered from NSHQ but be prepared to defend yourselves in case of attack.'[4]* By that time three air force squadrons had completed or nearly completed movements to Nova Scotia from the western and central parts of the country. These, however, added little to the capabilities of 5 Squadron, as they were all equipped with civilian aircraft or obsolete military types. There were still only two destroyers on the east coast. On 31 August, HMCS *St Laurent* and HMCS *Fraser* had hastily cast off from Vancouver, where the ships were participating in the Pacific Exhibition, for a high-speed two-week run to Halifax by way of the Panama Canal. Because of uncertainty about Japan's attitude and the possibility that German warships might operate in the Pacific as they done in 1914, HMCS *Ottawa* and HMCS *Restigouche* remained on the west coast until October, when the Royal Navy (RN) was able to station a cruiser in British Columbia waters.

Among the most important measures was prompt action by the Canadian government to allow NSHQ fully and immediately to carry out its responsibilities in the control of shipping. On 26 August, when Britain brought naval control of its merchant shipping into effect, the Canadian government did the same for the small fleet of Canadian-registered vessels. Meanwhile Commander Brand at NSHQ presided over mobilization of the control system for the whole of Canada and the United States, aside from ports in Florida and in the Gulf of Mexico. An official from Ottawa flew to the United States to deliver up-to-date confidential instructions to the British consular offices at American ports. Retired naval officers who had registered for service in the event of war took up their stations at Canada's main ports on both coasts to organize the control of shipping and other defensive precautions in accordance with the plans Commander Brand had so recently refined.

None of this haste was wasted. On the evening of 3 September, hours after Britain's declaration of war, *U-30*, one of the German submarines that had taken up war station in the western approaches to the British Isles, torpedoed and sank the unarmed liner *Athenia*, en route from Liverpool to Montreal. The U-boat commander had violated Hitler's orders not to 'sink on sight.' The German leader still hoped that with a display of restraint he could negotiate Britain out of the war. Nevertheless, the Admiralty took the incident as evidence of a new 'unrestricted' submarine offensive against merchant shipping, and ordered sailings in convoy. NSHQ arranged for the consular offices in the United States, and the shipping-control authorities at Canadian ports, to direct shipping to Halifax, which had been selected by the Admiralty as the main assembly point for the heavy traffic bound from North America to the United Kingdom.

HX 1, using the designator for Halifax convoys that had been adopted during the First World War, sailed without fanfare in the early afternoon of 16 September 1939. The 18 merchant ships were slow to take up their cruising positions in short columns on a broad, six-kilometre front as they emerged single file from harbour, but then did well keeping station. *St Laurent* and *Saguenay* provided close-in anti-submarine protection, cruising just ahead of the convoy in positions off each side of it. The British cruisers HMS *York* and *Berwick* screened from about nine kilometres away, in case one of the heavy German surface raiders had in the last days of peace taken up station in the western Atlantic. Overhead, one or two of the Royal Canadian Air Force (RCAF) flying boats from Dartmouth circled during the first 24 hours of passage, after which, at a distance of about 400 kilometres from shore, the convoy moved beyond aircraft range. On the evening of 18 September, when the convoy was more than 700 kilometres out and clear of the coastal area where the enemy could most readily locate shipping, the warships turned back to port. HX 1 continued unescorted

The British cruiser HMS *Berwick* in 1939 and three Canadian midshipmen serving in the ship: From left to right, F. C. Frewer, J. C. O'Brien and J. A. Charles. (Courtesy of F. C. Frewer)

until, on 29 September, it approached the southwest coast of Ireland, whereupon British warships joined to bring it through the area of greatest danger.

This rendezvous was crucial. The RN in September 1939 had fewer than 200 destroyer and equivalent escort types in total, and most were needed for reconnaissance and strike work with the main fleet forces. Yet in 1918 some 200 destroyers and equivalents had been required for escort of the main Atlantic merchant ship convoys alone. Tight schedules therefore had to be set for the score of destroyers and other vessels suitable for ocean anti-submarine work that could be squeezed from other pressing commitments. This dictated every step of the assembly and sailing of convoys from North America, and created enormous pressures, especially on the naval control of shipping staff at Halifax. Nevertheless convoys sailed from Halifax every few days in what almost immediately became a well-organized routine, even as the number of ships arriving for each sailing increased to 40 and 50. British officers sent to help found there was nothing for them to do.

Much of the credit for the excellent organization at Halifax belonged to Commander Richard H. Oland, RCN. He had entered the Royal Naval College of Canada in 1913 and, like the rest of his class, saw wide-ranging service in British warships during and after the First World War. He left the navy in 1930 to become a successful businessman, but volunteered to return to service in the event of war and was assigned for duty as the Naval Control Service Officer at Halifax.

One of the chief secrets of Oland's success at running the convoy control organisation was the depth of his knowledge of the kind of lives led by seamen. It was not just a question of being courteous to the old commodores and masters and sympathising with their problems — he had a clear picture in his mind of the conditions faced by every member of a ship's crew from the pantry boy upwards. He reckoned that if a freighter was to sail on time in convoy, to meet the buffetings of nature as well as the violence of the enemy, then her crew were entitled to reasonable comfort and consideration ashore and as decent food at sea as could be got. As a result everyone trusted him and his organisation never let them down.[5]

This tribute came from Rear-Admiral Sir Kenelm Creighton, RN, one of the retired senior officers who volunteered to serve as 'convoy commodores.' A convoy commodore sailed with a small signals staff in one of the merchant vessels of a convoy, and was responsible for the good order and navigation of all of the merchant vessels; if naval escorts were present, the senior commanding officer dealt with the convoy commodore to coordinate defensive measures. Despite advanced age and prestigious rank, the convoy commodores willingly endured the rough conditions in many of the merchant ships in which they sailed. And, like the merchant sailors, they faced much greater danger than the crews in escorting warships, because the plodding cargo carriers were the enemy's principal target. Oland wrote a warm account of the commodores for a local newspaper. This piece is steeped in the profound empathy that fuelled overwork in relentless pursuit of greater efficiency at the port of Halifax and contributed to Oland's death by a heart attack in 1941 at the age of only 44:

Through the years like all sailors, high or low, they no doubt dreamed of their retirement to a little home by the sea … This happy life they have left to go to sea again, to face sudden death.

My first recollection of them was when I saw three elderly men in naval uniform, slowly climbing the stairs to the Control Office [in Halifax]. Weathered, grizzled, they had a look of command … for all their weariness and veteran aspect. Each wore on his chest a blaze of ribbons; each on his sleeves carried the broad band of commodore.

Half way up they paused, like ageing horses on a hill. 'The old pump,' said one, 'isn't quite as good as it was.' Three pairs of eyes, amazingly young in wrinkled faces, interchanged glances of agreement … These are the elders of the sea who command our convoys.[6]

Within weeks of the passage of HX 1, the Halifax convoys had much more formidable defences against surface raiders. This threat was greater than it had been in the First World War, rather paradoxically, because the German surface fleet was much smaller. The goal of German naval expansion in the 1930s had been to recreate a major battle force that could directly challenge the British fleet. That hope had disappeared with the early outbreak of war with the Western powers. The most useful employment now for the few — but individually powerful — big ships that had been completed was to slip them out of the North Sea, under the cover of darkness and foul weather, for commerce raiding. The menace became evident in October, when the powerful German 'pocket battleships' *Admiral Graf Spee* and *Deutschland* began to strike independently sailed shipping in the Atlantic. Unlike the submarines, which still hovered off Britain, these ships were well positioned to devastate the unprotected convoys at mid-ocean. On 16 October two battleships and two cruisers, the vanguard of the RN's 3rd Battle Squadron, arrived at Halifax. These heavy ships, which were soon reinforced by others, began a transatlantic shuttle,

... too undependable for extended over-water flying: a 1920s vintage Westland Wapiti biplane at Halifax in January 1940. (Courtesy of C. Vincent)

... the RCAF's only modern maritime bombers: a Supermarine Stranraer flying boat. (Courtesy of C. Vincent)

covering convoys through the whole passage to Britain. Additional heavy forces, assigned actively to hunt the German surface raiders, periodically operated from Halifax as well.

The minuscule Canadian maritime forces did their part effectively, but the activities at Halifax alone had stretched them to the limit and beyond. During the war scare in the fall of 1938, Rear-Admiral Nelles had described the situation on the east coast as 'near tragic.'[7] He was referring not to the main difficulty — the shortage of ships — but to the lack of everything from base facilities to the equipment needed to convert civilian vessels for patrol duties. The tight financial constraints on rearmament, and the priority to be given to west-coast operations, had left almost nothing for the Atlantic. Because the government had not provided additional funds for the defence programme until early 1939, little could be done by the time war broke out.

Captain Massey Goolden, a retired RN officer who had been flown from his home in British Columbia to take command at Sydney, Nova Scotia (designated as the second principal base on the east coast), *found that the existing defences of the Port consisted of … five seaplanes, at present without bombs, [and] two R.C.M.P. launches armed with Lewis [machine] guns.'*[8] The Northrup Delta float planes were a civil type, operated by 8 Squadron RCAF, which specialized in aerial photography. Experienced coastal aircrew from Dartmouth came to Sydney to give on-the-job training for maritime patrol duties. The air force base facilities consisted of a clearing beside the Sydney River; workshop space and quarters for the personnel had to be rented in the city, several kilometres away. The naval facilities included the government wharf on the waterfront and offices in a commercial building. The crews from the Royal Canadian Mounted Police (RCMP) marine section at Sydney, and elsewhere in the Maritimes, were a valuable resource, for the navy had organized their training since early in the 1930s. Most of the 200 personnel had enrolled in the Royal Canadian Naval Reserve (RCNR) and immediately come out on active service. On mobilization the RCMP vessels were commissioned into the navy, or assigned as rescue boats for the RCAF, but were too small to provide the continuous patrol needed in the approaches to ports. In the absence of any anti-submarine armament at Sydney, Goolden had his staff manufacture improvised depth charges by filling steel barrels with blasting powder; these were rolled off the stern of the RCMP vessels.

Still, in Newfoundland such resources appeared luxurious. Newfoundland was a separate dominion until 1949, equal in status to Canada. During the Depression, however, the government had gone bankrupt, and Newfoundland had to revert to a British dependency, under the rule of a British-appointed governor. Britain had let it be known to Canada in the latter part of the 1930s that its forces had no resources whatever to provide local protection for Newfoundland. Canada would have to supply most of what was needed. Dominating the Canadian Atlantic coast as Newfoundland did, it was obviously in Canada's interests to supply this protection. That is exactly what had happened during the U-boat crisis of 1918: the RCN anti-submarine flotilla had screened much of Newfoundland's shores, as well as those of the Maritime provinces and the Gulf of St Lawrence. In the late 1930s, however, Mackenzie King would have none of it. He had pledged not to make military commitments that would compromise Canada's ability freely to decide on participation in war.

In September 1939, Captain C. M. R. Schwerdt, a retired RN officer who had been serving as the governor's secretary, found himself virtually alone as Newfoundland's naval defence force. Assisted by three reserve officers (one of them a St John's lawyer who worked as a volunteer without pay), he had to carry out the control of ocean shipping from all of Newfoundland's ports, decode and encode all secret communications, and recruit 625 Newfoundland fishermen needed for service in the RN. These were all the responsibility of the Admiralty, but there were no means in place for the Newfoundland government to make direct charges on a British department. Schwerdt found himself constantly fighting these bureaucratic battles while at the same time bargaining with the manager of the Newfoundland Hotel (the only suitable fireproof building in St John's) for a discount rate on the two rooms used by the little naval staff! In the summer of 1940 one of the officers warned the besieged Schwerdt, quite unnecessarily: *'You know, Sir, we began last Fall with a wheelbarrow, today we need a good big truck.'*[9]

Newfoundland's needs, together with those of the whole of the Canadian seaboard, were not the only ones crying for attention from Ottawa. The most pressing situation was in the Caribbean. These heavily travelled waters were distant from the north Atlantic centre of Britain's sea power and therefore a likely place for German raiding operations. Indeed, seeking protection from RN cruisers, many German merchant ships had interned themselves in neutral ports in and around the Caribbean. These ships could then dash out to supply raiders, or mount guns and

Rear-Admiral P. W. Nelles, chief of the naval staff, coming aboard HMCS *Restigouche*. (DHH, 0-1785)

become raiders themselves. In response to calls for help from Admiral Meyrick, in mid-September 1939, as soon as the first reinforcement of two destroyers had reached Halifax from British Columbia, the RCN assigned one of these ships for duty in the Caribbean. All that Meyrick immediately wanted for Newfoundland was an initial, thorough air reconnaissance to make sure the enemy had not hatched something in these remote waters so readily within reach from northern Europe during the last weeks of peace. Two Delta float planes from Sydney carried out this mission in a week-long series of flights from inlet to inlet around the whole of the coast of the big island, beginning on 4 September, six days before Canada was at war. Thereafter, the Deltas' patrols regularly took in the south coast of Newfoundland, where the concentration of shipping was the heaviest.

* * *

For once, Canada's maritime forces improvised in the knowledge that they had the government's full support. Things would get better. The air force benefited first, thanks to heavy government investment since 1937 and access to the United States' burgeoning military-aircraft industry. Construction of the new airfield at Dartmouth was sufficiently advanced by October 1939 for flying operations to begin. It was none too soon, for the tarmac of the Halifax Flying Club strip, in use as an interim facility, had a dangerous tendency to break through under the weight of loaded military aircraft.

More importantly, during the last week of August 1939 the government had lifted the prohibition on aircraft purchases in the United States. The British government, with a vested interest in improved air coverage in the Canadian-Newfoundland area, released 10 Lockheed Hudson bombers from its own orders in the United States. After hasty conversion training at Rockcliffe, Ontario, adjacent to Ottawa, 11 Squadron moved to Dartmouth in early November 1939 and began operational flying soon after that. With a top speed of nearly 250 knots, and an effective operating range of 650 kilometres, the Hudson performed fully a third better in these critically important categories than the Supermarine Stranraer flying boats in 5 Squadron, until then the RCAF's only modern maritime bombers.

Fortunately, the US Army was still willing to assign machines from its own orders for early delivery to the RCAF. The first of 20 Douglas Digby bombers began to arrive in Canada in December 1939, and, in April 1940, 10 Squadron gratefully began to operate the new aircraft at Dartmouth. The unit had been at Halifax since September 1939, but had scarcely been able to fly operations because its 1920s vintage Westland Wapiti biplanes had proved too undependable for extended over-water flying. The Digbys were larger than the Hudsons and, although somewhat slower, were able to remain airborne for 10 to 12 hours, as compared to six or seven for the Hudsons. This enabled the Digbys to linger longer than the Hudsons to cover shipping, or to press somewhat beyond the 650-kilometre range of the latter.

By the spring of 1940 there were other important developments. Construction of the airfields at Sydney and at Yarmouth, at the southern tip of Nova Scotia, were approaching the point where flying would be possible. Canadian manufacturers, with the benefit of the pre-war contracts, were beginning to deliver Bristol Bolingbroke aircraft, a Canadian variant of the British Bristol Blenheim light bomber. Although lacking the range and carrying capacity of the superior US machines, they were useful for maritime work. With the lifting of the government's ban on orders from the United States, it had also been possible to negotiate a contract with Consolidated Aircraft of San Diego, California, for 105 PBY flying boats. This machine was also known as the Catalina, the name given to the variant built for the Royal Air Force, and the Canso, the name of the variant built for the RCAF. The flying boat could remain aloft for up to 24 hours and patrol to ranges of 1000 kilometres while carrying a substantial bomb load. The first batches of Cansos would be completed in San Diego, but work began to set up production facilities at Boeing Aircraft of Canada in Vancouver and Canadian Vickers in Montreal to manufacture the later batches with assistance from Consolidated. It would be a year, however, until the RCAF received its first of the long-range flying boats — initially a single squadron of Catalinas from British orders in the spring of 1941, and then Cansos from the Canadian order beginning in the fall of that year.

The most striking development in the first months of the war was the change in the government's attitude towards naval shipbuilding. Prior to August 1939 the high costs and need for close collaboration with Britain had been fatal liabilities given the government's emphasis on financial constraint and the avoidance of binding ties to British rearmament. The new political calculus of war turned all this on its head. The King government, not wishing to send a large land army overseas, wanted to emphasize industrial production for the Allied cause and operational roles as close as possible to home. In the matter of

... woven from thousands of metres of heavy steel cable: anti-submarine nets at Halifax. (National Archives of Canada, PA-105924)

Corvettes under construction at Davie Shipbuilding, Lauzon, Quebec, April 1941. (Canadian Forces Photographic Unit, PMR 83-1674)

shipbuilding, King's desires meshed perfectly with Britain's needs, as the RN was desperately short of anti-submarine and other types of coastal patrol vessels. The Admiralty quickly advised the Canadian government to build these vessels in quantity to both protect Canada's own shores and provide others for Newfoundland and the Caribbean. Rear-Admiral Nelles, for his part, warned that even the largest of his pre-war recommendations now bore no relation to what was needed. The immediate U-boat offensive in Britain's western approaches led him to predict a repetition of what had happened in the First World War:

The enemy will be forced [by the strengthening of anti-submarine measures in British waters] to work further afield if he is to cut off the flow of munitions and foodstuffs from Canada and Eastern United States ports to Great Britain. We must, therefore, be prepared, in addition to the patrol and minesweeping services, to escort all shipping with properly equipped A/S [anti-submarine] vessels, not only from the Convoy Assembly Ports on our Eastern seaboard to the open sea, but also (1) in the St. Lawrence River below the Isle of Orleans ... and (2) along our coasts to and from the Eastern United States Ports.

If this is not done we must expect heavy losses of important shipping and cargoes within sight of our own shores.[10]

What ships were needed for this work, and did Canada have the capacity to build them? No one knew, because the government had discouraged industrial collaboration between the RCN and the Admiralty. British authorities, ignorant of the prostrate state of Canadian shipbuilding, expected Canada would be able to manufacture sophisticated ships and get any technical assistance required from US industry. The RCN, unaware of the extent to which British industry was over-extended, counted upon large-scale British help. The Canadian service, moreover, having always been trained and organized on the basis of British equipment, was extremely reluctant to embrace quite different US types.

The first break in the fog of ignorance and uncertainty came just as war was breaking out, and in an unusual way. The Canadian Manufacturers Association, fed up at the dearth of armament orders, sent a large delegation to Britain in July 1939 to try to drum up business. Major-General A. G. L. McNaughton, who since his retirement from the military in 1935 had been president of the National Research Council of Canada, encouraged the delegation and used his contacts within the British military to open doors for the industrialists. The government, under pressure to make a gesture of support for busi-

ness, allowed McNaughton to accompany the delegation. McNaughton was acting out of concern at the manner in which the powerful head of the civil side of the Department of National Defence, although a former officer, was ignoring the advice of the military staffs about the industrial aspects of rearmament. In fact, McNaughton withheld some of the masses of information the delegation gathered in Britain until he had assurances that the offending official would be removed.

The delegation brought back the startling news that the Admiralty had sponsored the design of two new warship types suited to Canada's circumstances. The most important of these was the anti-submarine 'whale-catcher,' so named because it was based on the design of ocean-going whale-hunting vessels, a good model given the parallels between whale and submarine hunting. Sir Winston Churchill, who became First Lord of the Admiralty (the government minister responsible for the navy) on the outbreak of war, found a more warlike name from one of the smaller classes of true fighting ships in the age of sail: 'corvette.' At 60 metres in length, and with a displacement of 860 tonnes, the corvette was nearly three times the size of the trawlers that had been adapted for similar military use during the submarine crisis of the First World War, and which had been the main type in the Canadian flotilla. Most importantly, it was a commercial design that could readily be produced by shipyards, like those in Canada, that did not have the expertise demanded by the finer tolerances and precision demanded by naval designs. The other new type was the Bangor-class minesweeper, a naval design simplified for building by commercial yards. At 610 tonnes, it was over a third larger, and therefore more seaworthy, than the most recent type known in Canada. The greatest virtue of these vessels for manufacturing was also its leading drawback in terms of operations. Both were powered by simple piston-driven reciprocating steam engines, not the more powerful steam turbine equipment whose precision engineering was beyond the capability of Canadian firms. The penalty paid was in speed, a maximum of 16 knots. Both classes would become principal anti-submarine types during the crisis of the Battle of the Atlantic, and the powerful diesel engines U-boats used when cruising on the surface would enable them to outrun these hunters.

Churchill called corvettes and vessels designed for mass production the 'cheap and nasties,' but their construction was a daunting project in Canadian terms. The cost was over $500,000 a ship, which raised protests from the Department of Finance that

only a few should be built. Mackenzie King himself, in a revelation of his change since the outbreak of war, blasted aside these objections in Cabinet:

I went over some of the recently received telegrams from Britain, and pointed out how there was a danger of Finland being defeated. Norway and Sweden passing to the control of Germany and Russia, and that we might find ourselves where our own coasts might be attacked on the Atlantic, and I thought quite possibly, before the year was out, on the Pacific, and our own position such that we could not get munitions from Britain …

… the last thing the people would forgive would be any shortage at a time of need.[11]

Early in February 1940 the government approved the construction of 90 corvettes and Bangors, the maximum number it appeared Canadian industry could produce in an all-out two-year effort. Included in the orders for 64 corvettes were 10 placed by the Admiralty. RN technical officers, sent to Ottawa to arrange contracts in Canada and the United States, were shocked at the state of Canadian industry:

The ignorance of all the firms concerned as regards almost every kind of warship equipment, and especially as regards the quality required, was appalling, except in the case of Canadian Vickers, some of whose older employees had served at Barrow [the British shipbuilder]. For instance, drawing-office staffs were of the most meagre description and had practically no knowledge or experience of Admiralty requirements. In consequence, the Mission was flooded with inquiries regarding materials, methods of manufacture and design, even of such details as door-switches, signal-flag lockers, galley ranges, lagging, etc. Inspection was nominally carried out by the Canadian Offices of the two British Registries, Lloyd's and the British Corporation; but a long time elapsed before it was realized that their ideas of inspection differed very greatly from those of the Admiralty, and that their methods were of the sketchiest description and relied largely on the abilities and good intentions of the contractors and their almost non-existent Inspection Departments …

Hence it soon became evident that one of the principal duties was, and for a long time would be, the education not only of the contractors but of the Registries. There is no doubt that this proved a considerable surprise to the E.-in-C.'s [Admiralty Engineer-in-Chief's] Department, who had no idea at all of the primitive nature of the firms in question …

Yet other troubles were caused by the fact that, for the sake of the dollar exchange rate [heavy purchases in Canada and the United States had already depleted Britain's reserve of dollars], and because manufacture in

Canada had not been considered and started, a large proportion of the auxiliary machinery for these ten ships had been ordered from the United Kingdom. Delays were caused by losses in transit, and by the constant failure of British firms to keep their promised dates of despatch …[12]

The British officers were also appalled at the inability of the Admiralty to provide essential information about their own designs.

The U.K. drawings from which the ships were built, and particularly the machinery drawings, were sometimes incorrect, often insufficiently detailed, and had not been properly checked and amended in Admiralty before issue. For instance, they were often several years old, with the result that amendments made in the shops during manufacture had not been inserted, or they had not been brought up to date in regard to later Admiralty practice.[13]

One of the top British officers in Ottawa, Engineer Rear-Admiral H. A. Sheridan, became so frustrated at delays in provision of corvette drawings that he begged for the RCN's intervention: *'I have requested these and been rudely rebuffed … I would like you to shake up the Home Departments if you can.'[14]*

These difficulties reflected profound problems that would bedevil Canadian naval shipbuilding and equipment procurement through the whole war. British industry relied on large numbers of skilled workers who would take designs as guidance, and solve problems in the production models on the shop floor. Because the Admiralty and industry were working flat out in a crisis situation, moreover, there was often no time — or domestic need — to draught revised plans. By contrast, North American industry, geared to mass-production methods that demanded far fewer skilled tradesmen, required precise designs. The problem was still greater with the many precision components required for the simplest ship, such as pumps, electrical generators and weapons systems. British standards for everything from screw threads to materials specifications and operating electrical current were different from Canadian and American ones. Thus either special production had to be arranged in North American factories or delays had to be accepted in deliveries of equipment from Britain's beleaguered firms.

It was clear that the ambitious naval building programme offered no hope of early support to the thinly stretched forces in the Atlantic. The situation there was desperate. Only 14 vessels were available for coastal patrol, most of them converted civilian ships, some of them veterans of the RCN's First World War flotilla. The Canadian government there-

fore did what it had done during the earlier conflict: dodged US neutrality laws against the purchase of ships by belligerent nations. Lieutenant-Commander J. W. R. Roy, RCN, went to US ports in civilian clothes, posing as a yacht broker. The Department of External Affairs then arranged for patriotic yachtsmen to purchase 14 vessels Roy had found, and sail them to Canadian ports for transfer to the RCN. This was a band-aid solution. Nelles reminded the government, *'At the end of the last war, we had some 125 small craft.'* Even with the US yachts, there would be scarcely enough for the immediate local defence of Halifax and Sydney: *'The defence of shipping in the St. Lawrence simply cannot be coped with, a situation I feel certain the Government would not wish to countenance.'*[15]

The navy's fears that U-boats would come to the Canadian coast as early as the summer of 1940 were by no means exaggerated. In January 1940 the German naval staff recommended an attack in the Halifax approaches. Hitler rejected the idea only because an operation so close to American waters might help precipitate the United States' entry into the war.

The crisis of 1940 was different from what the Canadian navy — or anyone else — had expected. It came sooner and was far, far graver. Offensives by the German forces quickly, in April, conquered Norway, and, in May, sliced through the Low Countries and northern France. The French government surrendered on 23 June. Italy had come into the war on Germany's side on 10 June.

CHAPTER III

A NEW WAR, A NEW NAVY, 1940–1941

Urgency due to possibility in near future of sea-borne invasion of United Kingdom … Largely by means of destroyers that such invasion would be opposed and sea-borne trade in home waters maintained. Recent developments and the attitude of Italy have left the United Kingdom sadly lacking in available destroyers in home waters for these tasks. Furthermore, submarines in the near future certain to be very active against shipping but more especially in waters adjacent to the United Kingdom …

> Vincent Massey, Canadian High Commissioner in the United Kingdom, telegram to the Government of Canada, 23 May 1940[1]

One wonders if the Canadian destroyers will come back. We may find our own coasts left bare in giving our last possible aid to the Mother country. That, however, to my mind, is right. We owe to her such freedom as we have. It is right we should strike with her the last blow for the preservation of freedom.

> Prime Minister William Lyon Mackenzie King, 24 May 1940[2]

These orders were, of course, extremely secret … Our ships' companies knew that we were going somewhere because of the large quantities of stores which were suddenly taken onboard. Most of them, especially in RESTIGOUCHE, thought that it would be the West Indies. You can imagine their surprise, therefore, when they were told we were going to the British Isles. You could have heard a pin drop for about thirty seconds and then everybody started talking at once. Many people were bewailing the fact that they had left their greatcoats and warm clothing at home …

> Commander Horatio Nelson Lay, RCN, commanding officer HMCS *Restigouche*[3]

On 24 May 1940, the day after German forces reached the Channel coast, HMCS *Restigouche*, HMCS *Skeena* and HMCS *St Laurent* sailed from Halifax for Devonport in southern England. HMCS *Fraser*, the destroyer on duty in the Caribbean, rushed to Bermuda, refuelled and followed on 26 May. That left only one destroyer, HMCS *Saguenay*, available for service on the Canadian coast; HMCS *Assiniboine* and HMCS *Ottawa* were undergoing refit.

After the week-long transatlantic run, the warships were rushed into dockyard for modification in light of recent combat experience. One of the two sets of torpedo tubes, the destroyer's traditional main armament, was removed to allow space and weight capacity for additional anti-aircraft guns and depth-charge armament. It was a striking confirmation of Commodore Hose's faith in the destroyer's great flexibility.

On 9 June, when the crews had scarcely had time to try out the newly fitted weapons, the Canadian ships began runs to the French coast to evacuate Allied troops. These were hair-raising missions in which the ships had to pull in close to shore and remain immobile while personnel were brought out in small boats, even as German troops advanced towards the shore. *Fraser* and *Restigouche* were returning from the last of these missions when, on the evening of 25 June, disaster struck. In a close manoeuvre at speed, *Fraser* crossed the bows of a British cruiser, HMS *Calcutta*, whose prow sliced the Canadian ship in half. Of the expanded wartime complement of 172 in *Fraser*, 47 were lost or later died of injuries; at least

19 of the 33 British personnel known to have embarked from the French coast were also lost. In the confusion of the evacuation, other people may have been taken on and then killed in the sinking. Losses would have been heavier without the swift and thorough rescue work of *Restigouche* and *Calcutta*.

The loss of a ship under any circumstances is the most devastating thing that can happen to a commanding officer. It was especially so for Commander W. B. Creery, RCN. He knew the ship and its people intimately, having commanded for two years. Present on the bridge at the time of the accident, he bore full responsibility. Interestingly, in view of the scant public support the navy had received during difficult times in the First World War, Creery was sustained by letters of appreciation and support from towns *Fraser* had visited in British Columbia while stationed there before the war and from the parents and wives of lost crewmen, almost all of them westerners:

As the father of one of your Boys I wish to express my deep thanks for your kindness towards him while he was under your command. That boy sure worshiped you and when on leave in November 1939 could not talk of anything else but the Captain and the officers of the Fraser. I would appreciate it if any of the Fraser Survivors have any photo of my son if they can lend them to us so we can have something to treasure. I will have prints made and return them all. If this is not possible owing to War regulations rest assured Sir that we will understand any token of him will be cherished. God man he was so damned proud of the 'Fraser.'[4]

Thank you so much for your kind letter of sympathy. I can't tell you what a horrible shock my husband's death was to me. I too thought he had every chance of recovery, especially after I received his telegram to say he had arrived in England safe and sound and a letter would follow.

… It seems so cruel that a man so fine in every way should die away from all he loved …

I would be most grateful if you could give my heartfelt thanks to all who were with George when he needed them most. My greatest sorrow was that I could not be there myself. I would also like to thank those who so kindly sent wreaths. I could not even do that because I had no way of knowing when or where he was buried.

May I wish you and those who are left of the 'Frasers' ships company the very best of luck on your new ship.

Please let me thank you again for your kind letter.[5]

Even before the last voyage to France, the Canadian ships had begun to carry out anti-submarine and shipping defence duties on the ocean routes to the west of Britain. Cut off from continental Europe, Britain was almost utterly dependent upon transatlantic shipping. The U-boat force now numbered only 21 ocean-going submarines, three fewer than there had been at the outbreak of war. Nevertheless, access to French ports on Britain's doorstep brought the Germans even greater success than had the all-out effort in September 1939, when British defences had scarcely been organized. The prompt redeployment of shipping from the south and east of England to the northwestern and Scottish ports, itself an enormous achievement that required fundamental reorganization of both the land transport networks and the shipping and port services, did not overcome the new German advantage. Nearly 350 merchant ships were sunk by U-boats during the last six months of 1940, as compared to 200 during the first nine months of the war. The submariners called this their 'Happy Time.'

The escorts, depleted by the need to keep many destroyers on anti-invasion duty on the east coast, often operated more as an ambulance service than an anti-submarine force. The Canadians quickly gained a reputation — which would grow throughout the war — for compassion, a willingness to risk themselves to save others. The largest rescue was one of the earliest. On 2 July, *U-47*, renowned for its destruction of the battleship HMS *Royal Oak* inside the British fleet anchorage at Scapa Flow in October 1939, torpedoed the liner *Arandora Star* off Northern Ireland. The ship was bound from Liverpool carrying 1299 German and Italian internees and German prisoners of war, whom Canada had agreed to take into custody, and a crew and military guard of 347. *St Laurent* (Commander H. G. DeWolf, RCN) arrived about seven hours after the ship went down:

Ten lifeboats, all fairly well filled, formed a group, while the area to Windward (Westward) for two or three miles was littered with rafts and small wreckage, to which were clinging many survivors, singly and in small groups.

The ship was stopped in the centre of this area, and all boats [were] sent away with instructions to pick up individuals from the water and those with poor support while the ship was manoeuvred among the rafts and heavier wreckage picking up groups of three and four. This part of the work was painfully slow. Very few survivors were able to help themselves to any extent, and in many cases it was necessary to have a man over the side to pass a line around them and hoist them bodily inboard. Some were very heavy.[6]

St Laurent lingered for over two and a half hours, at great risk in an area where a U-boat was known to

be present, until every survivor, 859 people, had been picked up. R. P. Welland, an officer in *St Laurent*, recalled the sequel:

Covered with oil. They had been in the water about 8 hours and by the time we got back to Greenock [Scotland, early on 4 July] ... at full speed, 32 knots, 62 of them had died. I remember the number. DeWolf had told me, I was now a junior lieutenant, 'You, Welland, take 2 strong sailors, and you're in charge of Category 2 people' I said, 'Category 2, sir,' he said, 'Yes, dead.' The ship was a shambles. Within an hour of picking those people up, not one lavatory in the ship worked. The whole thing was covered by oil. People had been throwing up ... You can imagine. There were 50 people in the ward room all lying down in rows, like a slave ship, and all in pretty poor shape, and dying all the time. I and my two sailors went around and collected the people who were dead and stacked them up on the Y gun deck. That's a lot of dead people. We had no doctor on the ship but there were two doctors among the survivors. They had been in boats and they were invaluable. They must have saved 200 lives.

... We did the best we could. Everybody gave all their clothing, all the blankets, all the canvas sheets, hammock covers, to wrap these people in to keep them warm, because most of them were on the upper deck. There wasn't room for that number of people down below, so they were wrapped up on the upper deck with the ship doing 32 knots and the spray coming over.[7]

The Italian internees later sent word to Naval Service Headquarters (NSHQ) in Ottawa of their *'profound gratitude'* to *St Laurent's* people *'for all they did in their endeavour to save the shipwrecked and for the kind attentions which were afterwards accorded ...'[8]*

St Laurent shared in retribution a month later, the RCN's first major blow back at the enemy, although no one realized it at the time. The Canadian ship and the British destroyer HMS *Sandwich* joined the incoming convoy HX 60 on the morning of 4 August, about 540 kilometres off Northern Ireland, the limit to which anti-submarine escort could be provided at that time. *U-52* had made contact with the unscreened convoy the night before, sinking two ships, and was able to get into position for a submerged attack that sank a third shortly after the destroyers joined. *Sandwich*, rushing towards the stricken ship, made an asdic contact that *St Laurent* picked up as well. The two warships carried out a total of nine coordinated depth-charge attacks, of the type described in the prologue to this book, during a three-hour hunt. There was then no further contact and no other evidence that the submarine was still present.

In fact the crews of the warships doubted that they had accomplished anything, for the action of the heavy ocean swell against the hulls of the destroyers had seriously interfered with the performance of the asdic throughout the operation. As we now know from German records, the experienced *U-52* had been so severely damaged it had immediately to limp home and was out of action for four months while under repair.

U-52's fate demonstrated why convoys were so effective against standard daylight submarine tactics. Unfortunately for the Allies, Admiral Karl Dönitz, commander of the U-boat force, was a pioneer of anti-convoy tactics. He had lost the submarine he had commanded while attacking a convoy in 1918, and worked on the problem ever since, especially since taking command of the reborn U-boat force in 1936. The solution was to concentrate large numbers of submarines for mass attacks on the surface at night. Submerged, the U-boats were nearly immobile, dependent upon the limited battery capacity and slow speeds of the underwater electrical propulsion, and therefore vulnerable to the Allies' underwater detection equipment. On the surface, by contrast, the submarines' powerful diesel engines delivered speeds in the order of 18 knots, enough to outrun many of the escorts. Darkness, moreover, afforded the surfaced U-boats the protection of near invisibility. The submariners could clearly see the tall silhouettes of the merchant ships and escorts against the horizon, while the low profile of the submarine, hidden in the shadows, could not be seen from the ships. The submarine in fact would have the freedom to penetrate close to or inside the convoy, making multiple attacks at point-blank torpedo range of 1000 metres or less before withdrawing at speed. Dönitz's ambition was to overwhelm convoy defences by having several submarines striking simultaneously: the U-boats were to operate like a swarm of fast surface torpedo boats, the original concept that had given rise to small, torpedo-armed warships in the late 19th century. The ability to submerge, and thus escape, would be used only when an escort had sighted the U-boat and was closing for the kill. In the confusion of the mass submarine attack the Allied warships would not have the opportunity to mount the long, methodical hunts that were usually necessary to damage or destroy a U-boat, and the darkness would make the task that much more difficult.

Group operations by U-boats would also solve the basic problem of attacking convoys: finding them. Deployment of U-boats in individual search zones widely distributed across expected convoy routes

greatly increased the chances of one of the submarines making a sighting. It would then be the job of that U-boat to shadow the convoy, following on the surface at a distance at which the crew could see the ships but at which the Allied seamen could not see the low hull of the submarine. The shadower was to make an immediate sighting report by radio to U-boat headquarters and regular reports thereafter. Headquarters could then instruct other submarines within supporting distance to close the convoy. When sufficient submarines were lurking in the vicinity of the convoy, Dönitz would give the order for a mass attack once darkness had set in.

The German admiral had an extremely personal style of command, insisting upon regular reports from all of his boats about everything from the weather to technical problems, as well as any shipping encountered. In addition to orders, he passed along words of encouragement or admonishment, useful recent experiences of other submarines and important family news such as the birth of a child to one of the crew members. Thanks to modern radio communications, the admiral and his small, hand-picked staff of highly experienced officers were able to keep their fingers on the pulse of operations at sea, responding quickly to any significant development.

Dönitz recognized that in theory all of this signalling exposed the U-boat communications to decryption by Allied intelligence. It was well known that the British had broken German naval radio codes during the First World War. The Germans were confident, however, that there was little danger that the British could repeat this success. The German forces now used ciphers generated by 'enigma' machines. At the heart of the machine, which resembled a typewriter, were three mechanical rotors with 26 electrical contacts connected by complex wiring. Each time a letter was hit on the keyboard, the rotors moved, each at a different rate, creating entirely new circuitry and thereby selecting virtually random replacement letters for broadcast. The message could be decoded only by typing it into another machine with identical initial settings for the rotors and a system of patch cords. The German navy was the most rigorous of the three armed forces in security procedures and made the maximum use of the equipment's many variable settings. According to mathematical probability, it was virtually impossible (using any known technique) to decode messages, and a certainty that no one could do it quickly enough to interfere with the operations referred to in the messages. Dönitz had every right to be confident about the security of his centralized command system, but only for the time being.

The Germans had no choice but to adopt group tactics and tackle the convoys in the late summer and fall of 1940 if they were to sustain the 'Happy Time.' The Royal Air Force (RAF) Coastal Command was concentrating its strength over the new focal area of shipping, north of Ireland, making it increasingly difficult for U-boats to run on the surface there, where it was easiest to find shipping. Further out at sea, beyond the 360- to 540-kilometre limit of regular air patrols, the shipping was dispersed, requiring group tactics for coordinated searches. Then, too, Britain was bringing an increasing proportion of shipping into convoy, reducing the stream of independently sailed ships.

The RCN organized the most important of the new convoy series, SC, which began to sail from Sydney, Cape Breton, on 15 August 1940. This was reserved for 'slow' ships that could make between seven and nine knots. The question of convoy was always a finely balanced one that traded off lost shipping capacity, because of the considerable delays inherent in group sailings, against ships lost to enemy action. With the urgent demands for sustaining a national economy, week in and week out, shipping capacity lost through delays was every bit as serious as actual sinkings. Experience in the First World War had shown that one of the greatest problems with convoys was that they could move no faster than the slowest ship. To try to minimize the disruption to trade, the HX series was limited to ships faster than nine knots but slower than 15. Ships of 15 knots or better were seldom convoyed unless they were carrying troops, because even submarines freely moving on the surface at their best speed had little chance of catching them. Slow ships, by contrast, were the most vulnerable. The British wanted to keep them off the dangerous north Atlantic route but discovered there was no choice because of the new dependence on North America, especially for bulky items like grain and timber. Such was the confusion of that summer that the Canadians, who were to make all the arrangements for the slow convoys, found out about it only at the end of July, and by accident. Shipping control officers in the United States reported that masters of slow ships had heard rumours that they were to be convoyed, and refused to sail unless this was the case. Puzzled, the authorities in Ottawa queried the Admiralty and discovered the rumour was true. Commander Richard Oland made arrangements to expand the shipping-control staff under Captain Massey Goolden at Sydney, and the 40 merchantmen of SC 1 were assembled and sailed without difficulty.

Signalling by flashing lamp in HMCS *Restigouche.* (DHH, N-104)

HMCS *Chambly* and sister corvettes en route to St John's to establish the Newfoundland Escort Force, May 1941. (NAC, PA-115350)

The British hoped to expose the slow merchant vessels on the transatlantic run only for a few months, until stocks were built up. The inexorable demand for shipping put paid to that idea. The Admiralty's intention of keeping the slow convoys small, no more than 30 ships, fell by the wayside as well. No fewer than 53 ships presented for SC 2, and 47 for SC 3. Thus the SC convoys became one of the largest permanent series, and continued until the war's end. It also had one of the most tragic histories, for precisely the reasons the Admiralty wanted to spare the slow ships from danger. The actual speed of the convoys was often six knots or slower, and the two-week crossing at that painful pace — compared to 10 days or less for the HX series — gave the U-boats ample chance to find them and get in position for attack. As fate would have it, the RCN would be responsible for escorting the vast majority of these vulnerable convoys during the most difficult months of 1941 and 1942.

Canadian warships were also present for two of the earliest assaults on the slow ships, giving the RCN its first experience of the brutal efficiency of the U-boats' surface, night attacks. On the evening of 14 September *St Laurent* and two British destroyers joined the incoming SC 3. The Canadian ship swept astern of the merchantmen. Leading the convoy was HMS *Dundee*, the ocean escort that had shepherded the merchant ships through the whole passage from Sydney. *Dundee* was only a sloop, a 900-tonne vessel without the high speed and heavy armament of a destroyer, that had been pressed into this perilous role because no better warships were available. The British destroyers swept ahead of each flank of the convoy. The moon highlighted the ships from the south, allowing *U-48* to approach unseen in blackness from the north, get past the British destroyers and fire a torpedo spread that blew the stern off *Dundee*. It would take many months for Allied officers to appreciate fully how close surfaced submarines could come at night, and how long they could remain with almost perfect invisibility. In this case, the captain of the senior British destroyer, which was standing by the wreck of *Dundee*, assumed that the attacker had fired from out on the dark flank and quickly retreated back in that direction. He ordered the other two destroyers on a sweep out into the blackness, leaving the convoy virtually undefended for three hours. During that time *U-48* kept in close contact, striking twice more and destroying a merchant ship each time. In the vastness of the darkened convoy, spread over 50 or more square kilometres, there was no method for rapid and full communication. The senior British destroyer did not learn of the renewed attacks and recall his consorts from their futile hunt until it was too late for them to help.

The British destroyer's calls for assistance also brought HMCS *Ottawa* (recently arrived from Canada), HMCS *Skeena* and HMS *Arrow* to the scene. These three ships had just parted company with a convoy outward bound from Britain (and were scheduled to reinforce SC 3 later in the day for the run back to port), but were able to dash ahead and arrive an hour and a half after the last sinking. Commander E. R. Mainguy of *Ottawa* was, as the senior officer present, now in charge. So great was the confusion, however, that he could not get clear information as to what had happened. *St Laurent* took *Dundee* in tow for a few hours before the shattered hulk sank, while the other destroyers rounded up the badly scattered convoy. Meanwhile, *U-48*, during its withdrawal, sank a fourth ship that had fallen behind the main body of the convoy.

All four Canadian destroyers had much the same experience some 10 weeks later, but under more trying circumstances. After escorting a fast outward-bound troop-ship convoy, the warships joined the incoming SC 11 on the morning of 22 November. The weather was miserable and getting worse, with winds of over 50 kilometres per hour, seas of three to four metres in height, and deteriorating visibility. By evening the destroyers were barely under control: at the convoy's slow speed of seven knots, the long, thin hulls of the warships could not maintain course under the battering of the breakers and wind. *Ottawa* kept in position only by running at a higher speed straight forward for a few kilometres and then running straight back. Western Approaches command warned that the convoy had been located by U-boats, probably on the basis of direction-finding bearings on their radio reports. A hard turn soon after dark made a confused situation worse, as the struggling merchant ships became more scattered. *U-100*, commanded by the ace Kapitänleutnant Joachim Schepke, remained in contact and torpedoed six merchant ships in three attacks through the night. Although it was now standard procedure for a ship to fire an illumination rocket when it was hit at night, in the spray-swept blackness the escorts saw nothing of the first attacks, and in the later ones saw only flashes that were too indistinct for the destroyers' crews to discern from which part of the convoy they came. HMS *Enchantress*, the sloop that had carried out the transocean escort, may have been within 1400 metres of the submarine at one point but, although firing starshell, could not see a thing. On at

The explosion blew off the bow to a length of 10 metres and started
a raging fire: HMCS *Saguenay* after the attack by the Italian submarine *Argo*,
December 1940. (NAC, PA-114155)

… every survivor, 859 people, had been picked up: HMCS *St Laurent* rescues the passengers and crew of
the torpedoed liner *Arandora Star*, July 1940. (Courtesy of C. P. Nixon)

least two occasions destroyers were unable to respond promptly to calls for help because they had been pushed several kilometres out of position by the seas. In a particularly sickening roll, *St Laurent* subsequently lost two men overboard, only one of whom could be recovered. During daylight on 23 November, Coastal Command provided air cover, an almost certain method of forcing a shadowing U-boat to submerge and lose contact with a convoy. It says much for Schepke's determination, and for the vulnerability of the slow-moving SC convoys, that he nevertheless managed to hang on. *U-100* torpedoed a seventh merchantman that night in conditions that were as difficult for the escorts as they had been the night before.

The Canadians, however, had no monopoly on ill-fated convoy-escort missions. On other occasions, when Dönitz succeeded in his ambition of concentrating several U-boats for coordinated night attacks, losses had been far worse. On 17–19 October 1940, seven U-boats sank 22 of 34 ships in convoy SC 7.

The RCN's small flotilla, meanwhile, suffered a further tragedy at the end of a saga that highlighted Britain's perilous state. The Admiralty, despite the Royal Navy's (RN) shortage of destroyers, responded favourably to Canada's request to purchase a replacement for *Fraser*. Before any transfer arrangements could be made, one possible ship, HMS *Delight*, was sunk in a German bombing attack on Dover. That left HMS *Diana*, which was recommissioned as HMCS *Margaree* on 6 September and went into drydock on the Thames for refit just as intense air attacks on London's docklands began. Bombs struck close by *Margaree's* berth, but the ship escaped damage during its month-long stay. Then, on its first major voyage, escorting an outward-bound convoy from Londonderry, Northern Ireland, the destroyer was cut in half by one of the merchant ships on the night of 21 October. No one on the bridge survived, so it will never be known precisely what happened. It seems that the warship fell back into the convoy in poor visibility during a rainstorm. The front part of the ship, containing most of the accommodation spaces, sank immediately, with 140 of the ship's 176 personnel. Sadly, many of those lost in *Margaree* were survivors of the earlier collision that destroyed *Fraser*.

The RCN suffered its first major casualties from enemy action during the early hours of 1 December 1940. HMCS *Saguenay*, which had begun its tour in British waters in October, was torpedoed by the Italian submarine *Argo* during convoy operations. The explosion blew off the bow to a length of 10 metres and started a raging fire. Luckily the hit occurred just as the watch was changing over and many of the crew had come up from the forward accommodation. Casualties were therefore light — 21 killed and 18 injured — in view of the grievous damage. The quick, professional response of the crew controlled the fire and saved the ship, which made port with the assistance of tugs. Reconstruction of the forward part of the ship took nearly six months.

* * *

The sudden commitment of the destroyers to battle on the far side of the Atlantic was the leading edge in the transformation of Canada's maritime effort. Plans governing the speed and size of expansion, and the employment of Canadian forces, went through the shredder. So, too, did seemingly immutable assumptions about the country's place in the world and what it could do. Suddenly, the Atlantic looked much narrower than before, and not only because Canadian seamen were dying off the shores of France and Britain.

The U-boat offensive in Britain's western approaches was the starting gun in a race for more ships, more aircraft, more equipment, more seamen and more airmen. Now that convoys had become the focus of the assault, they had to be ringed by more escorts and covered by more aircraft through a greater and greater part of their long passages. This had to be achieved at least as quickly as Germany produced additional U-boats, even though the catastrophes of the spring and summer of 1940 forced Britain to begin the race far back from the starting blocks.

Canada could not avoid a leading role in meeting the gaping shortfalls. The country was Britain's largest ally, and the one best located geographically to give support. It would remain so until Hitler invaded the Soviet Union in June 1941. Although the heroic defence by the Soviets proved in hindsight to be the turning point in the war, in 1941 Germany seemed on the verge of another victory. Certainly the Soviet Union was in no position to help in the west — quite the reverse. Delivery of war supplies from North America for the Soviets was an additional strain on the Atlantic convoys. The lone struggle of the British Empire would not truly end until the United States entered the war in December 1941.

Canada had a vested interest in sustaining Britain. The chiefs of staff repeatedly reminded the government that the best guarantee of Canadian security was the survival of Britain, which dominated the sea routes from Europe to North America. The members of the government needed reminding. For all their patriotic sentiment towards the mother country,

Below: US destroyers, including USS *McCook* (number 252), arrive at Halifax in September 1940 for transfer to the British and Canadian navies. Above: HMCS *St Croix*, the former *McCook*, in December 1940. (NAC, PA-104474)

(DHH, H-255)

they were terror-stricken at denuding the coasts. The prime minister ruefully recalled his often-stated justification for rearmament since the mid-1930s: *'We had told the Commons that money had been spent on our coast defence. That they could feel security there ... Now when there came to be real danger to Canada itself, we were parting with the defence of our own country.'[9]*

King nevertheless knew that the country's exceedingly modest maritime forces were capable of carrying out nothing more than supporting roles behind the strategic cover provided by major Allied navies. We have seen that, since the First World War, Canadian security on the Pacific had increasingly relied on the United States Navy (USN). With the fall of France, and the possible early collapse of Britain, it looked as if Canadian security on the Atlantic might quickly become reliant on the USN as well. Britain's sudden change — from a leader of the Western European alliance to a besieged island on the periphery of a hostile continent — had made the still-neutral United States the main hope for ultimate victory. This was instantly clear in Ottawa. Reservations about excessive overseas military commitments began to fade as Canada witnessed France's defeat and the raining of bombs on London. It also damped down long-standing fears of US military hegemony in North America. On the dispatch of the destroyers to Britain, the prime minister quickly noted that *we should immediately acquaint the US with our position. Let them see how completely depleted we were of defence on both coasts.'[10]*

In fact, the Roosevelt administration was soon in touch. After secret military staff meetings, defence collaboration came out into the open with the establishment of the Canada-US Permanent Joint Board on Defence, on 18 August 1940. Roosevelt and King created the board simply by issuing a joint press release while meeting at the border town of Ogdensburg, New York. Both leaders liked the manner in which this informality signalled the growing ease of relations between the two North American countries. The board, which included senior officers of the armed forces of the two nations, was mainly concerned during the first months of its existence with American reinforcements that could be sent to Canada in the event Britain fell. From the Canadian perspective, cooperation with the United States was a method of drawing the Americans out of their isolationist shell. It allowed Canada to dispatch all possible help to Britain while keeping minimum forces at home, educating the Americans all the while about the full extent to which Britain was North America's best shield.

Winston Churchill, who had become prime minister of Britain in May, did not think so. He saw only a renewed emphasis on North American isolation. *'Supposing Mr. Hitler cannot invade us and his Air Force begins to blench under the strain,'* Churchill telegraphed testily to King, *'all these transactions will be judged in a mood different to that prevailing while the issue still hangs in the balance.'[11]* King, in the words of C. P. Stacey, the official historian of Canadian war policy, *'was now in the sad position of the cat who has killed a songbird and presents it to his mistress, fully expecting praise, and is bitterly surprised when instead he finds himself severely scolded.'[12]*

Both Churchill and King were edgy because critically important negotiations were then underway between Britain and the United States, and Canada was caught in the middle. On the Atlantic approaches to the United States was a string of British possessions, from Newfoundland in the north, through Bermuda off the Carolinas, to its Caribbean possessions in the south. France's collapse immediately heightened the US military's interest in acquiring substantial territory on the islands to establish bases. They would become a defensive cordon rather than potential springboards for Axis attacks. The Roosevelt administration linked this need with Churchill's plea for the 'loan of forty or fifty' USN destroyers to replace heavy losses among the RN's already short-handed destroyer force. American neutrality legislation forbade the transfer of US armed forces equipment to a belligerent, but Roosevelt thought he could get Congressional approval by presenting the destroyers as straight payment for the base sites. Such a bargain-basement price for valuable strategic territories might persuade Congress. This approach, in Churchill's view, would only strengthen US isolationism. He offered the base sites as a magnanimous gift, and wanted the US to volunteer the destroyers in the same spirit. These acts of good will would pave the way for American participation in the war. Each leader leaned upon King, who knew both of them, but he managed not to be dragged into either camp. The compromise reached by Roosevelt and Churchill in September was to treat the destroyers as payment for base sites in the Caribbean. Sites in Newfoundland and Bermuda were offered and accepted as gifts.

Destroyers for bases proved to be the first step in closer US alignment with the Allied cause. Secret British-US military staff talks in January to March 1941 (ABC, or American-British Conversations) laid the groundwork in the ABC-1 agreement for combined organization, strategy and spheres of responsi-

bility in the event of US entry into the war. There was a mushrooming of US military observer groups in Britain, and British staffs in the US. In March 1941 the Roosevelt administration's Lend-Lease Act provided virtually open-ended financial support and unlimited access to American resources to a nearly bankrupt Britain.

US collaboration did nothing to reduce pressures on Canada's maritime forces. Large-scale US rearmament did not begin until the summer of 1940. Warships and aircraft of the type needed for the Battle of the Atlantic were available in only limited numbers, and Britain had first call for these. For reasons of sovereignty, moreover, the Canadian government was determined not to be too dependent upon other nations for the defence of the country's seaboard, as had happened during the First World War.

At this same time, authorities in Ottawa greatly expanded the definition of Canadian coastal waters where Canadian forces should play a leading role. From the spring of 1940 the government treated the defence of Newfoundland as if the dominion was Canadian territory. The German airborne and seaborne assault on Norway in April 1940 caused the change. The achievement in leapfrogging forces more than a thousand kilometres to the north European Atlantic frontier, right under the nose of superior Allied sea power, instantly triggered enormous worry about 'stepping stones' in London and Ottawa, and, as we have seen, in Washington. British forces occupied Iceland in May 1940 to prevent another Axis leap. In mid-June Canada began to move 10 Squadron, Eastern Air Command's best-equipped unit, to Newfoundland Airport, located at Gander, in the northern part of the island. A battalion of Canadian troops moved into the airport to provide local security. In the words of Air Vice-Marshal G. M. Croil, inspector-general of the RCAF:

All points within a circle of 500 miles radius which has this air base at its centre are threatened. It will be seen that this includes Halifax and practically all of the economic and military targets on the Canadian Atlantic Coast. Because Newfoundland airport in the hands of the enemy would represent a threat to our trade and security we should occupy it in force at once and operate it as an advanced base for the protection of Canadian interests.[13]

The King government intended that American assistance, except in the worst case of Britain falling, should not eclipse the presence and authority of Canadian forces in either Newfoundland or the Maritime provinces. King did not offer base sites on Canadian soil to the US. Its forces would be welcome to use Canadian-built and -controlled facilities. After talks with the American services in July 1940, Captain L. W. Murray, deputy chief of the naval staff in Ottawa, reported that *'it is the expectation of the United States Navy that if they come to Canadian waters ports, local defence and A/S [anti-submarine] patrols connected with local defence will be carried out as now by the R.C.N. and under R.C.N. authority.'[14]* This was a principle enshrined in all of the subsequent Canadian-American plans and agreements developed under the Permanent Joint Board.

For the RCN the upheavals of 1940 meant that everything previously planned for the two-year expansion programme had to be done more quickly, while simultaneously a great many new demands had to be met. Base development was one of these unanticipated urgencies, one that really should have been properly addressed in the late 1930s. In the summer of 1940 improvements were still underway only at the navy's main bases, and not a great deal of progress had been made. At Sydney, Goolden's staff had not yet moved out of their rented commercial offices. At Halifax, the cramped dockyard was still little changed from when the RN had vacated it in 1904. Also, four new defended anchorages had to be established, at Gaspé, Quebec, Shelburne, Nova Scotia, and two Newfoundland ports, Botwood in the north and St John's near the southeastern tip. These were to serve as bases for local Canadian patrols, and, if Britain fell, as front-line operating bases for surviving elements of the RN's main fleet and reinforcements from the US fleet. Each anchorage required hundreds of personnel for repair and replenishment facilities and for port defences. One of the most manpower-intensive requirements was the installation and maintenance of anti-submarine nets at the entrances to the anchorages. These were woven from thousands of metres of heavy steel cable, suspended from massive floats, and anchored by enormous concrete slabs. Other substantial organizations had to be built up as well. Staffs at Montreal and Quebec City, for example, would be responsible for taking over corvettes, Bangors and other new craft as they came from the St Lawrence and Great Lakes shipbuilding yards. Trials had to be carried out, naval crews put on board, and the ships made ready for the initial passage to Halifax. There were similar, if smaller-scale, requirements for expansion on the west coast. Training facilities at Esquimalt fed personnel to the east coast, and the important British Columbia shipbuilding firms produced vessels for both coasts.

During the fall and winter of 1940 shipbuilding also began to accelerate and expand. In the words of

historian C. P. Stacey, 'the dollar sign' came off the Canadian war effort. The tight financial calculations that had governed the 90-ship programme no longer applied. The new rule was that no building slip should be empty, and therefore, as the first batches of corvette hulls were launched, the navy ordered an additional 16 corvettes and 20 Bangors. It had originally been intended that additional corvettes and Bangors — and in smaller numbers than these — would not be built until the third and fourth years of the war. The object now was to complete, by the end of 1941, more ships than had been included in the four-year programme, a goal that Canadian industry and the RCN would meet.

The most immediate pressure came from Admiral Sir Dudley Pound, chief of the British naval staff. He sent personal pleas for Canada to man as many as possible of the 50 American destroyers acquired under the 'destroyers for bases' deal. The RN was desperately short of manpower. Admiral Nelles offered to supply crews for four, but warned it would not be easy. The RCN was lacking in most of the technically expert personnel required: *'competent engineers, higher gunnery and higher torpedo ratings.'*[15] Pound persisted. The RCN agreed to take six destroyers, and ultimately a seventh. Yet further calls for help followed. The 10 corvettes building in Canada for the Admiralty had been given top priority and were completed in the fall of 1940. The RCN agreed to provide skeleton crews to deliver the vessels to the United Kingdom, giving the men experience and an opportunity to take courses at RN schools before their early return to Canadian service. The crews never did leave the ships, for the Admiralty asked the RCN to take over these 10 vessels as well.

These unheralded demands for a total of some 1500 seamen tipped the RCN into a training crisis. By May 1940 the navy had a total of 6528 personnel on active service, as compared to 2673 in late September 1939, but this initial expansion was easier than had been anticipated because over a third of the additional personnel were merchant seamen and former naval personnel who had unexpectedly come forward on the outbreak of war. These men were accordingly entered as temporary, hostilities-only members of the RCN (that is, the regular force) in the case of those with earlier service in the regular navy, and the Royal Canadian Naval Reserve (RCNR) in the case of merchant seamen. The active service strength in May 1940 included 2900 members of the Royal Canadian Naval Volunteer Reserve (RCNVR), the branch for those with no professional seafaring credentials, but many of these people had

joined the reserves and received training before the war. It was only in May 1940 that the navy began to confront the problem of providing a full training programme for recruits with little or no naval or marine background. Indeed the navy had gone slowly with recruiting since September 1939, for fear of swamping the limited training facilities at Halifax and Esquimalt, which had had difficulty keeping up with the modest expansion of a few hundred personnel during the last years of peace. Beginning in the summer of 1940 those facilities were well and truly flooded, as intakes of raw recruits (all entered as members of the RCNVR) leapt from 748 in June to more than 1645 in August. By September 1940 the strength on active service was nearly 11,000, of whom more than half were members of the RCNVR for the first time. The effort was possible largely because the summer weather at Halifax allowed many courses to be conducted outdoors, while temporary buildings were hastily constructed and the city's exhibition park was taken over as additional accommodation.

Among the early residents of the bleak quarters in the converted arena were British seamen who came in groups of a thousand to take over the destroyers that the USN delivered at Halifax in batches of six or eight through the fall of 1940. The ships became known as 'Town' class in British Commonwealth service, for the RN renamed them after towns and cities in the United Kingdom that had a counterpart in the United States, such as HMS *Montgomery* and HMS *Lincoln*. Since the early 1930s, the RCN had named its destroyers after rivers, and it continued the practice with the first six ex-US destroyers it accepted, selecting rivers on or near the Canada-US border: HMCS *Niagara, St Croix, St Clair, St Francis, Annapolis* and *Columbia*.

RN and RCN efforts to bring the warships into service at Halifax were something of a circus, featuring many minor collisions and equipment failures. Although the Americans had done everything possible to make the vessels fit, the warships were old, having been constructed at the end of the First World War, and many had been laid up for years. Built for speed for the destroyer's primary role of fleet torpedo actions, they manoeuvred poorly, with a hull narrower than British designs and the twin propellers set close together. The technology, moreover, was quite different from that in British warships, a difficulty aggravated by the fact that the British and Canadian crews were short of engineering personnel qualified to handle steam-turbine propulsion plants (one Canadian ship soon burned out a boiler). All of the

Acting Lieutenant-Commanders R. P. Welland and R. L. Hennessy in
HMCS *Assiniboine*, 1944. (Courtesy of R. P. Welland)

Rear-Admiral G. C. Jones,
the Rt. Hon. Angus L. Macdonald,
minister of National Defence
for Naval Services, and Commander
E. R. Mainguy. (DHH, H-115)

Lieutenant-Commanders J. C. Hibbard,
H. N. Lay and H. G. DeWolf,
commanding officers of three of the
destroyers sent to England in May 1940.
(DHH, N-33)

ships required considerable modification for their new role, including the removal of equipment from the upper deck to make their high, narrow hulls stable enough for sustained operations in the north Atlantic.

The other part of Canada's new navy, the corvettes, which began to arrive from the shipyards late in 1940, were still less impressive as fighting ships. Commander O. M. Read, the US naval attaché in Ottawa, visited two of the first corvettes to be completed in Canadian shipyards under instructions from the Navy Department in Washington to see if the design would be a useful one for the American service. Read replied with a firm 'no': *'While this type of vessel might be one that the British had to accept, due to the circumstances confronting them, it was suitable only in a limited degree for escort and patrol work.'*[16] He reported, accurately, that early British experience in attempting to operate these small vessels as open-ocean escorts had quickly brought the Admiralty to have a larger, faster ship designed expressly for this role (this was the origin of the frigate type, which began to come into service in the RN in 1942).

In March 1941 *Westaskiwin*, one of the first corvettes to be completed at west-coast yards, visited Long Beach, California, while on passage to Halifax, and welcomed aboard a group of officers from the battleship USS *Utah*. The US officers made a detailed and prescient report. The Canadian personnel evidently spoke at some length about the wild motion of the ship in seas of any height:

Due to the short length of the ship and shape of the bow, these ships have a tendency to ride over normal swells and have the greatest trouble in a short choppy sea or in a cross sea ... According to statements of officers on board the ship has an excessive roll reaching as much as forty-five degrees in a heavy sea, and a very quick motion and a jerk at the end of the roll.

Yet the crew also reported that the ship, despite the discomfort, had ridden well during cruises off British Columbia *'in some of the worst weather experienced in many years'*. The American officers' conclusion was quite positive; all of the criticisms would be amply borne out during the next two years of warfare in the north Atlantic:

This type of vessel being new has many discrepancies to be corrected. It seems that every effort was made to keep the plans as simple as possible in order to expedite construction, however it is considered with a little extra work and expense the efficiency would have been increased far out of proportion to the time and expense now necessary for these improvements ...

An excellent vessel for convoys up to twelve knots,

except for the excessive roll it is an excellent seagoing boat, economical, and with slight improvement in the ventilating system, very livable. Use of either four inch gun or pom-pom would be impossible in rough weather as the roll of the ship is too great. The magnetic compasses are inadequate and handicap submarine triangulation to a great extent. In order to make triangulation more accurate and fast the ship should be provided with some type of gyro compasses. With the degaussing equipment and other metals on board the magnetic compasses are subject to rapid change and even then are not accurate. Also some faster means of intership communication should be provided ...[17]

The crews of the corvettes included far fewer qualified and experienced personnel than the naval staff had planned. The pool of regular-force and former merchant-service officers and ratings had been severely depleted by the need to man the former US destroyers. In most of the ships only the commanding officer and two or three ratings were from these categories; the rest were members of the RCNVR, many of whom had scarcely been to sea before. R. P. Welland, a regular-force specialist in anti-submarine warfare whom we last saw in HMCS *St Laurent*, was now in charge of a party that provided training for the newly commissioned ships:

A corvette would come up the river from some building yard like Sorel [Quebec], the crew having been shipped [up from Halifax to take over the ship] a week before. They would arrive at the working up base in Pictou [Nova Scotia]. In many cases they didn't know how to light the boiler fires. If by chance the corvette's one boiler happened to go out they weren't capable of lighting it, so ... [w]e taught those people how to ... get the boiler cranked up. From the top to the bottom we organized the ship. We had those ships three or four days and they were sent out into the Atlantic Ocean.

... The captain was usually ex-merchant marine and at least could find his way across the Atlantic. The crew had done some training and the anti-submarine ratings had had a course but they didn't know a hell of a lot. We all knew we were pushing them right into that war as rank amateurs.[18]

The RCN ships at least had some dignity to their names, which were drawn from Canadian towns. This was a successful attempt to give people across the country ties to the navy. In many cases crew members from the ships visited their name towns, and the townsfolk themselves organized supplies of warm clothing and other amenities for the crews. All British corvettes, by contrast, including the 10 built for the RN in Canada, were named for flowers common in British gardens. That said, HMCS *Trillium*

and HMCS *Mayflower* (both corvettes built in Canada for the RN and then transferred to the RCN) did have a more pleasant ring than HMCS *Wetaskiwin* (which inevitably became 'Wet Ass Queen' among the fleet) or HMCS *Norsyd* (the shortened form of North Sydney).

The Canadian government had not been entirely altruistic in accepting the ex-US destroyers in the fall of 1940. Mackenzie King, before the destroyers-for-bases deal came together, had had the naval staff approach their American counterparts to see if Canada could purchase four destroyers for the defence of the east coast. Each movement further west by German submarines and surface raiders during the fall of 1940 sharpened the prime minister's profound concern about the thinness of the maritime forces in Canadian home waters. He wanted to keep all of the ex-US destroyers there, and also to bring back the group in British waters. Angus L. Macdonald, the former premier of Nova Scotia who joined the federal cabinet in the new portfolio of Minister of National Defence for Naval Services in August 1940, tended to agree with the prime minister. Admiral Nelles, however, again persuaded his political masters that the ships could more effectively defend the country in British waters. Despite the losses of *Fraser* and *Margaree*, and the severe damage to *Saguenay*, the RCN continued to keep up the full group of four destroyers, and the government agreed to reinforce them with four of the ex-US destroyers. The first three set out at the end of November in the midst of a heavy storm that forced one ship back with serious damage. The next two arrived in the United Kingdom on 31 January and 2 February 1941. The 10 corvettes built in Canada for the RN came over with skeleton Canadian crews in groups between December 1940 and March 1941. It was at this time that the Admiralty intimated that the RCN should take the ships over permanently, to help alleviate the RN's manpower shortage.

Neither the corvettes nor the ex-US destroyers were prepared, in terms of equipment or the training of the personnel, to undertake quickly a full schedule of operations. After the ships had undergone considerable dockyard work, and the crews had had additional training, they began to enter operations in March 1941. The ships had completed just a few convoy missions when a new thrust westward by the U-boats completely changed the deployment of the RCN.

On 20 May 1941 Admiral Pound again sent an urgent personal message to Admiral Nelles. The time had come to provide convoys with anti-submarine escorts in the western part of the central Atlantic so

that they would have protection against U-boat attack through the whole of their passage. Within 24 hours, the Canadian naval staff agreed that St John's, Newfoundland, would be the best base for the new escort force, and undertook to send all 12 of the RCN corvettes that were ready for service (or soon would be) to join the new force. The Admiralty, in fact, wanted Canada not only to supply these ships, but also to commit all 10 RCN corvettes and eight RCN destroyers then serving in British waters. In view of this large Canadian contribution — about two thirds of the whole of what would be known as the Newfoundland Escort Force (NEF) — the Admiralty nominated Commodore L. W. Murray, RCN, to take command.

Murray, like all Canadian regular officers, was well known in the British service. A short while before, he had gone to London to head a small liaison staff created in the expectation that a substantial part of the Canadian fleet would continue to operate in British waters; his work had confirmed his good reputation within the RN. The highly competent Captain Schwerdt was still in St John's and would be available to join Murray's staff. The Admiralty also sent Captain E. B. K. Stevens, RN, who had considerable experience of anti-submarine warfare at Western Approaches command, to fill the key appointment 'Captain (D[estroyers]),' the officer directly responsible for the efficiency and well-being of all the ships and crews of an escort force. A British destroyer depot ship was dispatched to St John's, where there were very limited waterfront facilities, to provide repair services to the escorts pending construction of a base.

The Canadian government readily agreed to the large new commitment and assumed much of the responsibility for the development of base facilities on a far grander scale than the modest defended anchorage scheme of 1940 that the RCN was just beginning to execute in the early months of 1941. The government's willingness to take on a huge new undertaking at St John's is not surprising. At a stroke, Canadian naval forces were being brought closer to home waters, and Canada's special interest in Newfoundland was being recognized and strengthened.

By the time Commodore Murray arrived at St John's, on 13 June 1941, Canadian and British warships had already begun the new escort run. Newfoundland escort groups accompanied HX and SC convoys to the vicinity of Iceland, where RN groups took over for the rest of the passage. After refuelling at Iceland, the Newfoundland group then met convoys outward-bound from Great Britain and escorted them across the Atlantic to the vicinity of Newfound-

land. The convoys from Great Britain were designated 'ON'; every second one was reserved for slow ships as a counterpart to the eastbound SC series.

The difficult north Atlantic crossing in the small corvettes provided a harsh school for Canada's newest warships and their green crews. They were given some help by a new organization for convoy sailings. The fast HX series sailed from Canada every five or six days, and the slow SC series only half as often. The Admiralty therefore arranged for each SC convoy to join up with every second HX convoy off Newfoundland and sail with it. This in effect reduced the number of separate eastbound convoys to be escorted by a third, and allowed larger escort groups to be sailed so that the inexperienced and slow corvettes would have the support of two or three destroyers. Something that did not make life easier was the fact that both the SC convoys from Sydney and the HX from Halifax went into the Gulf of St Lawrence and followed the difficult Strait of Belle Isle route around the northern tip of Newfoundland. The spring fog and icebergs caused collisions and groundings that sank or seriously damaged merchant vessels in several convoys. There was a reason for this harrowing northern passage: During the latter part of May U-boats had begun to probe towards the southern part of Newfoundland.

In May and June the Admiralty had come into a wealth of information about U-boat movements. Captures of documents with 'enigma' settings and components of the machine from a U-boat and two German weather ships had finally enabled British intelligence to decrypt U-boat radio traffic. This invaluable intelligence came to be known as 'Ultra,' because of its ultra-secret sensitivity: Should the Germans ever get a hint that their 'enigma' cypher was broken, they could readily implement changes that might require months or years of additional work before another break-in would be possible. Using the new intelligence with prodigious care, the Admiralty was nevertheless able to route convoys clear of German submarine groups through the summer of 1941.

CHAPTER IV

THE FIRST BATTLE AT MID-OCEAN, FALL 1941

My memory of the Battle of the Atlantic is: lack of sleep, a lot of water, some awful nights and long watches.

G. H. Hayes, describing service in the corvette HMCS *Trillium* in 1941[1]

The period of grace provided by Ultra came to an abrupt halt with the passage of SC 42, which departed from Sydney on 31 August. The convoy was a large one: 62 merchantmen sailed from Cape Breton and another five linked up from Newfoundland. Nevertheless, the ocean escort that joined from St John's on 2 September numbered only four warships — one destroyer and three corvettes. The senior officer, Lieutenant-Commander J. C. Hibbard, RCN,

in HMCS *Skeena,* was highly experienced. He had commanded the destroyer since before its deployment to British waters in May 1940. Among the corvettes, HMCS *Alberni* and HMCS *Orillia* and their commanding officers were charter members of the Newfoundland Escort Force (NEF), although that gave them a scant few months' experience. *Kenogami* had been only recently commissioned and this was its first major mission.

The small size of the escort was no accident. SC 42 was the second slow convoy, in the summer of 1941, to sail after a major reorganization that ended the practice of combining the slow series with the fast HX. One frustrated convoy commodore spoke from

bitter experience about the difficulties of the combined sailings.

The practice of combining fast and slow convoys is disliked very much. In many cases, especially in motor ships, it is difficult for a ship in the fast convoy to 'steam' at the slow speed which is the limit of the slow convoy, and she steers badly. Also the tendency is for the slow convoy to be 'driven' to the maximum speed of its weaker members, which is hard on the personnel and machinery when doing a long passage, so that they are at their worst at the time that the ships reach the most dangerous area, and tend to straggle …. Furthermore the large convoy becomes very unwieldy and difficult to manoeuvre, and the benefit of the faster speed of the fast portion is lost entirely. If large convoys are not objected to by the Admiralty, though every Commodore I have spoken to looks upon 40 ships as about the limit, it would surely be better to sail a 'slow' convoy from Sydney at longer intervals, and not mix it up with a fast one, and, during the week the S. C. sailed a longer interval might elapse between the sailings of the H. X. convoys, if escort vessels are the difficulty.[2]

The notoriously bad conditions off Canada and Newfoundland, where the convoys linked up, was a further problem: *'A ship lost in collision with other ships, or icebergs, in fog, is just as much a loss as a ship lost by enemy action, and the practice of deliberately routeing convoys through, and making junctions in, areas known to be probably foggy is inviting disaster.'*

All of these difficulties were well known at the Admiralty and thought to be important. More particularly, the staffs in London did indeed dislike large convoys, because they seemed to risk too many eggs in one basket. Only in 1942, when the Admiralty began to draw on the advice of operations research scientists, would it become clear that the vulnerability of a convoy depended not upon the convoy's overall size, but rather on the length of the perimeter, which increases only as a fraction of area. That is to say that two convoys, each of, say, 40 ships and with four escorts, could be protected nearly twice as effectively by sailing them together with eight escorts. If the 40-ship convoy covered an area of, say, 60 square kilometres, giving a perimeter of 32 kilometres, each escort had to screen a perimeter of eight kilometres. Doubling the area of the convoy to include 80 ships would increase the perimeter to 44 kilometres, meaning that each of eight escorts would have to cover only 5.5 kilometres, a zone that could be protected much more effectively than one of eight kilometres given the short range of asdic and human eyesight, the only detectors then available. The difference,

moreover, was considerably greater than these figures suggest. With eight escorts it was possible to send one, two or even three to pursue U-boats sighted, without denuding large sections of the convoy perimeter of protection against unseen U-boats approaching from other directions. This sort of tactical pursuit was crucial to blunting the submarine attack, or, if only the U-boats pursued were in firm contact, altogether preventing or breaking an assault. Such pursuit, however, was a dangerous roll of the dice if it meant stripping the convoy perimeter of cover, as occurred in the attack on SC 3 in September 1940. The dispatch of two of three escorts on a mistaken chase had left the convoy wide open to repeated attacks in which the U-boat was able freely to come in to point-blank range.

In the spring of 1941 the Admiralty had overcome its dislike of large convoys because of difficulties in deploying sufficient escorts for the huge new task of transocean screening. The alternative to combined sailings could have been no escorts for some convoys. In August, as the new organization became better established and additional warships were deployed, the Admiralty once again sought convoys of a more moderate size, and, more validly, to allow faster ships to make quicker passages and thereby increase carrying capacity. The changes implemented before the departure of SC 42 included not only the ending of combined sailings. The lower limit for the fast HX series was raised from nine to 10 knots, and the upper threshold for the slow SC series was correspondingly increased. Although this cut down on the expanding size of the HX convoys, it of course brought these nine- to 10-knot ships into the SC series. To accommodate them, SC sailings were nearly doubled in frequency, to every six rather than every 11 days. The HX cycle was lengthened slightly, from every six and five days to an unvarying six-day cycle.

The effect, seen with SC 42, was to increase the burden on escort groups and disperse their efforts to the detriment of the slow convoys. Previously there had been two eastbound convoy passages every 11 days — one combined HX/SC convoy with a double escort group, and one HX with a single group. Now there were four sailings every 12 days: two HX and two SC, all with single groups. Although group strength was to be increased from five to six warships, giving a sailing strength of five ships once refits were taken into account, this increase had not yet been achieved when SC 42 sailed. As a result, each of the warships in *Skeena's* little group was responsible for trying to seal some 10 kilometres of perimeter: the convoy, in 12 columns of five or six ships each,

Merchant ships assembling for convoy in Bedford Basin, off the north end of Halifax. (DHH, HS-1106-15)

covered an area of about 100 square kilometres. It was an impossible task, all the more so as the merchant ships inevitably fell out of order at moments of crisis when emergency manoeuvres had to be made, greatly lengthening the perimeter.

That was one strike against the convoy. The second was the weather. A gale raged for four days, bringing the convoy to all but a standstill and forcing three merchant vessels to drop out. *Skeena* had to run ahead and then back at speed to maintain steering control, much as *Ottawa* had to do in the SC 11 battle. Late on 7 September, as the storm eased, *Skeena* signalled that the convoy was three days behind schedule. Now it emerged that there might be a third strike. SC 42 was heading into a northern concentration of U-boats that was moving westward towards southern Greenland. Admiral Dönitz, although not believing that the Allies had broken the 'enigma' code, thought it suspicious that his increasingly numerous and widespread U-boat patrols failed to find convoys. One possibility he considered was that air patrols from Iceland were locating his submarines with a secret device; hence the movement of his patrols westward beyond the range of air coverage from Iceland. The Admiralty picked up indications of the change from Ultra and routed most convoys to the south of the German search areas. SC 42, however, because of the long delay in the storm, did not have the fuel for such a long detour. Western Approaches, late on 8 September, ordered the convoy to alter to almost due north in an attempt to do an Arctic end run around the submarines. So close was Greenland that *Skeena* pulled out ahead of the merchantmen to watch for the coast and avert the danger of mass groundings.

U-85, the most westerly of the submarines, sighted the convoy as it made its way up the southeast shore of Greenland and began to shadow. The U-boat made a torpedo attack that was wide of the mark at the stern of the convoy on the morning of 9 September, but was then forced down by the escorts. That night, this submarine and four others closed in. Lieutenant-Commander Hibbard's report of proceedings gives a clear sense of the rapid pace of a convoy battle, in which decisions had to be made instantly on the basis of fragmentary, contradictory information, all under a veil of darkness. Captain E. B. K. Stevens, the RN officer serving as Captain (D) at St John's, commented: *'In view of the fact that this report was drawn up during the only night in a month which H.M.C.S. SKEENA spent in harbour, its lucidity commends particular attention.'*[3] This was considerable praise for Hibbard's professionalism:

12. At 0046 [i.e., 46 minutes after midnight] on the 10th September, 1941, S.S. 'MUNERIC', #14 [i.e., the fourth ship in the first column], reported [on radio] that she had been torpedoed on the port side. Gunfire was observed bearing 220° and rockets were fired. H.M.C.S. 'SKEENA' increased speed, illuminated the port bow and port side of the convoy by starshell and carried out a search.

13. At 0054, H.M.C.S. 'KENOGAMI' reported the probable sighting of a U-boat on the surface, port quarter of the convoy [i.e., the left-hand rear part], and was ordered to investigate.

14. At 0100, H.M.C.S. 'KENOGAMI' confirmed the submarine to be on the surface … H.M.C.S. 'SKEENA' increased to maximum speed available, ordering H.M.C.S. 'KENOGAMI' to indicate her position by starshell or light. H.M.C.S. 'KENOGAMI' reported having no starshell and no light was seen by H.M.C.S. 'SKEENA'.

15. At 0102, H.M.C.S. 'KENOGAMI' reported the submarine submerged and that she was in contact. H.M.C.S. 'KENOGAMI' was informed that H.M.C.S. 'SKEENA' was closing to assist. At 0110, H.M.C.S. 'SKEENA', astern of convoy … was unable to see H.M.C.S, 'KENOGAMI'. At that time H.M.C.S. 'KENOGAMI' reported lost contact.

16. H.M.C.S. 'SKEENA' saw rockets in the convoy, turned to rejoin and ordered H.M.C.S. 'KENOGAMI' to search for 10 minutes and then rejoin, picking up survivors on return, if a ship had been torpedoed. At this time it had not been confirmed that a ship had been torpedoed, no underwater explosion having been heard by H.M.C.S. 'SKEENA' and no ship seen sinking … It was later ascertained that S.S. 'MUNERIC' had been torpedoed and sunk at this time [loaded with iron ore, the vessel had sunk like a stone, with all 63 of its crew — the probable source of the confusion here about its fate].

17. When returning to the convoy, H.M.C.S. 'SKEENA' communicated with the Commodore [in SS Everleigh *at the head of the seventh column, the middle column of the convoy] who stated that he had sighted a submarine on his port bow after the explosion and gunfire …*

18. At approximately 0248, H.M.C.S. 'SKEENA', on the port bow of the Commodore, observed rockets on the starboard quarter of the Commodore. A report was received on [radio] from #95, name not known, that a U-boat had been sighted. The report was rebroadcast to the escort …

19. H.M.C.S. 'SKEENA' increased speed to 18 knots, turned across the bow of the Commodore and proceeded down between columns 7 and 8 [i.e., right

Douglas Digby number 740, the aircraft in which Wing Commander C. L. Annis made the RCAF's first attack on a U-boat in October 1941. (NAC, N10/163-1)

One of the first Consolidated Catalina long-range flying boats delivered to the RCAF, at Dartmouth in September 1941. (NAC, PL-5952)

down the centre of the convoy]. The convoy executed an emergency turn of 45° to port. Ships in columns 7 and 8 were steering various courses and full speed ahead and astern had to be used on the engines to avoid collision [Skeena, *in other words, was desperately manoeuvring to avoid being run down].*

20. Several ships informed H.M.C.S. 'SKEENA' by megaphone that a submarine was in sight in the convoy. At least four ships of the convoy were firing at a submarine between columns 7 and 8 at this time. Starshell could not be fired because of the consequent blinding effect on the [officers on the] bridge at a time when every moment was valuable.

21. Switched on fighting and navigating lights and managed to avoid collision, although it was only prevented on two occasions by a few yards … H.M.C.S. 'SKEENA' passed ahead of #73 and was between columns 6 and 7 … when the U-boat was sighted. #74 called by megaphone that a submarine was on her starboard beam. At about 0250, #25, S.S. 'WINTERS-WYCKE' [Winterswijk], blew up, followed approximately four minutes later by #42, S.S. 'TASCEE' [Tahchee], and #45, S.S. 'BARON PENTLAND', within about 200 yards of H.M.C.S. 'SKEENA' on the starboard quarter.

22. It had been the Commanding Officer's intention to ram the submarine inside the convoy, which action would have been taken if it had not been for the intervening navigating difficulties previously referred to. H.M.C.S. 'SKEENA' turned to port under the stern of #74 … On completion of the turn, closed the position where the U-boat had been sighted, illuminated with starshell and dropped depth charges within a few minutes (i.e. as soon as the distance of the ships in convoy made this possible)…The area was searched with starshell for twenty minutes and depth charges were dropped.[4]

These depth-charge attacks were 'blind,' the churning of the water by so many ships having made asdic useless. This was yet another bad result of U-boats being able to get past a too-thin escort screen on the perimeter of the convoy. Even if sighted by one of the escorts, the submarine had only to dive under the confused waters, which offered nearly perfect cover against detection.

Another assault followed before dawn on 10 September, when all of the corvettes were occupied picking up survivors. Daylight brought only a brief respite — and a weakening of the escort. *Orillia*, astern of the convoy standing by the damaged tanker *Tahchee*, did not receive *Skeena*'s order to return to the convoy. The corvette's commanding officer, a seaman with merchant-navy background, was determined to save the valuable ship, and managed to bring it into Iceland, but at the cost of depriving SC 42 of 25 percent of its already utterly inadequate escort. The incident was telling of the inexperience of the corvettes' crews. No order to return to the beleaguered convoy should have been necessary. For fully trained personnel it would have been an automatic reflex. Nevertheless, in daylight, the diminished escort was able to make a more organized response. *U-85*, the original shadower, made a submerged run through the screen and sank a ship, but *Skeena* and *Kenogami* responded with a two-hour asdic hunt that so badly damaged the submarine that it had to depart for home.

When the wolf-pack gathered for a fresh, full-scale assault on the evening of 10 September, help arrived as a direct result of Canadian initiative. HMCS *Chambly*, one of the charter members of the NEF, was now serving as a training ship, leading newly arrived corvettes through exercises to improve on the paltry 'work-ups' available to them at Pictou. Early in September *Chambly*'s commanding officer, Commander J. D. Prentice, RCN, saw indications of the northern concentration of U-boats on the NEF headquarters situation map. Prentice, a Canadian who had served in the RN for 22 years and retired in his native British Columbia in 1934, had come out with the Canadian service on the outbreak of war. A man of tremendous energy and professional talent, he seized the intelligence about the gathering wolf-pack to try out one of his many ideas: put to sea a roving force of corvettes that could rush to the assistance of any convoy that was attacked. With the blessing of Commodore Murray, *Chambly* hurried from St John's on 5 September, in company with HMCS *Moose Jaw*, a newly commissioned corvette that had been preparing for a series of harbour exercises. The quick change of plan was a shock. As the ships encountered the gale that had held up SC 42, most of *Moose Jaw*'s crew became seasick, some incapable of getting out of their hammocks. Commodore Murray's headquarters had ordered the group to head back towards Newfoundland to support SC 43, the following convoy, when word came on 9 September of the attack on SC 42, then some 24 hours away from the corvettes. Thanks to the presence in *Chambly* of Skipper A. F. Pickard, Royal Canadian Naval Reserve (RCNR), an experienced merchant navigator who knew the vagaries of magnetic compasses and did elaborate calculations for corrections, the corvettes arrived precisely where Prentice wanted to be, about 18 kilometres in advance of the beleaguered convoy. Submarines preferred to sweep back into convoys

from ahead, to give the advantage of speed. From other directions the submarines had to overtake the merchantmen, but from ahead the combined closing speed of the convoy and the U-boats allowed them to race through the columns, picking their targets and then making a fast escape in the convoy's wake. The timing of the corvettes' appearance was as good as Pickard's navigation. Rockets and starshells from the first attack of the night of 10 September were just lighting up the sky.

Almost immediately Prentice had an asdic contact. He used the tight turning circle of the corvette to sweep in for an unconventional snap attack, before the submarine had a chance to go deeper or change course. The damaged U-boat surfaced near *Moose Jaw* and began to run away at speed. This corvette fired its four-inch gun, but immediately an over-excited member of the crew jammed the mechanism. An amazing series of events then took place, not untypical of the almost 18th-century style of close-range combat that could occur in submarine warfare. In the words of *Moose Jaw*'s commanding officer, Lieutenant F. R. Grubb, RCN (one of the few regular officers serving in corvettes):

14. The next few minutes was spent in chase … At one time four of the submarine's crew made a determined move to the after gun. As our own [main] gun was still jammed, no action could be taken except to increase speed and try to ram before they could fire. This I did, although the chance was small, but, fortunately, someone on the conning tower ordered them back. The .5 inch machine guns were bearing at the time, but when the trigger was pressed, they failed to fire. A subsequent check showed no defects, so I assume that in the excitement the crew failed to cock them.

15. I managed to go alongside the submarine, starboard side to, and called on her to surrender. To my surprise, I saw a man make a magnificent leap from the submarine's deck into our waist [the mid-part of the corvette], and the remainder of her crew move to do likewise. Not being prepared to repel boarders at that moment, I sheered off. The submarine altered across my bows and I rammed her …

16. After the impact she moved across my bows at reduced speed. The gun being cleared by that time I opened fire again. The crew jumped into the sea as soon as the first round went, and I ordered fire to be stopped. I subsequently learned that the shell had passed low enough over the conning tower to knock down the men who were standing thereon …

18. The man who I had seen jump on board turned out to be the submarine's commanding officer. He was badly shaken and when he was brought to me on the bridge appeared to be worried at the amount of light we were showing in order to pick up survivors.[5]

Chambly put an armed boarding party on the submarine to attempt to capture it. The Germans, having opened valves to scuttle the vessel, could not be forced even at gunpoint to re-enter the submarine. Lieutenant Edward Simmons, *Chambly*'s executive officer, boldly struggled through the hatch into the conning tower, but saw a wall of water rushing through the compartments below. The party and the survivors from the German crew had to jump clear for rescue by the corvettes' boats as the U-boat quickly settled; one of the Canadians did not survive.

This was the RCN's first confirmed U-boat sinking. The superb leadership and tactical innovation of Prentice, the initiative of the few qualified personnel in the corvettes and the Germans' own inexperience — this was the crew's first war cruise — had compensated for shakiness among the many novice Canadians.

The victory, effective screening work close in to the convoy by *Skeena*'s group at this same time, and the promptness with which *Chambly* and *Moose Jaw* joined the screen merely delayed the onslaught. Another seven merchant ships were sunk by six U-boats during the night of 10–11 September. The worst of the ordeal ended after daybreak on 11 September, when large-scale reinforcements arrived. Within hours, two of the British destroyers that had joined, assisted by aircraft from Iceland that were now continuously overhead, sank *U-207* as the boat tried to shadow.

Among convoy actions, only the slaughter of SC 7 the year before had resulted in worse losses. All told, 15 merchant ships had been torpedoed during the 48 hours in which the RCN held the ring alone, nearly a quarter of the total number in the convoy. Only one of the victims had been salved, the tanker *Tahchee*, thanks to *Orillia*'s outstanding feat of seamanship. Down with the ships had gone 40,000 tonnes or more of cargo. The SC convoys were still carrying the bulky items whose urgent shortages in Britain were the reason for starting the series in 1940. Among the losses were more than a thousand truckloads of wheat, an equally large quantity of explosives and the chemicals required to manufacture explosives, enough timber (millions of board-metres) to build barracks for several thousand troops, and enough steel and high-grade iron ore to build several destroyers. Lost with the ships were over 160 merchant seamen, most of them in the iron-ore laden *Muneric* and the explosives-filled *Empire Crossbill*; the cargoes had doomed the entire crews of both vessels.

(NAC, PA-200132)

(NAC, PA-20014)

(NAC, PA-200133)

(NAC, PA-200118)

(NAC, PA-200127)

In a typical convoy mission during the winter of 1941, HMCS *Saguenay*, covered in ice, comes into St John's and puts to sea with the eastbound SC 60.

(NAC, PA-200125)

(NAC, PA-200119)

(NAC, PA-200128)

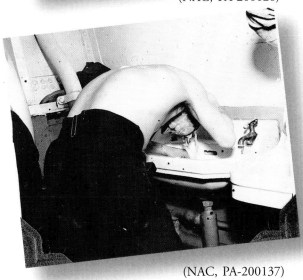

(NAC, PA-200137)

(NAC, PA-200124)

Saguenay arrives in Iceland and sails only two days later, escorting westbound ON 52.

Only two of the other ships suffered substantial loss of life, 10 men or more, thanks to the courageous rescue efforts of at least five of the merchantmen and the corvettes. The corvettes alone were crowded with a total of some 250 survivors, in addition to 35 German seamen from *U-501*. When *Orillia* began to tow *Tahchee* back to Iceland on 10 September, the little corvette was crammed with over 90 survivors from that and two other ships. A heavy price had been paid for this life-saving work by the escort. During the final attacks on the nights of both the 9th and the 10th, the escort screen had been reduced to *Skeena* alone because all of the corvettes were picking up survivors. That was not Hibbard's intention. He had meant for the corvettes only to screen merchant ships as they did the rescue work. Unsurprisingly, given the fact that cumbersome cargo vessels straggling in the wake of a convoy surrounded by U-boats were sitting ducks, several of the vessels pressed on when they saw that corvettes were at hand to save the survivors. The real answer would be to have specially equipped rescue ships fitted for swift recovery of men from the water, as the British had begun to do earlier in the year, but none had been assigned to SC 42.

Probably the fairest assessment of the convoy battle came from Captain Stevens at St John's. *'This is an appalling tale of disaster, but I feel that it is impossible to criticise any single action of the Senior Officer, Lieutenant-Commander J. C. Hibbard, R.C.N.; on the contrary I consider that he handled what must have appeared to be a hopeless situation with energy and initiative throughout, probably thereby averting worse disaster.'*[6] The last statement was unquestionably true: The small escort had responded effectively to several of the attacks, and in so doing destroyed one submarine and knocked another out of the battle. Stevens and the other officers in Commodore Murray's headquarters could well have claimed some of the credit for their support of Commander Prentice's inspired idea that had resulted in RCN reinforcements arriving a critical 12 hours before warships could reach the scene from Iceland.

What has to be kept in mind is that the outnumbered escort showed initiative throughout the nearly continuous 48-hour battle, even though the crews had already been exhausted in the four-day gale. W. H. Willson, then a young officer in *Skeena*, clearly remembered the paralysing fatigue over 40 years later:

I was so God damn exhausted I could hardly think straight … I'd been up for the first [watch, 8 pm to midnight] and the middle [midnight to 4 am] and I had to go on the morning [4 to 8 am] and I'd probably have to get up for an alarm, at nine o'clock [that same] morning. A series of sinkings and continuous ringing of that bloody *bell. Get out of your cart and come up. People don't realize there is a point at which you cease to function with any rational approach at all. You're just going through the motions and that's what you can do to a crew if you take them and put them at action stations, run them around for an hour, send them below, twenty minutes later call them up to action stations again: and that's how fast ships were going up, one goes up here, one goes up there. By that time you had submarines in the middle of the fleet, firing out in all directions.*[7]

Such was the strain on Lieutenant Grubb, who was making his first cruise in command and with a nearly completely inexperienced crew, that he had to be hospitalized when *Moose Jaw* reached Scotland: *'For some days I had been suffering from acute pain in my chest and stomach and was unable to keep down any food.'*[8]

The people who most appreciated the RCN's efforts were the masters of the ships in the convoy, very experienced mariners not easily given to praise. When SC 42 reached Lockewe, Scotland, on 17 September, they 'unanimously and spontaneously' asked the naval control service officer there to pass word directly to the commander-in-chief, Western Approaches, of their *'appreciation of the work of the escort vessels in endeavouring to protect Convoy S.C.42 against the heavy and concentrated attacks made on the Convoy by the enemy.'*[9]

* * *

One thing the battle had demonstrated beyond question was the inadequacy of a four-ship screen. Emergency measures scraped together additional escorts for the slow convoys following SC 42, but refits could be delayed and schedules tightened for a few weeks at most. Where were the warships going to come from to sustain the increased effort? It was a tricky question, not least because the whole Allied organization for the Battle of the Atlantic was undergoing a fundamental change.

The Americans had come in. The United States Navy (USN) took charge of the area west of Iceland to allow the Royal Navy (RN) to concentrate in the eastern Atlantic. Beginning with HX 150, which sailed from Halifax on 16 September, the USN escorted all the fast convoys as far as the waters on the longitude of Iceland (26 to 30 degrees west), where they met British escort forces. The Admiralty handed control over convoy routeing to the west of Iceland to the Navy Department in Washington, although the Admiralty, with its more complete intelligence, continued to make 'recommendations' that the American

staff almost invariably followed. The commander-in-chief Atlantic Fleet was Admiral Ernest J. King, USN, a brilliant officer who had made so many enemies by his uncompromising, even brutal, manner that he was saved from retirement only by Roosevelt's recognition of his ability. The president, who had been undersecretary of the navy during the First World War and still regarded the navy as his preserve, had personally selected King to handle the difficult situation in the Atlantic. King delegated north Atlantic escort to commander Task Force 4 (from January 1942, Task Force 24), Rear Admiral L. E. Bristol, USN, a highly regarded but more pleasant officer from South Carolina, who flew his flag at the US base still under construction at Argentia, Newfoundland.

The USN exercised 'coordinating supervision' over the Royal Canadian Navy (RCN) escort forces in accordance with the terms for Anglo-US cooperation worked out in the American British Conversations early in 1941 (the ABC-1 agreement). This meant that the USN's direction, exercised through Bristol, would be limited to telling Commodore Murray when and where escort groups were required. It would be entirely up to Murray to assign the groups, which would remain under Canadian control for all other purposes, including maintenance, the provision of crews and training.

None of this had been foisted on Canada. As soon as Roosevelt intimated that he might be willing to have American warships carry out convoy escort, the RN and USN had begun to make arrangements in which they consulted the Canadians. Early in July, the naval staff in Ottawa quickly recommended approval, and the prime minister immediately agreed. Aside from the desperate need for American assistance, the ready Canadian cooperation is not surprising. The command arrangements with the USN would be virtually identical to those that Canada had worked out with the RN in order to ensure respect for Canadian sovereignty and the distinct national status of Canadian naval forces. Interestingly, the safeguards for the autonomy of RCN forces, although so similar to Anglo-Canadian practices, originated in the principles the US Chief of Naval Operations, Admiral Harold R. Stark, had 'insisted' upon for his own navy from the beginning of the ABC meetings. At that time it had seemed that the main German offensive would continue in European waters and Stark was set on *preventing the distribution of US naval forces amongst the various units of the British Navy in British Home Waters.'*[10] The US Navy was treating the RCN as they themselves wished to be treated.

From the beginning of the negotiations in the summer of 1941 the Americans made it clear they wanted the full Canadian escort force to remain in Newfoundland to look after the SC convoys. This the Canadian government and the navy were always willing to do. In late August, the British and Americans asked the Canadians themselves to confirm the commitment they were prepared to make. The naval staff in Ottawa explained quite fully:

We have thirteen destroyers of which eight are long leg [i.e., long range] and the only ones really suitable for the Newfoundland-Iceland escort. These ships will form the destroyer section of C.C.N.F.'s force [Commodore Commanding Newfoundland's force]. At the same time it is necessary to maintain a small destroyer force at Halifax for the local escort of battleships and valuable ships of over fifteen knots speed, a commitment corvettes cannot fulfill.

We estimate that about one third of the destroyer force will be continuously out of action for refit and repairs — Western Approaches had 50% out of action during the last winter — and at the present moment only eight of our thirteen are in operation. From this it will be seen that we can give nothing more in destroyers.

The corvette situation is as follows: C.C.N.F. has a total of approximately twenty-five Canadian Corvettes under his command for ocean A.S. [anti-submarine] escort duties and I am prepared to keep this force up to its present strength.

We are quite prepared to accept the responsibility of providing A.S. escort for S.C. convoys with the above force. If circumstances warrant, the corvette force may be increased but this would entail weakening of other R.C.N. dispositions and can only be decided on after an appreciation of the situation existing at the time...'[11]

Commander O. M. Read, who had recently served as the US naval attaché in Ottawa, advised the navy department that there would be no difficulty dealing with the RCN. He spoke well of the senior officers ('*They are active, capable and good companions'*), but warned of '*one weakness — common to all ... they are afraid US–UK activities will shove the small growing new Canadian Navy off to one side.'* Even that, however, made them good allies: '*They are seeking all the recognition they can get and are willing to work to any limit to prove their case.'*[12]

Almost immediately the RCN was called upon to test those limits. The changes the Admiralty made in the SC series, which enlarged them and doubled the frequency of their sailing, do not appear to have been discussed in the negotiations with the Americans. The full extent of the increased effort required to protect the slow convoys became apparent only with

the attack on SC 42, well after negotiations had been concluded and precisely when the USN was struggling to take over the HX series. The USN had taken the Canadian willingness to continue its part of the NEF for the SC convoys as a blanket commitment to take care of that series.[13] From the Americans' point of view, Canadian and British agreement after the battle for SC 42 that the escort of the slow convoys had to be doubled in strength was purely an internal Commonwealth matter. Admiral King, to whom the Canadians appealed at least twice for help, did not believe his forces could keep up with more than the HX series. Although the American escort groups were made up entirely of destroyers, King, the consummate professional, was acutely aware that even the best warships and personnel could not overnight be catapulted from a peacetime basis to flat-out war operations in a demanding new role quite different in many respects from normal employment for destroyers. Admiral Pound in London professed to be mystified as to how the increased needs for the SC series had slipped through the cracks. *'We had expected,'* he signalled to Nelles in mid-September, that when the USN began escort operations

we would be able to withdraw all R.N. escort ships from Newfoundland and use them to augment escorts in Western Approaches area and also for Sierra Leone convoys which are very thinly escorted at present.

It came as rather a blow when we heard that the Canadian forces were to provide escort for all S.C. convoys … We had expected the U.S.A. to escort a larger proportion and that the Canadians would have been allocated possibly every other S.C. convoy.[14]

So convinced was Pound of the Canadians' obligation to keep nothing more than their existing forces at Newfoundland that he believed earlier plans to assign newly built Canadian corvettes to British waters still held good.

The RN, for its part, left five destroyers and seven corvettes in the NEF. At least half of these ships were unavailable, however, because of refit or unforeseen major breakdowns, especially among the destroyers, which were trouble-ridden ex-US 'Towns.' The Canadians, meanwhile, stripped corvettes from the meagre forces at Halifax and Sydney to reinforce Newfoundland. As the last 20 corvettes of the 64 ordered in the first 1940 programme completed during the latter part of 1941, they were also sent to Murray's command. These measures more than doubled the RCN's commitment. In short, despite the arrival of American help on the mid-ocean run, the crisis of the SC convoys compelled the RCN to continue to rush recently commissioned ships into intense operations.

Tragedy continued to haunt the SC series. Although evasive routeing of convoys around U-boat concentrations on the basis of Ultra intelligence continued to be a brilliant success, SC 42 proved to be the beginning of a worrisome development. So many U-boats were now at sea that it was becoming trickier to find safe routes in time to direct convoys clear of danger. Delays of a day or two in discovering periodic changes in the settings on the 'enigma' machines could prove fatal. At the same time the many submarines now on passage to and from patrol areas were making chance sightings of convoys that had in fact been routed clear of the patrol areas assigned by U-boat headquarters.

The slow speed of the SC convoys allowed the Germans to take the greatest advantage of these opportunities. After a chance sighting of convoy SC 44 west of Greenland, five U-boats sank four merchantmen and the corvette *Lévis*, the first Canadian warship to be lost to enemy action, on the nights of 19 and 20 September. This was another large convoy of over 60 merchant vessels, with a small escort: the British 'Town' destroyer *Chesterton* (Senior Officer), the Free French corvette *Alysse*, the British corvette *Honeysuckle* and three Canadian corvettes — *Agassiz* and *Mayflower* in addition to *Lévis*. The first warning of danger was the explosion of a torpedo in *Lévis*. It hit about three metres back from the stem, in the stokers' mess, killing almost all of the occupants. The captain, dazed by the explosion, precipitately ordered abandon ship. Remarkably, much less experienced junior officers and a group of ratings seized the situation. They remained to search the smoke- and steam-filled compartments for injured survivors, and to shut down the boilers and set the depth charges to 'safe' to prevent explosions should the ship begin to settle. *Mayflower*, already noted as one of the best of the Canadian corvettes, took the damaged escort in tow. Next day, however, the damaged bulkheads gave way. *Lévis* slipped under the sea. The officers who investigated the loss were shocked to discover yet another shortcoming of Canada's hastily built corvette fleet: the ships had not been supplied with damage-control equipment, especially the timbers needed to shore up bulkheads, and the crews had received no training in damage control.

A delay in finding changed German 'enigma' settings resulted in SC 48 being intercepted by a large pack of U-boats south of Greenland on 15 October. The original escort — the Canadian 'Town' destroyer *Columbia*, four Canadian corvettes, and a British and Free French corvette — was rapidly and massively reinforced on 16 October. This did not, however, halt

The first warning of danger was the explosion of a torpedo in HMCS *Lévis*: the corvette sank soon after these photographs were taken. (Courtesy of Ken Macpherson)

the attacks, as had happened in the case of SC 42. Losses included nine merchant ships, a British destroyer and corvette, and severe damage to the US destroyer *Kearney*, which produced the first American casualties in the Battle of the Atlantic.

Columbia, under the command of Lieutenant-Commander S. W. Davis, RCN, a regular RN officer who had retired in Canada and answered the call in 1939, had not reached the convoy until daylight on 15 October, after the first attacks. Because destroyers did not have the endurance for the full slow-speed crossing, extended as it was by evasive routeing, they often departed St John's a day after the rest of the escort. Steaming direct at economical speed to conserve precious fuel, the destroyers then joined the convoy as it neared the danger area, thus reducing the risk that extra steaming in the event of an attack would drain the tanks dry. In *Columbia's* case, bad weather and diversions of SC 48 as the shore authorities desperately tried to keep it clear of the large number of submarines prevented the destroyer from making contact until four days later than intended. As the destroyer neared, the crew sighted *U-553*, the U-boat that had inflicted heavy losses the night before, in the distance on the surface. The destroyer did not open gunfire, so as to get as close as possible. After the submarine dived, *Columbia* dodged a torpedo and made depth-charge attacks. The warship did not linger for an extended hunt. Davis correctly broke off to take charge of SC 48's beleaguered corvettes, but the hurried attacks on *U-553* were more effective than was realized at the time. In the words of Kapitänleutnant Karl Thurmann, the U-boat's commanding officer, *'I quickly go to great depth. 3 depth charges in a very tight pattern land [directly above the plunging boat]. Everything that can be knocked out is.'*[15] The damage proved to be superficial, but the submarine had to lay low while making repairs and was unable to regain contact with the convoy for a full 24 hours.

No one could have known how well the Canadian destroyer had done, but the travails of HMCS *Shediac*, a fifth corvette assigned to SC 48, were clearly evident. On 10 October, SC 48 had altered course at night and left the Canadian warship behind. The corvette had not picked up the course change signal because its communications equipment was incomplete and faulty. These problems made it impossible for *Shediac* to rejoin the convoy. Another corvette, HMCS *Baddeck*, performed well throughout the SC 48 battle, but its crew was in an agony of fearful anticipation all the while because of serious defects in the engine, the result of errors in construc-

tion, that could have caused a complete breakdown at any time. The ship was subsequently out of action for months when the problem proved to be beyond the limited facilities at Iceland and St John's: the machinery had to be virtually rebuilt at Halifax.

Faulty construction very nearly brought the loss of the corvette HMCS *Brandon* only a week before *Baddeck's* ordeal. *Brandon*, under the command of Lieutenant-Commander J. H. Littler, RCNR, was in company with the escort group for SC 46, having broken off for Iceland after turning the convoy over to British escorts for the eastern part of the voyage. As Littler recalled:

It was quite dark at 1600 and an easterly gale was brewing with the scud beginning to fly. As a squall of sleet swept across our group I received an urgent message from the chief engineer to the effect that we must stop immediately since the engine room was being flooded from a crack in the main injection piping [that brought in seawater for distillation and use in the boilers; in fact the problem originated with a badly fitted joint in the system]. So I gave the order and then tried to raise the ships which were on our starboard beam. We failed to get an answer before they were out of sight … The water was by now up to the main bearings [of the propeller shaft], and the auxiliary lighting and all pumps had failed. All hands were ordered to the [manual] pumps and also to form and operate a bucket chain… We were now lying beam on to a steep and vicious sea, but the ship was behaving splendidly, although sorely pressed over with the force of the gale …

The following 36 hours was a serious fight for life … At first the water gained; then we had a controlled level which slowly dropped to the point when the chief engineer could go underwater and find the crack in the great copper pipe … Now the spare bits of piping which [the chief engineer] had … collected in various dockyards came into their own. The leak was temporarily fixed so that we could concentrate on getting underway. By then a full gale was blowing, with sheets of spray covering the ship to the funnel top and masthead …

… I rather wondered at the way we were greeted on arrival in Valfjord [in Iceland]. Everyone was distinctly pleased to see us which was a bit unusual for our little ship. It transpired that we had been reported missing, and when Coastal Command aircraft could not find us … we had been presumed lost through enemy action … When I related the story of our experience to [the officers of the repair ship] Hecla who had seen the miracle worked by my valiant CERA [chief engine room artificer J. C.] Griffiths, congratulations were the order of the day; subsequently he was awarded a well-merited 'Mention in Dispatches.'[16]

The ship had been saved by the initiative and talent of a man who only months before had been a civilian with no marine experience. In Littler's words:

This small Welsh-Canadian, aged 55 or so, CERA Griffiths, had been the chief engineer of the Hamilton Power Company of Ontario, and his two sons were officers in the Canadian Army. Not to be outdone, and scorning a commission since it would have meant a shore job, he joined the Navy as an engine room artificer ... In the early days, I seldom saw Griffiths but that he was lugging aboard some salvaged piece of piping, or pieces of machinery which he felt could be put to good use ...[17]

Before Commodore Murray's command had a chance to recover from the battles between Greenland and Iceland, a new menace rapidly appeared much closer to home. Dönitz, during the last two weeks of October, dispatched four U-boats to watch off the Strait of Belle Isle. British and Canadian radio intelligence soon detected the deployment, and the departure of SC convoys was switched to the south, around Cape Race. Meanwhile, the Royal Canadian Air Force (RCAF) in Newfoundland launched a heavy schedule of patrols from Gander and Botwood, while rushing into operation a newly built airfield at Torbay near St John's. At least two of the U-boats were forced down by the appearance of aircraft.[18] In one case the air crew, flying a Digby from 10 Squadron at Gander, sighted the submarine. They made Eastern Air Command's first attack in which the presence of a U-boat can be confirmed.

I turned to Redman who was in the navigator's seat behind me, pointed and said: 'That's a submarine.' He jumped up, looked over my shoulder and said: 'It sure is.' He practically flew into the second pilot's seat as I told him to put the engines into 'manual rich.' At the same time I reached down and jerked open the bomb doors with the pilot's emergency release handle. As Redman adjusted the mixture I increased the boost and r.p.m. on the engines. The engines gave a slight cough and I looked to see that Redman in his excitement hadn't put the mixture into 'idle cut-off' position. When I looked up again I couldn't see the submarine. I yelled 'where is it?' and he pointed ... Only its conning tower was visible and it disappeared into a wave as I watched. The vortex of its dive was plainly visible and the shadowy darkness of its hull showed for a few seconds. As the vortex and bubbles built up towards the east I was able to decide what had been troubling me all along — the direction it was moving and therefore at which point to aim in the attack.

By this time, which I should judge to be 20–30 seconds after first sighting, we were in a 30–40 degree dive as I turned to the left ... to make a quartering astern attack. Remembering to aim short and ahead and estimating a six-second interval between release and detonation, I released the bombs in salvo, by means of the pilot's emergency release, when at a little less than 300 feet indicated on the altimeter ... The strong wind ... had caused me to undershoot somewhat.[19]

The bombs did not detonate. At some point in the long flight a member of the crew had set the weapons to 'safe.' As the official historian of the RCAF observed, this lapse was symptomatic of the difficulties under which the command was still struggling to establish itself. No 10 Squadron, like all the others on the east coast, suffered chronic personnel shortages and constant turnover of available personnel as experienced air crew and staff were transferred to form new units and carry out special duties such as the ferrying of aircraft and testing of new equipment. Training in the maritime role, moreover, was still carried out within the squadrons themselves. There was no 'operational training unit,' the finishing schools that fine-tuned the skills of air crews before they joined front-line units in other air forces. In this particular case, because 10 Squadron had too few crews for all its aircraft, the pilot, Squadron Leader C. L. Annis, was a member of command headquarters in Halifax who happened to be visiting. He volunteered to help with the big push, and was thus flying with a crew unknown to him. The error with the bombs was precisely the sort of lapse in detailed procedure that thorough training and highly developed teamwork among crews should have made impossible. Soon after the attack, the weather closed in and grounded aircraft for several days; this was a pattern that would become all too familiar during critical moments when the enemy was within reach.

As SC 52 made its way along the supposedly safe route past Cape Race on 1 November, British intelligence realized with horror that a large pack of U-boats was approaching closely from the east. One of the periodic delays in discovering new 'enigma' settings seems to have been responsible for the slow discovery of this major German movement. The Admiralty staff ordered an emergency change in course to the north. Contact had already been made by one of the boats from the Strait of Belle Isle, which had moved south in search of better hunting. On the night of 2 November the convoy came under attack, losing two steamers. Soon after, the US Navy Department and the Admiralty agreed it was hopeless for SC 52 to continue, having been fixed by a large concentration of submarines at the very outset of its voyage. SC 52 received orders to make for the Strait

of Belle Isle, now clear of submarines, and to return to port. The U-boats destroyed another two merchant vessels, and two others were subsequently lost in groundings in the straits. This was the only transatlantic convoy of the war that was forced back to port by enemy action.

HMCS *Ottawa* in the fall of 1940. Clockwise from top left: Signalman William R. Acheson; ratings in their mess deck; the ship's company; officers in the ward room; Commander E. R. Mainguy.

(DHH, HS-6492)

(DHH, R-614)

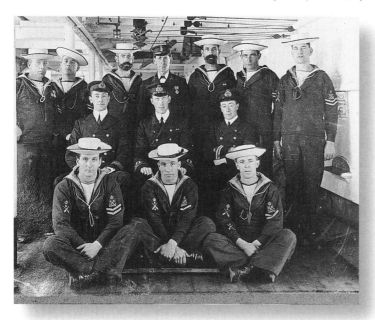

(DHH, 0-4430)

(CFPU, PMR 73-150)

The long struggle for maritime forces. Clockwise from top left. Future leaders on the Royal Naval College of Canada soccer team, 1913: Richard Oland is third from left, rear row; H. E. Reid is second from right, front row; C. R. H. Taylor is far right, front row. A boy seaman and a stoker in HMCS *Niobe*, c. 1911. The Quebec City division of the RCNVR on weekend training at Camp Valcartier, 1937. The instructional staff in *Niobe*, 1910.

The long hull was knife-like … The crew … had to be squeezed [in]: HMCS *Patriot* and its people during the 1920s. (DHH)

(DHH)

(NAC, PA-104481)

(NAC, PA-105573)

(DHH, 0-6488)

(DHH, S-90)

(DHH, WRN-172)

Staff officers. Clockwise from top left: Captain Richard Oland and his funeral in Halifax, September 1941; Captain Massey Goolden; Commander F. L. Houghton; Captain E. S. Brand (seated) and Commander H. D. Simonds, RN.

(CFPU, PMR 92-548)

(CFPU, PMR 90-193)

(NAC, PA-179887)

(CFPU, PMR 83-382)

Ships' officers. Clockwise from top left: Lieutenant-Commander D. W. Piers; Lieutenant Alan Easton; Lieutenant-Commander W. H. Willson (top right) and the officers of HMCS *Kootenay;* Commander J. D. Prentice.

(CFPU, PMR 77-380)

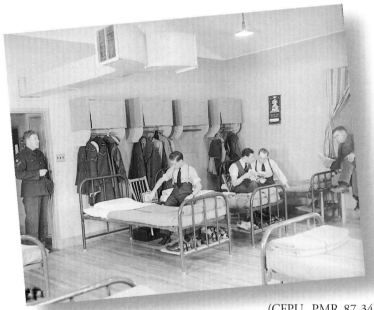

(CFPU, PMR 87-34)

(NAC, PL-21786)

(CFPU, PMR 77-177)

Eastern Air Command. Clockwise from top. A Lockheed Hudson escorting the Bay of Fundy ferry *Princess Helene.*
Wing Commander C. L. Annis. Squadron Leader N. E. Small. Airmen's quarters, RCAF Station Sydney, Nova Scotia.

HMCS *Clayoquot*, one of the stalwart Bangor minesweepers pressed into long-term escort duty on the Atlantic coast and in the Gulf of St Lawrence. (DHH, E-1198)

Clayoquot sinking after an acoustic torpedo attack by the schnorkel U-boat *U-806* off Halifax, Christmas Eve 1944. (CFPU, PMR 83-305)

An acoustic torpedo from the schnorkel U-boat *U-1223* blew the stern off HMCS *Magog*, deep in the St Lawrence estuary, October 1944. (NAC, PA-153486)

Crew members in *Clayoquot* when the ship first commissioned on the west coast in 1941. (DHH, West Collection)

What a power of the elements — and the God that made *them:*
HMCS *Trillium,* September 1943. (NAC, PA-37474)

In the officers' wardroom of HMCS *St Laurent,* February
1941: F. C. Frewer, R. Balfour, C. P. Nixon, D. H. Fairney.
(Courtesy of C. P. Nixon)

Stokers' mess, HMCS *Sherbrooke,* 1941.
(PA-200123)

Ship's company, HMCS *Chambly,* 1941.
(NAC, PA-11535)

CHAPTER V

THE BATTLE ON CANADA'S SHORES, FALL 1941 – SPRING 1942

I am very gravely concerned about the running of the ships of the Newfoundland Escort Force, particularly the amount of sea-time, relative to rest periods, which is being imposed on the corvettes …

Recently corvettes have escorted convoys Eastbound for sixteen days and then after between four and eighteen hours in harbour have returned with Westbound convoys, this voyage lasting between fourteen and sixteen days. This is quite unacceptable.

There seems to be a strong tendency to estimate the endurance of these small ships principally on their fuel carrying capacity. This is not only fallacious, but positively dangerous.

The factor which will ultimately control their ability usefully to keep the sea, is that of the endurance of personnel, particularly that of Commanding Officers.

It is essential to remember … that for the most part Commanding Officers have not one other officer on whom they can completely rely; furthermore many of these ships are grossly under manned, which imposes extra duty on men who are already suffering most arduous conditions …

Unless very urgent steps can be taken … I must report that grave danger exists of breakdowns in health, morale and discipline.

Captain E. B. K. Stevens, the officer responsible for the efficiency of the escorts based at St John's, sent this strong warning to Commodore Murray on 16 October 1941,[1] the second day of the battle for SC 48. Commodore Murray passed it to Naval Service Headquarters (NSHQ), with his unqualified endorsement: *'It shows very clearly the state of affairs existing in the Newfoundland Escort Force.'*[2] Murray himself had signalled headquarters just the day before, declaring that he had to have 10 more corvettes (an increase of strength, in this type, to 59 vessels) to ease the strain on the force.

The SC 52 fiasco at the end of the month inspired still darker assessments at St John's. On 4 November, Commander J. D. Prentice, the most experienced and qualified of the corvette captains, produced a report that showed a superb grasp of what was required to fight the wolf-packs and, in the same breath, demonstrated how far short Royal Canadian Navy (RCN) corvettes fell in every category.

It is honestly believed that unless immediate steps are taken to improve the material and the training of the ships of the Newfoundland Escort Force, it will shortly become impossible to run convoys in the face of the enemy's present attacks upon these convoys west of 30° west.

The majority of the R.C.N. corvettes ... have been given so little chance of becoming efficient that they are almost more of a liability than an asset to an escort group.

The Commanding Officers have apparently been given no instruction in convoy work and little chance to train their Officers ... most of whom are without sea experience of any sort. The result is that ships are seldom in station in low visibility and are continuously losing their convoys even on moonlight nights. In many cases ships cease zig-zagging for fear of collision under conditions of weather and visibility which make it imperative that they should continue to do this for the sake of their own safety alone.

One fundamental problem, from Newfoundland's perspective, was ham-fistedness on the part of the authorities in Ottawa and Halifax in their efforts to bring new ships into service. Whenever Newfoundland ships had to go to Halifax for repairs — which was frequently, because of the limited facilities at St John's — the Halifax authorities, with Ottawa's approval, raided the vessels of their experienced personnel in order to man newly constructed ships. As Prentice put it: *'In the best ships, ship's companies arrive at a certain average state of efficiency in spite of the complete lack of sea experience or training of the personnel only because they are keen, energetic and work as a team. As soon as that team is broken up, the ship again becomes inefficient ...'*

Ships within each escort group had to be forged into a well coordinated team, and in this respect the situation was even worse because of the brutal schedule the ships were having to meet. Routine maintenance and unexpected breakdowns, which were too common among the hard-driven escorts, could be managed only by constantly shuffling ships from group to group: *'It has been impossible to keep any escort group together for more than one convoy. In most cases it has been impossible to hold a meeting of Commanding Officers before sailing. This has prevented the development of even the most rudimentary form of cohesive action ...'* Prentice sharpened the point: *'It is as though we were attempting to play against a professional hockey team with a collection of individuals who had not even learned to skate.'*[3]

Murray passed this report to Ottawa, with a more detailed one of his own. He cited the case of HMCS *Orillia*, a veteran of the Newfoundland Escort Force (NEF), commanded by Lieutenant W. E. S. Briggs, Royal Canadian Naval Reserve (RCNR), *'one of the more intelligent, experienced and trustworthy'* of the corvette commanding officers. Because of transfers at Halifax, and an injury to the executive officer for whom no qualified replacement was available, Briggs was once more the only experienced officer in the ship. He would have no choice but *'to spend on the bridge as much of every 24 hours as his constitution will stand.'*

This, coupled with the necessity of acting as Executive Officer of the ship, A/S Control Officer, Gunnery Officer and cypher staff, is more than the best constitution can be expected to support over a period of 28 days, with only a short break of a few hours in harbour in the middle.

... we are asking a lot of the morale of an inexperienced crew, to expect them to be happy, and remain fighting fit and aggressive, in a ship in which they know their safety from marine accident alone, and not from any action of the enemy, depends upon the ability of the Captains to remain awake.

It should also be remembered that this fortitude is being expected from men who have seen gasoline tankers disintegrate in five seconds, less than half a mile away from them, and who have also been through the harrowing experience of seeing men with little lights on their shoulders bobbing up and down in the water and shouting for help ...

Only the desperate operational situation which exists off our coast at the present time persuaded me to allow 'ORILLIA' [to] proceed ... She is quite unfitted to meet the enemy, and in no other Service would a unit be placed in the firing line before the officers had mastered

the use of their weapon. She has been allowed to proceed, however, because her presence will fill a gap in the A/S screen visible to the enemy, and her presence may result in saving the lives of many merchant seamen, in which case the sacrifice of the health of one Commanding Officer would be justified.[4]

Fortunately, the German high command had begun to wind down north Atlantic U-boat operations soon after the SC 52 action in early November. Over the protest of Admiral Dönitz, the priority became the Mediterranean, to support the land and air forces fighting in North Africa.

As Captain Stevens feared, however, the onset of winter storms was at least as punishing as further combat. On 10 December the destroyer HMCS *Restigouche*, in company with six corvettes, including the hard-pressed HMCS *Orillia*, sailed from Iceland to pick up the westbound convoy ON 44. Soon a gale began to build, and by the 13th it was reaching hurricane strength. The escort group abandoned the search for the convoy and 'hove to' for two days, each escort manoeuvring the best it could to survive. The fabled buoyancy of the corvettes, which made them such uncomfortable vessels in even a moderate sea as they bounced over the waves, was now a godsend: '*Miraculously, the bows would rise, so that only the top of the sea would come crashing inboard …*'[5] By contrast, the long, slender hull of *Restigouche* was nearly torn apart. The commanding officer, Lieutenant D. W. Piers, RCN, still had almost every detail fresh in his memory 40 years later:

Just about dusk [on 13 December] … the wind now whistling at … 100 knots, the mast blew over … and down it came slowly. It was a metal mast, and it bent … it didn't hurt anybody … and the shrouds [guy wires] came each side of the funnel …

And on each side of the funnel there are siren wires, operated from the bridge … and these shrouds caught both of the steam sirens and they both went off at the same time with the most devilish sound you've ever heard, with the howling of the wind, and both of these sirens going madly out of tune, and shrieking … The next thing that happened to poor old Restigouche, was one of the funnels was knocked over, and salt water came down the funnel into the boilers and put out one of the boilers … But then a more serious thing happened. An enormous sea came inboard, tore one of the carley [lifesaving] floats adrift … lifted it up high above the ship … it landed on the quarter deck and as it landed it hit a hatch going down to the steering compartment, sheered [sic] off that hatch and left it open to the sea … and we had the prospect [as the steering compartment flooded] of being without steering … in

these horrible conditions. *Well the first thing we had to do there was get somebody aft. And Davy Groos [Lieutenant D. W. Groos, the executive officer] and Stew Moore [Sub-Lieutenant S. G. Moore], a great big strong fellow, they took a party down on the quarter deck [and rigged special lifelines to allow Moore to reach the open hatches and cover them with canvas] … then a big wave came and hit [Moore, driving him against the depth-charge rails] and broke his leg … The next report that came through … was, Captain we're sorry to tell you but there's some ugly noises underneath the fo'c'sle mess deck. The ammunition cases are rattling around. And they took the lid off the ammunition [magazine] up forward and found it was flooded. The pounding [of the seas] had pushed the [hull] rivets in … and there it was, filling up with water [to a depth of seven feet] … Well, there was only one thing for it … we organized the whole of the ship's company into [a] bucket brigade. The pumps were just swamped.*[6]

At dawn on 14 December, as the wind began to abate 'somewhat,' the destroyer swung about through the mountains and valleys, at the risk of being broadsided by a large wave and capsized. The dangerous manoeuvre succeeded, and the ship was running ahead of the seas, thereby avoiding further severe battering. The destroyer was now pointed towards Scotland, a fortunate turn of events and not only because of the excellent shipyards there. The crew's happy anticipation of Christmas leave in Canada had been replaced by fear that the ship might have to return to the barrens of Iceland for the festive season. *Restigouche* underwent more than two months' refit and repair at Harland and Wolff's yard near Glasgow, and did not return to service until early March 1942.

Restigouche's ordeal was only the worst case of storm damage in the winter of 1941 that knocked dozens of other ships out of action for days or weeks. Even when quick repairs were possible, the vessels became more prone to breakdowns in the harsh seas. The Newfoundland force was able to cope because Murray's earlier calls for help had brought some results. Additional RCN corvettes increased his strength in this type to 56 by early December, these including roughly 47 Canadian, three Free French and six British vessels. Meanwhile the Admiralty took account of the situation in Newfoundland in a reorganization that began in mid-December. Instead of six groups, each supposed to provide eight escorts per convoy (a figure that was increasingly honoured more in the breach than the observance), there were now seven groups, each to provide six escorts per convoy. As the convoy cycle required regular operations by six

groups, this in effect created a spare group that eased the schedule for all the others.

All the while the staff at NSHQ were examining the warnings and criticisms from Newfoundland. Senior officers agreed that the situation was *'deplorable but inevitable,'*[7] given the *'adoption of a policy of rapid expansion'*[8] of the RCN. There had been no alternative, however, a fact emphasized by the Americans' recent discouraging response to another British bid for help in the north Atlantic. The Canadian achievement had been impressive. In just over six months, from May through mid-November 1941, 42 corvettes and 13 Bangors had been commissioned. In mid-November another 12 corvettes, 18 Bangors and many smaller vessels were nearly ready for commissioning. The difficulty was that by November the entire supply of experienced seamen — the regular force (RCN) and the former merchant mariners of the Royal Canadian Naval Reserve (RCNR) — had long since been used up for key positions in ships. That left only the mostly inexperienced members of the Royal Canadian Naval Volunteer Reserve (RCNVR). Quick as the volunteers' progress had been in many cases, an attempt to catapult them into leadership positions, without further time at sea to let them integrate theoretical training with hands-on practice, would be doomed to failure. There was no choice but to continue to remove experienced personnel from the fleet to provide the principal officers, petty officers and ratings in new ships. As the Director of Naval Personnel put it, *'the Navy must still be regarded largely as a "training" Navy for the whole of the year 1942,'*[9] while the RCNVR found its sea legs. The naval staff, however, endeavoured to ensure that Murray did not in future receive completely raw new ships. Plans were to provide the newly commissioned vessels with eight weeks of basic 'work-up' training at Halifax, and then assign them for a month of escort operations between Nova Scotia and Newfoundland before committing them to the arduous transatlantic run. Less than three weeks after the naval staff informed the coast commands of the new working-up scheme, enemy action again left no choice but to rush additional ships to sea as quickly as possible.

* * *

The United States' entry into the war against the Axis powers following the Japanese attack on Pearl Harbor on 7 December 1941 gave Admiral Dönitz the opportunity he had been aching to grasp. The essence of his strategy, as we have seen, was to seek out Allied shipping where it was most weakly defended. He had been encouraged by the results of the brief operation in Newfoundland waters in the fall of 1941, and was sure there were richer targets in Canadian waters. The real prize would lie in US waters, where most north Atlantic shipping originated — and where there would inevitably be a delay before the Allies could organize defences. German efforts had previously been limited to the eastern approaches to Newfoundland for fear of precipitating further American participation in the war. That restraint was now gone. Dönitz successfully argued for limiting the effort in the Mediterranean (heavily defended waters where the U-boats were suffering losses for meagre returns) and making a push into the North American coast.

Dönitz launched two operations in the western Atlantic. Paukenschlag ('tap on the drum,' but popularized in English as 'drumbeat') included five large type IX U-boats. These submarines, designed for distant cruises, were to attack traffic off Sydney, Halifax, Boston, New York and Cape Hatteras, North Carolina. Less well-remembered today was the second operation, by six smaller type VII U-boats known as group Ziethen (presumably named for 18th-century Prussian General Hans J. von Ziethen, who played a key role in Frederick the Great's victory at Leuthen in 1757). These shorter-ranged submarines were assigned to the waters off southern Newfoundland. Dönitz's expectation was that the two groups of U-boats would not need to risk themselves in coordinated attacks on convoys. Rather, they could hunt alone, each destroying large numbers of independently sailed merchant vessels, much as had been possible during the extremely profitable 'Happy Time' off Britain's shores in the summer and fall of 1940.

The submarines laid low and did not make radio transmissions as they arrived at the end of December and the first part of January. The intention was for a large number of boats to strike simultaneously in different sectors on 13 January, and thereby disorganize the limited defences. Ultra intelligence derived from Dönitz's signals, however, revealed to the Allies the movement of U-boats towards the waters south of Newfoundland. As always, the first concern was the safety of the main north Atlantic convoys.

The weak point in the convoy system, because of the priority of the Newfoundland force, was coverage of the initial passage from Halifax and Sydney to the meeting point off eastern Newfoundland where the mid-ocean escorts joined, and where the U-boats now appeared to be headed. Since the attack on SC 52 close to Newfoundland early in November 1941, the RCN had made increasing use of the short-ranged 'Town'-class destroyers, some corvettes, and

Convoy conference: ships' captains meet for instructions before sailing. (NAC, PA-180530)

... boats were filled with corpses: after the torpedoing of the passenger ship *Cyclops* in January 1942, many survivors died of exposure. (CFPU, PMR 87-100)

Those fortunate enough to be rescued: survivors, at Halifax, of a winter torpedoing, January 1942. (NAC, PA-105675)

newly built Bangors (which stood in for Halifax and Sydney corvettes needed to reinforce Newfoundland), to provide three or four escorts for each convoy. During the second week of January this figure rose to five or six escorts per convoy. Air forces available included 37 Royal Canadian Air Force (RCAF) bombers in Nova Scotia, all concentrated at Halifax and Sydney, and a total of 31 US Army, US Navy (USN) and RCAF bombers in Newfoundland, at Gander in the north, Torbay near St John's and the USN air station at Argentia in the south.

The first attack by a Paukenschlag U-boat came earlier than planned, on the night of 11 January 1942. *U-123*, on its way to New York, sighted the British passenger ship *Cyclops* about 320 kilometres south of Halifax, and could not resist torpedoing such a choice target. Although the ship went down quickly, all but two of the 181 people aboard got away in lifeboats and on rafts, and the radio operator succeeded in dispatching a distress signal. The Bangor HMCS *Red Deer*, then on patrol off Halifax, responded but could not reach the scene until early the following afternoon. Mercifully, calm weather had kept the rafts and boats within close proximity of one another so that the minesweeper could quickly locate them. At least two of the boats were filled with corpses, however: 97 people had died of exposure.

While *Cyclops*'s survivors awaited rescue on the morning of 12 January, an RCAF Bolingbroke on a routine patrol from Sydney sighted another Paukenschlag boat, *U-130*, about 50 kilometres from that port in the Cabot Strait. The submarine dove in time to escape the two 125-kilogram anti-submarine bombs, but the commanding officer, Kapitänleutnant Ernst Kals, was shaken. This incident, and follow-up air searches from Sydney, brought him to report 'heavy air cover.'

Kals left the strait for the route between Cape Breton and Cape Race and, on the night of 12 January, sank the steamers *Frisco* and *Friar Rock*. Neither ship was able to broadcast distress signals. A passing schooner rescued one boat with six of *Frisco*'s survivors on 14 January; the second boat, with nine men aboard, was never found. One of *Friar Rock*'s boats had capsized soon after launching, dooming the occupants. The second boat was not found until 17 January, when it was sighted 200 kilometres southwest of St Pierre by the destroyer HMS *Montgomery*. There were 12 frozen corpses on the bottom of the boat and seven men still living after the four-day ordeal.

The Captain gently brought the destroyer alongside and two seamen climbed down into the boat to secure lines around and to assist in getting the unconscious survivors aboard. One poor fellow … was naked from the waist down and although still alive was coal black with frostbite, ice even covering his legs and lower abdomen.

The … men were taken below, placed upon mattresses on the wardroom deck, where their clothing was cut away and themselves wrapped in blankets.

As they regained consciousness from the warmth, their bodies became racked with the pains of recirculating blood … One man, the chap who'd been unclothed … never came around and died the following day in a Halifax Hospital.[10]

The Ziethen submarines had their first success on the night of 14 January when *U-552* torpedoed the freighter *Dayrose* within 25 kilometres of Cape Race. The ship dispatched a distress signal, which brought out four RCN escorts from St John's. They received support from two US destroyers and USN aircraft from Argentia, but got no trace of the submarine and found only four survivors from the ship's crew of 42. The tanker *Toorak*, which *U-86* torpedoed in daylight on 16 January, within 20 kilometres of St John's, had a happier fate. The operations office at St John's was able to divert three British destroyers and aircraft to the scene. *U-86* had departed, but *U-552* attempted to strike and was driven off by the sweeps of the destroyers while the warships shepherded the stricken tanker into port.

The RCN reacted to the sinkings in coastal waters exactly as it had done in the summer of 1918. Port authorities immediately organized coastal shipping into informal convoys and sailed them with whatever warship was available. The first informal convoy departed on 15 January, and by the end of February at least 40 had sailed between ports in Newfoundland and between Newfoundland and Halifax. Much of the burden fell on the recently commissioned Bangor minesweepers, which had been assigned for their designed role at Halifax and St John's but were becoming an integral part of the escort fleet. Later in the war, Reverend (later Archbishop) George Anderson Wells, on taking up his appointment as Principal Chaplain (Protestant) of the RCN, made a run from Halifax to St John's in the Bangor HMCS *Medicine Hat*:

The Captain … showed me to his own 'cabin' which he was giving over to me for the voyage. It was not a cabin, really, simply a cupboard with a shelf six feet long and about two and a half feet wide on which a bed was made. There was a curtain over the doorway, because it was too small for a door to swing either in or out.

Wells concluded that 'the minesweeper is the lowest form of ocean-going ship, for no craft could be planned

with less consideration for the convenience of officers and crew.'[11] Soon after, he sailed in one of the corvettes, renowned for their crowded discomfort, and found the accommodations *'luxurious compared with a minesweeper.'[12]*

The modest improvised coastal convoys supplied excellent protection, losing only one ship during the intense January operations. Other than on this single occasion, the presence of the escorts induced such caution among the submarine commanders that they did not press in close enough to make successful attacks. This effective defence was achieved even though the ill repair of many of the warships, their poorly trained men, and the difficult asdic conditions in Canadian and Newfoundland waters meant that the escorts' counter-attacks did not destroy or seriously damage any of the submarines. As the war diary of the RCN's Newfoundland command remarks, almost with surprise: *'It is realized that the escort of the coastal convoys, which is more often than not one mine sweeper only, is quite inadequate; yet as far as can be seen it appears to have the requisite deterrent effect.'[13]*

These well-conceived and prompt defence measures could do nothing to help merchant vessels already making passage without escorts, and there was an unusually large number in the western part of the north Atlantic during the last part of January 1942. A vicious storm, centred at about the longitude of Greenland, had peaked on 11 January with winds of more than 200 kilometres an hour. Several transatlantic convoys were scattered (and HMCS *Saguenay*, caught in one of the worst areas, suffered damage that knocked the ship out of action for three months). The Ziethen U-boats, although suffering nearly as much as the escorts and merchantmen, found many targets among the dozens of merchantmen that had to make their way independently in the wake of the storm. Other U-boats that were crossing the central ocean at mid-month to relieve the original members of the western Atlantic groups were able to locate and sink lone merchantmen hundreds of kilometres out at sea. By the end of January, 20 ships had been destroyed in the Newfoundland area (including *U-130*'s two victims), 15 of them west of 50 degrees west and five out as far as 40 degrees west in the central ocean.

The U-boats had little success close along Nova Scotia's shores during January. *U-130*'s two early attacks east of Cape Breton were the only ones Kapitänleutnant Kals was able to make. He did not seem to realize that the SC convoys had shifted to Halifax for the winter; the sailing of local traffic in convoy between Nova Scotia and Newfoundland also ac-

counted for his lack of success. After a heart-stopping near-approach by two escorts (the warships in fact do not seem to have sighted the submarine), Kals gratefully abandoned the bitterly cold seas off Cape Breton and headed for US waters. *U-109*, the Paukenschlag submarine assigned to the area south of Halifax, had much the same experience as *U-130*, with unnerving appearances by aircraft and escorts and little merchant-ship traffic to be seen. The submarine sank one vessel off Shelburne, and its torpedoes may have contributed to the sinking of another ship in the same area. U-boats following the original groups had more luck further out to sea, beyond Sable Island. *U-553* destroyed a tanker that was sailing independently from the Caribbean. In the midst of a gale on the last day of the month, *U-82* managed to contact a fast troop-ship convoy and sink the British destroyer HMS *Belmont*, one of the escorts. In the heavy seas the warship's consorts did not realize it had gone down. There were no survivors. Among those lost were six RCN ratings who had been serving in the ship.

The shift of the U-boat offensive into North American waters compelled the Allies fundamentally to reorganize the Atlantic escort forces. Senior commanders on both sides of the Atlantic had for months been considering how the forces and convoy routes could be rearranged for greater efficiency, to allow merchant ships and escorts to get through the hard winter conditions. The new need to build up forces on the North American coast, and assist the USN in dealing with a critical shortage of destroyers now that it was embroiled in war on two oceans, left no choice but to implement far-reaching changes quickly. The British and Canadians had already taken an important step to ease the strain on the NEF. From mid-January the SC convoys no longer made the punishing northern run towards Iceland, but followed a more direct southern route; a further advantage was that the escort groups could proceed to the British base in Londonderry, Northern Ireland, where conditions were far better for both men and ships. Soon after, senior Canadian, British and American officers agreed to integrate more closely the escort forces of the three navies, and to run all convoys on the shorter, southern route between Newfoundland and Ireland. This could be managed with fewer warships than the Iceland route, freeing some British and Canadian ships for the route west of Newfoundland and allowing the Americans to redeploy their destroyers. The initial proposals would have split off the RCN's long-range destroyers from the RCN corvettes. The Canadian service protested vehemently

and successfully at a staff conference in Washington on 22 and 23 January:

The RCN representatives [Commander H.N. Lay from NSHQ and Captain R. E. S. Bidwell from Commodore Murray's staff] pointed out that these proposals dislocated all the present operational and administrative arrangements for all types of convoys. They also pointed out the desirability of R.C.N. long-legged destroyers continuing to work with R.C.N. corvettes in the Newfoundland Escort Force, so that the present group system and training could continue, and that there should be the least disruption of the present R.C.N. arrangements for the operation and administration of the N.E.F. at St. John's.[14]

The navy was determined to maintain a prominent national presence in the north Atlantic.

In the new organization that took shape in February 1942, the US escort groups and the NEF were combined into the single Mid-Ocean Escort Force (MOEF). The most important changes were the relief of large numbers of US destroyers and the return to the north Atlantic run of substantial Royal Navy (RN) forces, available in part because the short route to Londonderry allowed reductions in the British groups that operated between Iceland and the United Kingdom. There were initially 14 groups, but needs on the US coast and in the Caribbean soon reduced this to 12. These included five British 'B' groups, four Canadian 'C' groups and three American 'A' groups, each of which was to have a sailing strength of two destroyers, or equivalent vessels, and four corvettes. Despite the national A, B and C designations there was quite a bit of mixing. The Americans had yet to build significant numbers of 'cheap and nasty' escorts and therefore provided only the destroyer component of the A groups; the corvettes were RCN. Because the RCN was short of long-range destroyers, British destroyers fleshed out the C groups. There was not enough room at St John's for the large number of additional British ships. This base remained largely a Canadian operation, as the Canadians wished, and the B groups used the American facilities at Argentia for their western turnaround.

During the reorganization all three Allied navies agreed that the shipping defences provided by the RCN west of Cape Race had to be strengthened and put on an organized basis. This was the origin of the Western Local Escort Force (WLEF), primarily an RCN commitment, which began to operate in mid-February. Until this time, as we have seen, the Halifax command pulled together as many escorts as it could to accompany SC and HX convoys to the meeting point with the mid-ocean groups south of

Newfoundland. Incoming ON and ONS convoys, which had previously dispersed to the east or south of Cape Race, had since late January pushed on towards the Nova Scotia coast, straining the limits of the escorts' fuel. Even so, U-boats had succeeded in sinking some of the ships that had proceeded independently southward towards US ports. The principal mission of the new WLEF was to provide six permanently organized groups on the scale of the mid-ocean ones to accompany the eastbound convoys to the southeast of Newfoundland and then meet up with westbound convoys, escorting them into Halifax. The RN was to provide 13 of its short-legged ex-US 'Town'-class destroyers to supplement the RCN's five ships of this type. The 30 corvettes required were to come from the existing Halifax force, the reductions possible in the RCN component of the new MOEF, and, in the short term at least, continued employment of Bangors as substitutes for the corvettes.

Continued losses to ON convoys explain the haste with which the WLEF escort cycle began to operate. The week before, on 9 February, U-boats stationed off Newfoundland sank the respected veteran Free French corvette *Alysse,* part of the escort for ONS 60 and one of the merchantmen that had just broken off from the convoy to make its way independently to Florida. In these circumstances, two of the mid-ocean escorts with sufficient fuel remaining, the corvettes HMCS *Sherbrooke* and HMCS *Barrie,* decided to keep the main body of the convoy together right through to Halifax. The convoy was less than 80 kilometres from the entrance to the port when, during the night of 14 February, one of the U-boats patrolling off Nova Scotia sank a merchant ship that had fallen back from the group. At that point the two corvettes had been at sea for 16 days, responded to U-boat warnings in the eastern Atlantic and undertaken counter-measures and rescue work after the sinkings off Newfoundland. One can practically hear the long sigh in *Sherbrooke*'s report of the recovery of survivors from the torpedoed vessel so near to the safety of Halifax.

The American-escorted ON 67 suffered much heavier losses on 24 February. In one of the few co-ordinated attacks during the first four months of 1942, a group of U-boats bound for North America combined with two submarines on return passage to sink seven ships in the convoy when it was in the western part of the central ocean, about 1100 kilometres southeast of Cape Race. Some weeks before, the Allies had lost their most powerful tool for routeing convoys clear of submarine concentrations. At the beginning of February the Atlantic U-boats

Commodore L. W. Murray (with the broad stripe on his sleeves) in HMCS *Assiniboine*, flanked by the ship's officers. (Courtesy of R. L. Hennessy)

changed from the three-rotor 'enigma' machine to a new model with four rotors that multiplied the difficulty of decipherment. The resulting blackout of Ultra intelligence for Atlantic submarine operations would last for 10 months.

Many of the escorts promised by the British for both the MOEF and the WLEF did not arrive until well into March, and the RCN had difficulty in meeting its expanded commitments. Even with reinforcements, the pressure did not ease. Requirements for the defence of shipping in Newfoundland, Canadian and northern US waters continued to increase.

These needs did not reflect continued German perceptions of Canadian and Newfoundland waters as a soft spot. The local convoys promptly established by the RCN in January 1942, combined with the air and sea patrols, had resulted in far fewer sinkings per U-boat in northern waters as compared to American waters where defences were less well organized. Almost immediately in February the weight of the German offensive shifted to US waters and into the Caribbean. During that month, aside from the nine ships sunk in the two attacks on convoys far out on the ocean approaches to Newfoundland, only nine ships were sunk in Canadian waters. In March, the grand total, including Newfoundland's ocean approaches, dropped to eight ships, and in April to only three. By contrast, some 45 ships were sunk along the US east coast and in the Caribbean during February, over 75 in March and over 50 in April. This was the U-boats' second 'Happy Time.'

Most of the sinkings in Canadian waters during February and subsequently occurred in the waters off southern Nova Scotia, among unescorted ships coming from or going to US ports. In March, therefore, the WLEF began to run a large, new convoy between Halifax and Boston (the XB-BX series), and in April the force also started to escort the incoming ON and ONS convoys through to Boston. This was the beginning of the 'Triangle Run' — Halifax to St John's (with an SC or HX convoy), back to Boston (with an ON or ONS convoy), then Halifax (with a BX convoy) — that figures as prominently in the memories of Canadian veterans as the north Atlantic run. Nor was that all. The persistence of U-boats in the Canadian and Newfoundland areas, despite meagre returns, required that the informal local convoys be placed on a regular schedule with adequate escorts assigned. As spring approached and preparations began to move the SC convoys back to Sydney, new local convoys had to be established to bring that entrepôt into the network.

Eastern Air Command, which had played such an important part in demoralizing *U-130* and *U-109* in January, achieved at least nine attacks in which the presence of U-boats can be confirmed from February through the end of June. In the spring of 1942 the command was undergoing a modest expansion and improvement of its capabilities. A new Hudson squadron, No 113, was stationed at Yarmouth for direct coverage of the threatened southern waters. At Sydney, No 119 Squadron's Bolingbrokes were being replaced by the superior Hudson.

* * *

What neither Eastern Air Command nor the RCN got was the breathing space needed for training, proper maintenance and upgrading of equipment, and regular rest for personnel. On-the-job training continued to be conducted while operations continued in the northwest Atlantic winter conditions that so appalled the U-boat crews. NSHQ's plan of December 1941 for two months of concentrated training and exercises for all newly commissioned ships went by the board; they were rushed to sea.

Frank Curry, who served as a rating in the corvette HMCS *Kamsack* during this period, offers some insights into how people coped.

It was like entering paradise when Kamsack finally made port ... Perhaps it was knowing that we would return to the war at sea again in a matter of days that made shore leave so precious: the warmth of English pubs, the mugs of bitters, the human companionship, the wet canteen, the public house, the bootlegger in a dark alley, the girls, the dance halls or on the streets of any port.

Sometimes, the release we sought was no more complicated than a soccer game. With our ship tied up for a few hours, and no shore leave, the crew got hold of a soccer ball and turned the getty in a field, for the wildest game. It was a no-holds-barred soccer, with plenty of kicking and butting, as we released every pent-up feeling, battered each other into bruised submission, and finally climbed back aboard to collapse, exhausted yet restored ...

Sometimes, the release came in a good old-fashioned brawl ... Such an occasion presented itself one time in the lovely old town of Lunenburg, Nova Scotia, where the good people had arranged a dance for our war-weary crew while our ship was tied up for a refit. The dance was a great success until the evening began to wind down, and the consumption of liquor escalated at such a rate that half the crew took to the streets and battled amongst themselves in a wild, terrifying night of blood, battered faces, broken noses and black eyes. It was as if

all the years of harsh and brutal living conditions had finally turned us into animals, who revelled at being able to hack each other into submission.

Often, through the long years of despair, our pent-up feelings found temporary release in man's oldest source of comfort — alcohol; in our case, the demon rum. Although the daily rum ration was supposed to be consumed as issued ... most crews seemed to get around the rules, and vast quantities of 120-per cent over-proof rum were stored throughout the ship in crew's lockers.

Much was carried ashore and consumed there, or sold; but enough remained on board to provide the basis for periodic breakouts, and they were wild. It was always a startling experience to return from shore leave to find a good part of the crew roary-eyed drunk and in a vile mood, the ship in a turmoil. Who could blame them? The breaking point was often very close for crews who had faced weeks and months of filth, cold and hunger ...[15]

Another memoir by a rating, Howard Williams, who joined his first, and very unhappy, ship during the expansion of early 1942, illuminates Commodore Murray's warning to headquarters that crews would quickly become ineffective if they lacked confidence in their officers. The vessel was one of the armed yachts that had been procured in 1940 only as a stopgap. Under the pressure of events in 1942, most continued to serve as full-fledged coastal escorts on a gruelling schedule. A new commanding officer in Williams's ship aroused simmering hostility by apparently trying to compensate for inexperience with rude pomposity:

'Mr Carroll [the experienced first lieutenant] should those ships be that far apart?' 'Captain as you can see one is heavily loaded down, it isn't unusual in such cases for it to fall behind a lighter loaded one.' 'I didn't ask for a long drawn out conclusion on your part' the Captain retorted. Silence fell over the bridge. Unlike Captain Evans giving direct instructions to the signal deck, Captain Johnson gave them to the Jimmy [the first lieutenant] to pass on to them.[16]

After a grim seven months in the ship, Williams went to the corvette HMCS *Midland*. When he came aboard, a member of the crew told him: ' "*The Captain Lt.-Commander Allan Taylor RCNR is a veteran Captain of many years' service on merchant ships both steam and sail. You'll find he's a great comfort in troublesome times during convoy duty.*" '[17] On one of the first escort missions, Williams found out what that meant:

Captain Taylor wearing a fleece lined jacket his spy glass perennially under his arm appears impervious to threatening elements surrounding the ship, he's no fair-weather Captain sitting in a swivel chair rivetted to the

bridge-deck, anyone watching can see he's conscious of every aspect of his ship. Gale force winds and sea bursting down the funnel, the up and down forward motion scooped up sea water deluging the entire ship ... Every once in a while the Captain got up and leaning forward on the dodger hung on with one hand while peering through his spy glass ... he surveyed [the] convoy ...

From [the] outset the Captain forewarned lookouts on the bridge to keep a sharp eye on merchantmen within sight of the ship, and if anything appeared minutely out of kilter he was to be informed immediately. The flag deck reported a Scandinavian ship straying ... Midland's speed [increased] immediately ...

'Captain Jorgensen' Captain Taylor hollered through the bull-horn ... 'Yumpin Yimminy, v'en d'you yoin d'noivy Ca'n Aloin Toila?' ... During the four days of [the] convoy plodding slowly forward [in the storm], at least five times Midland left her station to assist a merchantman back to his station, and in each case captains of merchant ships knew Taylor in a personal way. Anyone within hearing on bridge instinctively sensed a strong common bond of respect between them all.[18]

The combination of merchant service captains and largely volunteer reserve crews gave Canadian ships a distinctive character that could be daunting for professional naval personnel. Early in 1942, Lieutenant W. H. Willson, RCN, fresh from five years' training and service in British ships and Canadian destroyers that were still largely manned by regular force crews, was appointed first lieutenant in the ex-US 'Town'-class destroyer HMCS *St Clair*.

Gerald Baugh was the Captain ... He ... had been a Master with the CPR [Canadian Pacific Railway steamships] and an incredible ship-handler. He could do anything with that old four-stacker. Stick it into little places you wouldn't believe. He was merchant service all the way and conflicts we had were basically the merchant service/navy different approach. I felt the ship was pretty loose and slack ...

I was not at all happy with his sort of friendliness with defaulters who'd just made the most appalling mess of the Naval Discipline Act. Gerry would give them a little pat on the head and say, 'Well boys will be boys,' and that was it and I'd go away fuming and steaming.

Willson's efforts to tighten up routines in the ship inevitably produced serious tensions and, when the ship put into Sydney, he had the men organize a dance as a morale booster. One of the crew told Willson not to attend — ' "*Some of those guys are waiting for you ...*" ' When Willson ignored the warning and appeared at the dance:

One thug from the east end of Montreal, whom I came to know quite well later, he wasn't half as bad as

he looked, came up to me and said … 'we've got a little shed out the back with a couple of drinks. Would you care to come out and have a couple of drinks with us?' I pondered this one a minute and thought, 'Well, this is it. I guess this is going to be the big show. I don't know how I'm going to look tomorrow.' But I said, 'Sure thing.' He led me outside … and we struggled through bushes and up muddy paths … pitch black and he had a flashlight with him and I was … thinking God, I hope they know where to find the body. We came to this little shack … and inside were a couple of candles and a whole lot of bottles and about six guys standing around

drinking. We came in and there was a stunned silence when I walked in and one of them said, 'Will you have a drink, Sir?' I said, 'Sure thing.' So, they gave me a rum or something and we talked a little uneasily … I had my drink and then I said, 'Well, I had better get back to the dance …' 'Oh, okay Sir. Here I'll show you in … ' They took me back … and that was that … That ended that incident, but it did turn that crew around and we had a totally different relationship. There seemed to be more of a willingness to accept that things [had] to be done … pusser [i.e., in a correct, naval manner].[19]

CHAPTER VI

THE BATTLE OF THE GULF OF ST LAWRENCE, 1942

Since Jacques Cartier, sailors who enter the Gulf of St Lawrence by the Cabot Strait always have the same visual impression, that is to not know if they are still in the Atlantic or in the gulf ...

It is not therefore an ordinary entrance in which one sees the shores that extend into the distance, or one finds the waters of a different colour, brown with alluvial soil and less salty than the ocean. None of that applies in the gulf, for if sailors know that they have reached the continental plateau, they discover depths of more than 500 metres outside Gaspé ... Captains continue for several days to do oceanic navigation; it is not yet coastal navigation ... They sail in a gulf ... of dimensions comparable to the North Sea and Baltic.

... Two currents affect the circulation of water, the [frigid] Labrador current that circles Newfoundland clockwise and of which a part penetrates the gulf by the Strait of Belle Isle, and the Gaspé current which comes out of the river estuary and moves to the south east. Navigation is not easy: these are some of the foggiest shores in the world, winds change direction rapidly, and the seas make themselves felt.

The river estuary, in the shape of a funnel, is 575 kilometers long and 110 kilometres wide between Sept-

Îles and the Gaspé coast. At Pointe-des-Monts, the width contracts to 50 kilometres...[1]

Officers of the Canadian naval service have expressed the view that within a few months submarines may well be found operating within the gulf, and even in the St. Lawrence river. It is known that enemy submarines can leave their bases on the European continent, voyage to the shores of this continent, seek their prey for some days or weeks and return to their bases without the necessity of refuelling. If enemy submarines do operate in the gulf and river St. Lawrence, an additional burden will be thrown on the Canadian navy. Not only will our navy have the duty of assisting in escorting Atlantic convoys, but it will also have to assume the task of escorting convoys in the river St. Lawrence and in the gulf as well as along our coasts.

> Prime Minister William Lyon Mackenzie King, speech in the House of Commons, 25 March 1942[2]

The prime minister was speaking nearly two months before a U-boat appeared in the Gulf. Although he laid bare the thinking of the naval staff, he did not tell the Canadian public much that was new. Since Confederation, Canadians had responded to

the threat of war with fears about the vulnerability of the great sea and river route that leads to the heart of the nation. This was the route by which the country had been founded and fought over in colonial times. It had always been Canada's main artery of overseas trade. Except during winter months, when ice blocked the river and Gulf, Montreal was Canada's principal Atlantic port. During the late 1930s, as we have seen, the prime minister had capitalized on worries about the Gulf to win acceptance for rearmament.

In the spring of 1942 those worries were useful to him once more. Widespread support for overseas conscription, even among King's cabinet colleagues, forced the prime minister to hold a national plebiscite in April seeking release from his long-standing commitment never to impose this measure. This was a purely political manoeuvre. In view of the continued bitter opposition in Quebec, King had no intention of sending conscripts overseas. It was to this province that the original pledge really had been made. Although determined to hold the line on the contentious conscription issue, King was profoundly worried about Quebec's growing isolation from opinion in the rest of the country. He therefore stressed the menace to the Gulf — to Quebec's own shores — as a reminder that the war was not remote.

King's openness in March 1942 foreshadowed the large amount of detailed information that would appear in the press, and the House of Commons debates, throughout the battle of the Gulf in May to November 1942. This went considerably beyond the frankness that the government had intended. The Germans provided such an electrifying spectacle within clear sight of Gulf communities that censorship efforts often proved futile. Paradoxically, there were charges from politicians and newspapers that the government was covering up an important defeat, charges that have periodically reappeared ever since.

The second paradox is that although the government fully admitted a defeat in the St Lawrence, it was not entirely correct to do so. Sources that have recently surfaced show that the defence measures were much more effective than they seemed at the time, persuading the Germans to abandon the effort within a few short weeks of their greatest successes. The final paradox is that the greatest losses resulting from the battle of the St Lawrence in 1942 were produced by the navy's own lack of confidence in the defence measures. Certainly, the 21 ships sunk within the Gulf and the four others destroyed in the near vicinity were a serious loss. More important still, however, was the dislocation of trade caused by the navy's decision to limit severely the number of merchant vessels allowed to pass through the apparently indefensible Gulf.

The navy's worst nightmare since the first German U-boat offensive early in 1915, during the First World War, had always been a submarine loose in the Gulf and river. This inland sea, with its deep trenches and sinuous, thinly populated coastline, offered U-boats a thousand hiding places within easy reach of shipping routes. These routes, moreover, could be little varied through constricted passages at all three outlets from the Gulf: the estuary of the river and the adjacent passage between the Gaspé peninsula and Anticosti Island, the Cabot Strait and the Strait of Belle Isle. The Gulf was perfect for the sort of strike-and-hide ambush tactics for which submarines had been designed. Studies by both the Canadian and British naval staffs since at least 1918 had concluded that defence of the Gulf would require a half dozen destroyers or more and scores of smaller patrol vessels — a force fully as large as the one needed on the whole Atlantic coast outside the Gulf.

When in the late 1930s it became clear that nothing like the required resources would be available before the outbreak of war, the armed forces formulated a Gulf defence plan that laid out what could be done with what was actually available. The plan was updated annually in preparation for the spring thaw and re-opening of navigation. The picture had become more depressing each spring as demands on the armed forces outstripped their expansion. The plan rested upon two principles. Shipping would be convoyed, but, to minimize delays to trade and demands on escort forces needed elsewhere, this would not be done until ships had actually been sunk in the Gulf. Secondly, the air force would have to shoulder a great deal of the burden to relieve the over-extended navy. The naval staff emphasized this last point with their air force colleagues during the early months of 1942.

On the morning of 13 May 1942, newspapers carried detailed reports of the first sinking, scarcely 24 hours after the event.

A St. Lawrence River Port, May 12 (CP) …

An informant said over the telephone that residents for two miles around one fishing village were awakened last night 'by a terrific explosion that rocked our houses as though there was an earthquake. We saw lights suddenly appear in the distance offshore and we knew that something had happened to a ship.'

Early this morning, he said, two lifeboats drifted ashore bearing the forty-two crewmen from the torpedoed freighter. The boats were not equipped with oars and were carried ashore by wind and tide.[3]

... one hell of a ruckus: Flying Officer M. J. Belanger (right) and his crew made three near-miss attacks on *U-517* in the Gulf of St Lawrence. (CFPU, PMR 77-178)

The emergency response by these Curtiss Kittyhawk fighters at Mont-Joli, Quebec, to the torpedoing of a ship resulted in the loss of one aircraft and its pilot, Squadron Leader J. A. J. Chevrier. (CFPU, PMR 75-622)

In the following days the press reported further accurate information. Another group of survivors from the ship had drifted ashore later on 12 May, but it then became clear that six men had been lost in the torpedoing. A second ship had been hit on the night of 11–12 May (in fact just an hour and 15 minutes after the first) and gone down more quickly, with the loss of a dozen lives. The second crew, some clinging to small rafts and wreckage because there had been time to launch only one small boat, was picked up two hours later by passing freighters. Ironically, both ships, which had sailed from Montreal on the 10th, carried seamen who were taking passage to Britain after their ships had been torpedoed in the Atlantic. Neither ship had been warned of the danger of attack and, following usual procedure, would not have begun taking precautions until the next day.

The press did not report certain essential facts. The first victim was *Nicoya*, the second *Leto*, modern Dutch ships under charter to the British Ministry of War Transport. They had gone down off the north shore of the Gaspé peninsula; *Nicoya*'s people had come ashore at the little town of Cloridorme and the hamlet of L'Anse-à-Valleau. Naval personnel who rushed from the town of Gaspé by road to the scene reported instant cooperation on the part of the local population. Fishermen took one of the officers out in their vessel to reach one of *Nicoya*'s lifeboats, drifting nine kilometres off shore. Royal Canadian Mounted Police officers arrived to find there was nothing for them to do: '*Seeing that all the survivors were in good health and very well taken care of by the Rev. LeBlanc, Parish Priest of Cloridorme, and by the proprietor of Hotel Bernatche, we left …*'[4]

The ships' killer was *U-553*, still under the command of Kapitänleutnant Thurmann, whom we met under a barrage of depth charges from HMCS *Columbia* during the SC 48 battle and hunting in the ocean approaches to Nova Scotia in January 1942. The U-boat's arrival in the Gulf was not part of a grand strategic plan. Thurmann had again been assigned to the Nova Scotia area, but the submarine was suffering from equipment malfunctions and Thurmann on his own initiative decided to try less dangerous backwaters.

The defences were not so ill prepared as the press accounts and critical questions in Parliament suggested. This was possibly the result of a happy coincidence. During the night of 8–9 May an observer on shore at Cape Ray, Newfoundland, reported seeing a submarine heading into the Gulf. It was at this time that *U-553* actually entered through the Cabot Strait, but at no point was it anywhere nearly close enough

to the Newfoundland side to be observed at night. The sighting was therefore probably false, but accurate nevertheless. No flying was possible until 10 May because of weather, but Canadian and American aircraft from Gander then made a thorough search of the Gulf towards the Gaspé peninsula, the point the submarine might have reached. Late in the afternoon of 10 May, a United States Army B-17 bomber found *U-553* and made an attack that was wide of the mark. Air crews had by now made many attacks on what had seemed to be U-boats but which on further analysis proved to be fish or the flotsam that is so common in coastal waters. Information from detailed debriefings of the crews after they landed was needed to confirm that a submarine was actually there. Because of poor relations between the US Army and Navy and the Canadian services in Newfoundland — the root issue seems to have been disputes between the US services over control of maritime aviation — Canadian commanders did not get the confirmation that a U-boat was indeed present until late on 11 May, not long before *U-553* attacked.

Nevertheless, Eastern Air Command had dispatched special patrols of the Gulf from Nova Scotia stations on the morning of 11 May. Preparations had already been made to send several aircraft to the training airfield at Mont-Joli, Quebec, on the following day when word of the sinking arrived and hastened this action. The navy, for its part, responded to the sinkings by immediately holding shipping in port and sailing it in convoy. These measures worked. Thurmann was able to make no more attacks. He had earlier signalled headquarters about the large amount of steamer traffic and good prospects for hunting, but the message he sent on 21 May, shortly before his departure, was less encouraging: '*no shipping traffic, very alert air surveillance, warship patrols by patrol boats type Eagle …*'[5]

To say that the defences were shoestring would be to flatter them, and there was a scramble to assemble what little there was. The attacks had come soon after the spring opening of navigation, before preparations begun earlier in the year could be completed. A new, half-strength air squadron, No 117, was hastily spun out of an experienced squadron at Dartmouth for Gulf operations. The headquarters of the new unit was at the North Sydney flying-boat station, and three or four of its seven Canso and Catalina flying boats were detached to Gaspé, where flying facilities were hurried to completion. These were the only combat aircraft that could be permanently stationed within the Gulf. The rest of 117 Squadron's flying

boats at North Sydney, and a squadron of Hudsons at Sydney airport, provided coverage of the eastern reaches of the Gulf, but they also had to keep up heavy commitments on the Atlantic, south of Newfoundland and east of Cape Breton. The RCN's Gulf Escort Force, based at Gaspé and responsible for the principal Sydney–Quebec convoy series (SQ-QS), comprised only five Bangors, an armed yacht and three Fairmile motor launches. At Sydney were two Bangors, six Fairmiles and two armed yachts. This little flotilla had to escort the Newfoundland passenger and railway ferries across the Cabot Strait, and also convoy merchant ships to and from Corner Brook, the main port on the west coast of Newfoundland.

The Fairmiles, like the Bangors, had only recently come into service, and their employment posed special challenges. These 34-metre-long wooden craft had a good speed of some 20 knots and were equipped with asdic and depth charges. Their light hulls could easily get into difficulty in the Gulf's heavy weather and seas, however, and their gasoline engines and volatile fuel required very careful maintenance.

In July, after ice cleared from the Strait of Belle Isle and the Labrador coast, two other convoy series began in the Gulf. The first, LN-NL from Quebec City, supplied the construction of a large new Canadian air base at Goose Bay, Labrador. A force of four Royal Canadian Navy (RCN) corvettes stationed at Quebec City provided the escort. The second series, SG-GS, supplied US construction projects in the Canadian Arctic and Greenland. Based at Sydney, Nova Scotia, the convoys were escorted by ships of the United States Coast Guard, which had become a fully integral part of the US Navy for war operations.

The next U-boat after Thurmann's to operate in the Gulf, U-132 (Kapitänleutnant Ernst Vogelsang), entered through the Cabot Strait on 30 June. It had the advantage of complete surprise: nothing tipped off the Allies. Vogelsang pushed up to Cap-Chat, where the St Lawrence River estuary begins to narrow, some 180 kilometres further west than the point where U-553 had made its attacks. In the early hours of 6 July, the submarine torpedoed two ships in the Quebec-to-Sydney convoy QS 15 — 12 ships following a single escort, the Bangor HMCS Drummondville. The merchant ships had not kept station well, and there was pandemonium after the explosions occurred. Neither of the sinking vessels fired rockets, so the escort lost valuable time trying to discover what had happened, and where. Starshell turned up nothing, and the searchlight proved useless in the hazy conditions. Nearly two hours later the submarine struck again, hitting a third ship. This time Drummondville could distinguish the direction, and rushed to the scene, firing starshell and illuminating U-132 on the surface. The submarine dived as the Bangor raced towards it. Vogelsang had trouble controlling the boat because of the 'considerable damage' done by Drummondville's depth-charge attacks, and because of the layering of cold, dense water of the Gulf with warm, less dense water from the river that abruptly changed the buoyancy of the submarine. U-132 plunged very deep, to 180 metres, and hid there for 12 hours. (The pronounced temperature or 'density' layering of water that is common on the Canadian coast would prove on balance to be a blessing for the U-boats. Although the phenomenon complicated the underwater manoeuvres of submarines, it also interfered with the sound emissions from asdic, reducing the equipment's effectiveness or altogether blinding it, a difficulty that was not well understood at the time.)

Fog prevented flying boats coming from Gaspé, but at Mont-Joli, 100 kilometres from the sinkings, four Curtiss Kittyhawk fighters of the recently formed 130 Squadron scrambled into the darkness. One of the aircraft, flown by the squadron's commanding officer, Squadron Leader J. A. J. Chevrier, did not return from the mission. The grim news came later in the day: *Four eye witnesses had seen the [Chevrier's] aircraft crash dive into the water after circling... with a rough motor — the casualty signal was sent and next of Kin notified. Dragging operations commenced.*[6] No trace of the pilot or the fighter ever turned up.

The Halifax commands quickly sent six Hudsons to Mont-Joli and at least five corvettes to Gaspé. These forces vigorously pursued several contacts, all of them false. On 20 July, north of the Gaspé peninsula not far from where Nicoya and Leto had gone down, convoy QS 19 passed over the submerged submarine. U-132 was able to fire from within the convoy in broad daylight, fatally damaging one steamer. Although the convoy escort included a corvette, a Bangor and three Fairmiles, the submarine escaped detection. Possibly it benefited from the inability of asdic to penetrate the density layers in the deep water. Certainly it was helped by the confused lunging of steamers trying to flee the scene. The weather had also favoured the U-boat by preventing air searches along the convoy route that had been planned for that day and forcing cancellation of the close air escort for QS 19.

* * *

(NAC, PA-200323)

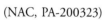

(NAC, PA-200330)

(NAC, PA-200335)

(NAC, PA-200325)

HMCS *Trail* joined … in a rescue effort that saved all but 13 of the 562 passengers and crew in *Chatham*, the first American troop transport to be lost during the war.

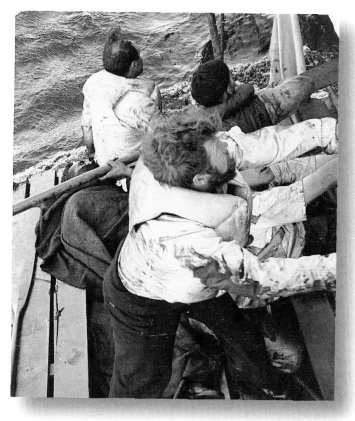

(NAC, PA-200322)

(NAC, PA-200324)

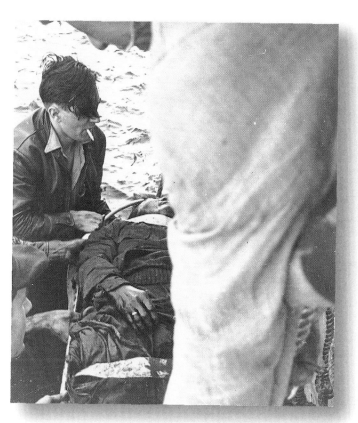

(NAC, PA-200334)

(NAC, PA-200327)

Very shortly, however, the airmen would have greater success off southern Nova Scotia. One of Eastern Air Command's most effective squadrons was also the newest. No 113, equipped with Hudsons, had been formed at Yarmouth earlier in the year. The commanding officer, Squadron Leader N. E. Small, was an old hand. He had joined the regular Royal Canadian Air Force (RCAF) to become a pilot in 1928, immediately after graduating from high school in his native Hamilton, Ontario. In 1937 Small left the service for commercial flying, but rejoined in the fall of 1939 and was employed as an instructor. A 'master' pilot, in the first part of 1941 he flew Catalina aircraft across the Atlantic for delivery from the United States to Britain, and then joined the RCAF's first Catalina squadron, No 116. Such was his impatience and keenness that during an early instructional flight, in which he was teaching other squadron personnel about the flying qualities of the machine, he made an attack on a suspected submarine (it was undoubtedly a false contact). The results were almost comical. Neither Small, nor anyone else in the unit, had yet received instruction on weapons and anti-submarine operations. One bomb hung up in the rack, the other failed to explode, and Small's improvised version of a U-boat warning signal caused bafflement at air control in Dartmouth. Nevertheless, his actions almost instantly removed delays in the provision of anti-submarine instruction to the squadron.

In the summer of 1942, Eastern Air Command was still in the grip of the conundrum the navy knew so well: trying to become more efficient and effective while meeting crushing operational demands with inadequate resources. Expert visitors from the Royal Air Force's Coastal Command, the most experienced maritime air force in the world, came to North America to help both Canadian and US airmen. Blizzards of paper from the British command laid out the details of how and why they operated as they did. Small, however, was apparently the only officer at the squadron level who managed to rise above the intense daily pressures to absorb and apply the latest information.

The essential message from Coastal Command was the overriding priority of prompt patrols in response to the latest naval intelligence on U-boat movements. Rather than attempt to cover every convoy, as the Canadian and US air forces were doing, the effort should be concentrated where the enemy was most likely lurking. A convoy well clear of areas where there had been recent U-boat activity could safely be left with minimal or no air protection.

Strength should be conserved for saturation of areas where the presence of U-boats was suspected, not only with coverage of shipping, but also with wide-ranging hunting patrols to search the entire area where the submarine might have moved to since the last contact. By this method, Coastal Command had so harassed U-boats operating off the United Kingdom that they had withdrawn in late 1940 and early 1941 beyond the range of regular air patrols. The Foreign Intelligence Section at Naval Service Headquarters, with its network of direction-finding stations, was by now producing timely and reasonably accurate bearings on U-boat signals. Nevertheless, because of poor communications between Ottawa and Halifax, the bearings arrived too late to be of use for quick-response air searches. Strong urging from the Coastal Command visitors helped overcome this problem in the summer of 1942, when Air Force Headquarters began to send the information in a voice code by commercial telephone to Eastern Air Command.

Small made sure his unit received this vital information promptly. He also brought two important Coastal Command innovations into his squadron. The Royal Air Force was one of the first armed services in the world to make full use of scientific analysis to improve operational efficiency, the beginnings of what came to be known as operations research. Maritime projects focused on the failure of aircraft to surprise U-boats in time to make an attack before they could crash dive, safe from any aerial weapon then available. The studies revealed that white-painted aircraft were the hardest to see from the surface of the water (on reflection, hardly a startling discovery given the light plumage of gulls and other fish-eating birds). Standard dark aircraft finishes were among the most clearly visible at sea. The studies also showed that lookouts at sea level had the greatest difficulty spotting high-flying aircraft: looking up strains the neck and the observer suffers from the sun's glare. Aircraft should therefore patrol at altitudes of up to 1500 metres, as compared to Eastern Air Command's standard of 300 to 450 metres.

No 113 Squadron's high-flying, white-painted Hudsons almost immediately had results in their aggressive hunts in the vicinity of recent direction-finding bearings. During the late morning of 31 July 1942, Small himself sighted '*a submarine fully surfaced approximately three miles ahead and one mile to port of aircraft's track.*'

The approach to the target was made at a slight angle to the submarines [sic] track and from astern. The submarine's crew was seen to be scrambling for the hatch as

the aircraft approached. The U-Boat was clearly visible, battleship grey in colour... The entire deck was visible when the depth charges were released and they were seen to explode very close to the hull ...

It was a model attack, Small having skilfully executed a hair-raising dive to 15 metres off the surface, the only way to ensure that depth charges were accurately dropped. The submarine had begun to dive just as the charges exploded. The aircraft circled. *'Fifty-five minutes after the depth charges were dropped, a heavy explosion was seen to take place at a point approximately 5 miles from the point where the depth charges exploded.'*[7] U-754 had been destroyed. That same day and on 2 and 5 August other 113 Squadron aircraft found and attacked the remaining three U-boats operating off southern Nova Scotia. None of these other attacks was successful, but it was a formidable demonstration of the effectiveness of the latest Coastal Command patrol methods.

* * *

The navy would need all the help it could get from the air force in the coming weeks and months. New German deployments and the relentless expansion of the U-boat arm were bringing Canada's maritime forces up against their greatest challenges of the war. A renewed wolf-pack campaign against convoys at mid-ocean had already begun in July 1942. Meanwhile, although strengthened defences exemplified by 113 Squadron's achievements had persuaded Admiral Dönitz to give up the offensive along much of the Canadian and US coast, he was still probing for soft spots. The essence of 'tonnage warfare' was to strike wherever ships could be destroyed with the fewest U-boat losses, and one such place was the Gulf of St Lawrence. U-553 and U-132's records of sinkings were only average compared to scores achieved during the early days of the offensive in North American waters, but in the summer of 1942 they looked very promising.

The assault began with yet another German concentration at the Strait of Belle Isle, where Dönitz's radio intelligence told him vulnerable shipping could still be found. U-513, U-517 and U-165 took up station there during the last week of August. Almost immediately, on 27–28 August, U-517 and U-165 attacked the American Sydney-to-Greenland convoy, SG 6. The convoy had been moving in two groupings, the US Army troop ship *Chatham* and one fast escort running ahead of the rest, beyond the reach of the cover supplied by RCAF aircraft from Newfoundland. The vulnerable troop ship was sunk in the preliminary attack. A subsequent attack on the main body of the convoy resulted in the sinking of the cargo ship *Arlyn*. A third ship, the tanker *Laramie*, was severely damaged but managed to return to Sydney. Behind SG 6 was the small Canadian convoy LN 6, bound for Goose Bay. Its escort, the corvette HMCS *Trail*, joined both the US Coast Guard escorts and RCAF aircraft in a rescue effort that saved all but 13 of the 562 passengers and crew in *Chatham*, the first American troop transport to be lost during the war.

U-165 and U-517 then proceeded south into the Gulf, though direction-finding bearings on the submarine's radio reports soon revealed their movements to Canadian naval intelligence. The extra air patrols mounted did not do much good. After fog shut down flying, U-517 sank the Canadian Great Lakes freighter *Donald Stewart* on the night of 2–3 September about 140 kilometres south of the strait. The escorting corvette, although preventing the submarine from torpedoing a second steamer, could not make asdic contact — a frequent occurrence, as we have seen, in the complex waters of the Gulf. The next day an RCAF Digby from Gander sighted and attacked U-517, but did no damage. The aircraft had been flying at only 275 metres, and the German lookout saw the bomber in ample time for the U-boat to get below the surface.

Eastern Air Command rushed bombers from Nova Scotia to Mont-Joli once more, and pressed aircraft from training stations all through the Maritime provinces into service over the Gulf. U-165 and U-517 meanwhile installed themselves in the river and estuary, where U-553 and U-132 had had success. The air patrols had in fact compelled the submarines to enter these narrow waters. As U-165 later reported, *'Getting targets'* east of Gaspé was *'difficult because of air cover, therefore went submerged during the daytime'* just off Cap-Chat.[8] In this area it was possible for the U-boat to find shipping in the constricted waterway without the long runs on the surface that would have exposed it to air attack. Poor asdic conditions made the danger of detection by naval escorts slight.

During the night of 6–7 September, U-165 sank one merchantman and the armed yacht HMCS *Raccoon* in convoy QS 33. The next day, further along the Gaspé peninsula shore, U-517 destroyed three more merchant ships in the same convoy. The escort had included, in addition to *Raccoon*, two Fairmiles and the corvettes *Arrowhead* and *Truro*. *Truro* had just been completed and was on its way to Halifax for basic work-ups; the inclusion of such unprepared ships in convoy escorts was one of the expediencies to which the RCN had to resort. There had been both

sweeps of the river and strong air escort for the convoy until dark on 6 September, but that was of little use against a U-boat already in a good ambush position. An aircraft took off in response to the sinkings at night, but in the thickening weather could not find the convoy. The weather continued to virtually wash out air coverage on 7 September.

Saddest among the losses was the destruction of *Raccoon*. The light hull of the yacht disintegrated with the impact of the torpedo. In the darkness and confusion, the explosion sounded like the detonation of depth charges and the other escorts took little notice. Because *Raccoon* did not have a radio-telephone and was habitually out of communication for long periods, it was not missed until the next day. Weeks later a few bits of wreckage washed up on shore, as did the body of Lieutenant R. H. McConnell, Royal Canadian Naval Volunteer Reserve (RCNVR), a noted McGill University football and hockey player *'who had been offered a professional contract, but elected to join the navy instead.'*[9] No trace was ever found of the remaining 32 crewmen.

These losses came close on the heels of another bold U-boat strike inshore on 5 September. When *U-513* had no luck at the Strait of Belle Isle, Dönitz dispatched the submarine along the Atlantic coast of Newfoundland, to Conception Bay, immediately west of St John's. There were no anti-submarine defences in the bay, only a coast battery for protection against surface attack at Bell Island, site of the large Wabana iron-ore mines. *U-513* torpedoed *Sagana* and *Lord Strathcona* at the ore-loading piers at Bell Island, manoeuvring so closely that the submarine's conning tower collided with the hull of one of the vessels. *Sagana* went down instantly, entombing 30 of the crew. *Lord Strathcona* also sank quickly, but the seamen had already begun to abandon ship with the hit on *Sagana* only 10 metres away; three men died.

At the time there were two other boats [merchant vessels] anchored in the roads which kept up a rapid fire [with their self-defence armament] in all directions, and all the while everyone in Lance Cove that had a boat was searching for survivors together with a large number of people in lifeboats from the steamers. Everything possible was done by these people who were moving around in all directions amongst the shells that were bursting with no apparent regard for their safety. There is great credit due these people for the manner in which they acted ...

I [William Russell, Head Constable of the local detachment of the Royal Newfoundland Constabulary] then had the three bodies brought up to the Police Sta- tion ... *Mr. [Reid] Proudfoot [of Dominion Steel] authorized me to purchase three caskets at a cost of $60.00 each and Mr. Andrew Murphy took charge of the bodies ... They were supplied with a complete new outfit, placed in their caskets and waked at the Police Station all night where a large number of people came to see them and brought numerous wreaths which will necessitate an extra hearse to take care of the flowers.*[10]

The bad news continued. On 11 September *U-517* destroyed the corvette *Charlottetown* with two torpedoes near Cap-Chat, within sight of horrified onlookers on shore. On the afternoon of 15 September *U-517* succeeded in another submerged attack close off Gaspé, sinking two ships in convoy SQ 36. The next day *U-165* struck the same convoy within the river mouth, not far from Cap-Chat, sinking one merchant vessel and fatally damaging a second. The submarines achieved these results against SQ 36's strong escort, which included a British 'Town' destroyer (one of two the RCN had recently brought in to the Gulf from the Western Local Eescort Force [WLEF]), two corvettes, two Bangors and two Fairmiles. The counter-attacks by the destroyer had inflicted only slight damage on *U-517*.

* * *

The Canadian naval staff had already recommended closing the Gulf of St Lawrence to shipping, and on 9 September the government agreed it should be done immediately. The impetus had come from yet another large new commitment, the Admiralty's urgent request that the RCN provide 17 corvettes to support the Anglo-American invasion of North Africa (operation Torch) scheduled for November. The naval staff had previously warned British shipping authorities that it would be necessary to shut down traffic in the Gulf if the limited defences available proved inadequate. This was already obviously the case, and the corvettes for Torch could be found only if the six sent to reinforce the Gulf convoys were redeployed.

Moreover, the Torch commitment was not the only one stretching Canadian naval resources. In September 1942 the WLEF was just taking on major new responsibilities. During that month, New York replaced Sydney and Halifax as the assembly port for transatlantic convoys. Completion of the coastal convoy system in US waters to counter U-boat attacks had eliminated the advantages of the Canadian ports whose position to the north of the US seaboard and proximity to the United Kingdom had made them the logical departure point prior to the German offensive against the North American coast. Ships from

The armed yacht HMCS
Raccoon. (DHH, 2784)

Fairmile motor launches (foreground)
and Bangor escorts at Sydney, Nova Scotia.
(CFPU, PMR 86-210)

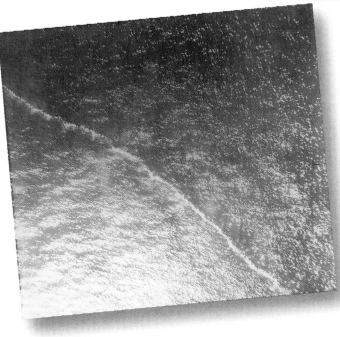

The oil slick and air bubbles left in the wake of an
unsuccessful air attack on a U-boat off Nova Scotia,
August 1942. (DHH, 181.003-D25)

any American port had been able conveniently to assemble at Sydney or Halifax, already a good part of the way to their overseas destinations. By the summer of 1942, however, ships departing from US ports in the coastal convoy shuttle lost precious days in each port of call awaiting the assembly of other ships for the next leg. Under the new system introduced in September, the transatlantic convoys departed directly from New York, where most United Kingdom-bound ships loaded. The Canadian trade came out in small feeder convoys from Saint John, New Brunswick, Halifax, Sydney and Newfoundland as the main convoy passed by Nova Scotia and proceeded out the Cape Race route. For convoys coming from the United Kingdom, the system worked in reverse, with groups of ships peeling off from the New York-bound main convoy to the Newfoundland and Canadian destinations.

The RCN's WLEF provided the escorts for the whole passage between New York and the meeting point for the mid-ocean escort groups just east of Newfoundland. This was an 1800-kilometre voyage, more than half the length of the 3300-kilometre run from Newfoundland to Northern Ireland. Because of the limited range of many of the WLEF warships, the escort groups had to change over at Halifax, one group coming out in relief as the other went in to refuel.

Even as the navy prepared to reduce its forces in the Gulf of St Lawrence, the air force decided to increase its effort there on the very largest scale it could manage. Early in September, Eastern Air Command had sent three Hudsons from 113 Squadron to the training airfield at Chatham, New Brunswick, handy to the eastern end of the Gaspé peninsula where many sinkings were taking place. Using the methods learned from Coastal Command, the aircraft were rewarded with attacks on *U-517* on 9 and 16 September. Both of these attacks were wide of the mark but Eastern Air Command was determined to push harder. The airmen turned the Yarmouth patrol area, where there were no known U-boats present, over to the US Army Air Forces in New England, and moved the rest of 113 Squadron to Mont-Joli and Chatham, giving a total of six Hudsons at each place. Other aircraft from mainland Nova Scotia reinforced the squadrons at Sydney.

Large convoys continued to move on the main Sydney–Quebec route until the end of September, and they received excellent protection. Although *U-165* had left, *U-517* was still hunting. On 21 September the submarine was shadowing convoy SQ 38 off Gaspé when the Bangor HMCS *Georgian* came

out of that port to join the escort. The Canadian warship sighted the partly surfaced U-boat and attacked with depth charges for two hours. The submarine was not destroyed (as the Canadian captain was convinced it had been), but damage forced it to withdraw from the shipping route for two days to make repairs. *U-517* then sighted convoy QS 37 north of the Gaspé peninsula on 24 September. The frequent appearance of aircraft, and no fewer than three attacks on the 24th and 25th, all by 113 Squadron Hudsons from Chatham, defeated the submarine's every effort to catch up to the convoy with fast surface runs. A single crew, headed by Flying Officer M. J. Belanger, made two of the attacks. Belanger, only 23 years of age in 1942, had served as a flying instructor for a year before joining the east-coast unit, a testament to his skill. A native of Quebec, he had been raised in Vancouver, and would later serve with 425 'Alouette' Squadron, RCAF, in bombing operations over Europe in 1944–45.

One of Belanger's attacks, as Small commented, would certainly have been lethal if Eastern Air Command had had depth charges filled with Torpex, a high-power new explosive that would not be delivered to the command for some weeks. The Hudson had struck by moonlight during one of the night patrols Eastern Air Command was mounting more frequently despite the dangers, given the state of aviation technology at that time. In the words of Kapitänleutnant Paul Hartwig, *U-517's* commanding officer: '*Surprised by aircraft. 2 powerful explosions astern. 3 bombs dropped; 3rd bomb right next to ship's side so that stern gets flooded over by impact. Presumably a dud.*'[11]

Hartwig pushed through to the Cabot Strait to try to intercept QS 37 there. Aircraft on patrol from Sydney were so omnipresent that the U-boat gave up and returned to its original hunting ground near Gaspé. The next attempt to strike, in the early hours of 29 September, was defeated by the effective screen of convoy QS 38 and damage done to the submarine's torpedoes by the Canadian forces' previous counter-attacks. Later in the day *U-517* was again depth-charged by a Hudson, with Belanger at the controls for a third time: '*The depth charges were seen to explode all around the hull slightly ahead of the conning tower. One large explosion occurred around the hull of the U-Boat. The U-boat's bow came up out of the water and all forward motion stopped.*'[12] Although the charges had in fact overshot, Hartwig himself described them as 'well placed.' A few days later, *U-517* headed for home, not signalling until clear of the coast for fear that the obviously efficient Canadian direction-finding system would bring out aircraft.

Historian Michael Hadley found that both the RCAF and the St Lawrence were still powerful memories when he interviewed Hartwig in the early 1980s.

Hartwig recalls the stress that RCAF surveillance ... and attacks caused his watch officers. Planes would unexpectedly swoop down on them, buzz them, drop out of a cloud, or skim low over the water out of the sun and drop bombs which, even when inaccurate, made 'one hell of a ruckus' ... All his officers had been badly shaken by such attacks and advised him of their preference to stand their watch submerged. They no longer felt confident about the patrol situation on the surface. This confirms RCAF suspicions at the time that at least one 'submarine should carry back to Germany a very flattering record of our aircraft's [sic] readiness off this coast.' ... On other occasions, patrol on the St Lawrence was so quiet they cruised on the surface with the forward hatch open. This was, of course, a serious risk, but one worth taking considering the need for fresh air and the marvellous tranquillity of the scene. The crew, as Hartwig recalls, also experienced moments during the beautiful Gaspé autumn that remained with them over forty years ... Many still recall a very early morning off a Gaspé shore. Only one small building in the tiny settlement showed any signs of life as the light of dawn began to hint at a new day: a shack with lights on, and smoke curling invitingly from its chimney. Conversation on the U-boat's bridge — between captain, officer of the watch, and engineer and look-outs — moved casually and even intimately between the ranks ... [There was] half-earnest, half-whimsical banter about launching the dinghy for a trip ashore. The desire remained a haunting dream.[13]

Encouraged by the successes of early September, Dönitz ordered no fewer than five additional U-boats to the Gulf area: three to enter through the Cabot Strait, and two to renew the watch at the Strait of Belle Isle. *U-69*, under the command of Kapitänleutnant Ulrich Gräf, the first to arrive, found the same strong defences in the Cabot Strait that had turned back *U-517* the week before. On 2 October, Gräf located a convoy near St Paul Island in the strait, but was prevented from attacking by the constant appearance of aircraft. The Sydney squadrons were out in full force because they had been alerted by the navy's direction-finding bearings on Gräf's convoy contact signal to U-boat headquarters. Finally, Gräf pushed far into the river. Although Eastern Air Command's Mont-Joli detachment was continuing careful coverage of the river, in the narrow waters *U-69* was able to find an ambush position. In the early hours of 9 October the U-boat sank the freighter *Carolus*, from the Goose Bay-bound convoy LN 9, off Métis Beach. Press reports that appeared a week later focused on the fact that the attack took place less than 300 kilometres from Quebec City.

Residents of the south shore communities adjacent to Metis Beach were awakened by the blast of the torpedo...

The subsequent hunt for the submarine, during which Canadian corvettes fired star-shells and dropped depth charges, led Octave Gendron to think his lighthouse home was under bombardment and to fear for the safety of his large family ...

When the torpedo blast occurred ... Gendron reported the incident to the nearby Royal Canadian Air Force Training Station and obtained permission to turn off his light. He thought the enemy was bent on smashing the lighthouse.

He loaded his whole household — Mme Gendron, eight children and Esther Leblanc, the local school teacher who boards with them — into his car to get them out of range.[14]

Although the escorts were unable to make an asdic contact, around-the-clock air coverage of the river drove *U-69* out of the area within two days. The submarine, which was unable to remain on the surface long enough to recharge its batteries for continued underwater operations, crept away back to the Cabot Strait.

Meanwhile *U-106* and *U-43* were also arriving in the Cabot Strait. Although neither radioed, increased air patrols resulting from the general alert following the sinking in the river drove both submarines under the surface. Unfortunately, convoy BS 31, from Corner Brook, Newfoundland, crossed the path of *U-106*'s hiding place on the morning of 11 October. The submerged torpedo attack destroyed *Waterton*, one of the two steamers. HMCS *Vison*, the armed yacht sailing as the surface escort, made a snap, blind depth-charge attack. Although not on target, it had an effect. A 117 Squadron Canso had been flying in support, and the U-boat commander, Kapitänleutnant Herman Rasch, had been acutely aware of its dive towards the scene as the torpedo detonated. He believed that the depth charges had come from the Canso, and interpreted the loud engines of the Fairmile launches that came out to help with the search as evidence that he was being pursued by a powerful hunting group of destroyers and aircraft. Although he knew the density layering he was encountering in the water protected him against asdic detection, he went very deep and stayed there for eight hours.

U-106 continued into the Gulf for a three-week mission, and *U-43* patrolled there for 11 days. Al-

though both found shipping, neither achieved any sinkings in the face of the RCAF's heavy patrols and more aggressive sweeps around convoys by the naval escorts. *U-106's* veteran commander said conditions were '*exactly like those in the [Bay of] Biscay,*' where the highly experienced British Coastal Command was conducting an all-out offensive against U-boats as they made their way to and from bases in France. Ober-leutnant H-J Schwantke, *U-43's* commander, was impressed by the appearance of naval patrols soon after air sweeps, believing that the Canadians had achieved a highly effective coordination of air and sea defences.[15] This was especially laudatory in view of the fact that at the end of September the navy had cut back the Gulf force to the Fairmiles, Bangors and armed yachts, to carry out a reduced cycle of Sydney–Quebec convoys; it had not been possible entirely to shut down traffic by large merchant ships because of the needs of major industries in the Gulf region that could not be serviced by rail.

The bitter irony is that the very success of the defences in paralysing the U-boats contributed to disaster through a series of dreadful coincidences. Having been forced out of the Gulf, *U-69* lingered in the western approaches to the Cabot Strait early on 13 October, awaiting grain ships that headquarters had warned would be passing there. The ships proved to be Swedish neutrals, so Gräf did not try to follow them. Fearing detection by the air patrols from Sydney, he lay almost immobile beneath the surface throughout the 13th. Moonless conditions that night allowed the submarine to surface, as fate would have it, close by the track of the Newfoundland passenger ferry *Caribou*, which was making the crossing from North Sydney to Port-Aux-Basques. So bad was the visibility that the escorting Bangor, HMCS *Grandmère,* had difficulty seeing the big ferry from its station 1500 metres off to one side of the stern. The low profile of the submarine was utterly invisible as it tracked the ships for three hours, closed to within 650 metres of the ferry and fired, at 3:21 on the morning of 14 October. *Grandmère,* seeing the explosion, rushed ahead. At a range of 350 metres it finally saw the submarine and altered its course to ram as *U-69* crash-dived. The submarine went deep and stayed there, knowing that asdic could not penetrate these complex waters. The first, and unquestioned, obligation of *Grandmère's* commanding officer, Lieutenant James Cuthbert, Royal Canadian Naval Reserve (RCNR), was to find the submarine — to protect his own ship and all others that might cross its path. He tried for 90 minutes or more, but got no asdic contacts. The historian Douglas How, reporting on an

interview he had with Cuthbert in the 1980s, captured the agony that not just he, but hundreds of escort commanders, confronted in the aftermath of a torpedoing:

What made the night of October 13–14 his worst experience in years at war was what happened after he saw both the dying Caribou *and the surfaced submarine. The hunt, the asdic, the frustrations, the knowledge that men, women and children needed help, the doubts, the tensions, the searching of his soul, they are what can still sear his mind nearly half a century later. 'Oh, my God,' he says, 'I felt the full complement of things you feel at a time like that. Things you had to live with. You are torn. Demoralized. Terribly alone … I should have gone on looking for the submarine, but I couldn't. Not with women and children out there somewhere. I couldn't do it anymore than I could have dropped depth charges among them.' There are pain and sadness in his face. He gestures with his hands, and he says, 'Judge me how you will.'*[16]

As *Grandmère* turned with relief to rescue the survivors, it faced another sickeningly difficult situation. The ferry had gone down so quickly that only one lifeboat could be properly launched. Many of the survivors were clinging to small life rafts and bits of wreckage, rapidly becoming numb in the chill waters of the Cabot Strait, and they were being scattered by the winds and currents in the darkness. The arrival of a Canso from Sydney just as dawn was breaking helped, as the aircraft located groups of survivors, dropped smoke floats to mark their positions and signalled to the minesweeper. Civilian vessels came out from Newfoundland, about 70 kilometres away, and naval craft and a fast RCAF crash boat came from Sydney, some 140 kilometres distant from the scene. A total of 237 people had sailed in *Caribou*: 73 civilians, 46 crew and 118 Canadian and American military personnel. Only 101 survived. Half of the military personnel and two thirds of the civilians, including at least five mothers and 10 children, were lost. All but 15 of the crew died, which is indicative of the heroic efforts they made to get disoriented passengers clear of the plunging hull. Captain Ben Taverner, two of his sons and five other pairs of brothers were among the crew members lost, ripping the heart out of many families in Port-aux-Basques and Channel, the towns in southwest Newfoundland for whom the ferries had long been a business and way of life.

While families grieved — all across North America — and officials and officers looked for answers, there was another disaster that seemed to make a mockery of the defences. After *U-518* and *U-183*, the subma-

rines Dönitz had assigned to the Strait of Belle Isle, found nothing in their lonely, cold vigil, they moved down Newfoundland's Atlantic coast. On the night of 2 November *U-518* slipped into Conception Bay, sinking two loaded ore vessels at the Bell Island loading piers, again with heavy loss of life. The RCN had mounted a light patrol, consisting of a corvette and two Fairmiles, at Bell Island after the first losses had been inflicted by *U-513* in early September. This was the only interim measure possible, inadequate as it was for the protection of the vast bay, fully open to the Atlantic. During the rest of November and December, amid the early cold temperatures and gales of the brutal winter of 1942, the anti-submarine and anti-torpedo nets being lifted at Sydney for the freeze-up season were rushed to Bell Island. The work went ahead even though several of the barges the navy chartered for the work were driven ashore off Cape Breton in the heavy storms.

U-518 continued into the Gulf of St Lawrence, and, on the night of 8 November, landed a secret agent near New Carlisle, Quebec, on the north shore of Chaleur Bay. Alert townspeople quickly warned the Quebec Provincial Police about the suspicious arrival on foot of a stranger early in the morning, when no bus service was running, and he was arrested. *U-518* accomplished nothing else in the remaining 10 days of its patrol of the Gulf. *U-183,* evidently especially leery of the defences because defects had developed in the submarine's machinery, probed the Cabot Strait early in November and again towards the end of the month, but did not enter the Gulf.

In short, the five U-boats sent to the St Lawrence in the fall of 1942 sank a grand total of five vessels, only three of which were in the Gulf. Dönitz then decided that the area had to be 'evacuated,' primarily because of the RCAF. The air defences and, as the U-boat captains themselves remarked, the more active surface escorts, had limited the submarines to, at best, a single chance to shoot, and only when they had just arrived in a new area. Further experience during the war would show it was almost impossible to stop a submarine that did not radio and that hid beneath the surface much of the time. The best that could be hoped for was to force the submarine to remain immobile under the water, and therefore rendered incapable of pursuing shipping and making multiple attacks. The unavoidable danger, especially with a submarine newly arrived in an area, was that it might be able to ambush the one or two ships that passed nearby. As was only dimly appreciated in 1942, the possibilities of such ambushes were that much greater in the Gulf, as in much of Newfound-

land's and Canada's inshore waters, because asdic was so often ineffective. The Canadian forces had done as well as it was possible to do, with extremely limited resources, in the face of one of the trickiest problems in submarine warfare.

Yet it did not feel like victory. In October the Quebec newspaper *L'Action Catholique* published a series of ferociously critical articles under the title 'Ce qui se passe en Gaspésie' ('What is going on in the Gaspé'). Prominent English-language papers reprinted it, with their editorial endorsement: 'What is going on in Gaspe and what in Ottawa?' was how the headline in the *Toronto Telegram* put it. Although *L'Action Catholique* was no friend of the Liberal governments in Ottawa and Quebec City, Adélard Godbout, the premier of Quebec, passed the pieces to his federal counterparts, declaring them *'the most complete and objective articles I have seen on the subject.'*[17] The *L'Action Catholique* series synthesized in a powerful, if less factual, way what MPs from the Gulf area had been saying since May. This portrayal of the armed forces in some respects mirrored the bad press the navy had received in the First World War: an archaic military hierarchy that constantly tripped on its own unnecessary 'red tape.' These charges appeared in mid-October, just as word got out of the loss of *Caribou.*

Although the government responded more quickly and effectively than it had in 1918, with detailed information to rebut extreme claims and inspiring stories about the attacks on U-boats that had taken place, the armed forces themselves had little sense of victory. No submarine had been definitely sighted, let alone attacked, since the end of September. The meagre intelligence available only confirmed that a good number of U-boats had come into the Gulf during the fall. What no one could know was that some very aggressive U-boat commanders had been paralysed for weeks on end, or that happy accidents like *Vison's* ill-aimed attack on *U-106* at the moment a flying boat swooped down had given the Germans the impression of crisp efficiency. Instead, as in 1918, the focus was on the dramatic and bloody sinkings that did occur and not on the ones that were averted or thwarted. Officers and men were painfully aware only of how much had gone wrong. The officers visiting from the British Coastal Command, and the experienced captain of one of the British destroyers committed in the Gulf, did not stint in their well-intended criticism of failures in the complex art of close air-sea cooperation.

For the navy, the apparently dismal performance in the Gulf area was the least of its difficulties. The

renewed German wolf-pack offensive on the transatlantic routes in the summer and fall of 1942 had made the Gulf a backwater. Strikingly, in view of the government's long-standing concern about home defence and the intense political pressure it was under to strengthen the Gulf defences, the King administration fully supported the naval staff's conclusion: Canadian forces had to be prominent in the front lines of the Atlantic war. The problem was that, in the fall of 1942, it appeared that the navy's premier mid-ocean force was doing as badly as the inexperienced, ill-equipped St Lawrence groups.

CHAPTER VII

THE SECOND MID-OCEAN BATTLE, SUMMER 1942 – SPRING 1943

The Captain turned and shouted 'Signalman! Hold on tight a big one's heading for us.' When Williams nodded to the Captain and turned facing seaward, [he realized] in terror [the ship was] in a trough between two gigantic grey walls of sea, ahead is like dense fog; completely walled in by sea … [then came] the mad swirl and thunderous crash … 'How do you feel signalman?' the Captain shouted … [Williams's] teeth still chattering he hollered back 'F-fine Sir.' The Captain bellowed 'If it's any consolation m'boy weather like this sure as hell keeps U-boats down.'

Howard J. Williams, signalman, HMCS *Midland*, February–May 1943[1]

Symptoms of jadedness — some called it sea-fatigue — were beginning to show on the surface. There were always fears, of course. But these fears could normally be held in check, could be stowed away in the recesses of the mind. Now, and more frequently, they were pushing to the fore. They were vivid pictures of the ship breaking up under stress of weather, of getting in among the ships of the convoy on dark, invisible nights, as had happened,

and being run down by a heavily laden merchantman, of being torpedoed and trying to abandon ship on a rough night.

The worst time was dusk, when the dull day was fading and another ominous night was bearing down. I hated the sight of the yellowish-grey light, the dun seascape, the cold, curling waves as the evening dissolved into blackness.

There were times when I had been unjustifiably irritable, intolerant, which made me angry with myself afterwards — and probably angered others more. It was stupid, but there it was! Yet it was hard to tell how acutely I had been affected. I wondered how good my perspective was in judging my own nervous behaviour. I felt certain I had had enough.

Alan Easton, commanding officer, HMCS *Sackville*, 'Autumn 1942'[2]

Admiral Karl Dönitz's quest for vulnerable shipping brought the main U-boat force back to pack operations against north Atlantic convoys again in the summer of 1942. In a sense, the Atlantic war had

come full circle. Improved defences in British waters during 1941 had driven the submarines to mid-ocean in pursuit of weakly defended convoys beyond the reach of aircraft protection. Improved defences in Canadian and US waters during 1942 produced the same result.

In 1942, most of the advantages at mid-ocean lay with the Germans. During the first nine months of that year, the operational U-boat force underwent its greatest expansion of the war, from 91 to more than 200 submarines. By the fall of 1942 there were usually some 100 submarines at sea in the Atlantic — 45 on patrol and 60 heading towards or returning from their operational areas. By contrast, Allied defences at mid-ocean were no stronger than they had been in 1941, and in some respects they were weaker. One crucial thing that had not changed was the absence of air protection in the western part of the mid-ocean area, between the limits of patrols from Iceland and from Newfoundland. A single under-strength Coastal Command squadron of four-engine Consolidated Liberator bombers, stripped of all non-essential equipment and bolstered with the installation of additional fuel tanks, had been able to produce dramatic results on occasion, with patrols as far as 1500 kilometres from Iceland and Northern Ireland. Because of the overriding priority of the Allied strategic bombing offensive against Germany, however, pleas from the maritime air forces for additional four-engine bombers suitable for 'very long range' conversion had no effect. As it was, the Canadian, US Army and US Navy (USN) bombers available in Newfoundland could not safely reach their theoretical patrol range of 1000 kilometres, because the sudden appearance of fog so often shut down bases on the island dominion. Aircraft had to retain sufficient reserves of fuel for long diversions that could take them to the Maritime provinces and eastern Quebec. The 'air gap' therefore often began within 800 kilometres of the Newfoundland coast, and frequently closer still. As the Admiralty's *Monthly Anti-Submarine Report* put it, in uncharacteristically despairing tones: *'There is still a black pit of excessive danger in the main traffic area north-east of Newfoundland and it seems clear that the German U-Boat command is making strategic dispositions to intercept S.C. and H.X. convoys so near as may be to Cape Race — in some cases actually well within potential air cover from Canadian bases.'*[3]

The intelligence advantage the Allies had enjoyed in 1941 was gone, and the balance had swung to the benefit of the enemy. While the Allies were still unable to penetrate the four-rotor 'enigma' used for U-boat operations in the Atlantic, German intelligence had reconstructed the British Convoy Cypher No 3, and was able to provide timely information on as many as a third of the ocean convoys in the summer and fall of 1942. The intelligence blackout for the Allies had not been critical so long as the Germans continued to focus on the North American coast. The organization of shipping into convoys and air patrols in response to direction-finding bearings had been sufficient to stymie the German lone-hunter tactics. These measures in coastal waters also prevented the assembly of U-boats into groups for coordinated assaults on protected shipping. At mid-ocean, however, direction-finding bearings did not provide information that was complete or accurate enough for evasive routeing of convoys around U-boat concentrations, which were becoming larger and more numerous. And, of course, there was no air support to hinder the organization of wolf-packs. A senior officer from the USN's Newfoundland command saw at first hand how uncertain the intelligence picture had become, when he visited London in September 1942: *'... went to the Admiralty Convoy room and the submarine room where the "daily guess" [U-boat location estimate] is made up. I was present when they decided on the diversion of a convoy. A Vice Admiral, a Captain and three Commanders took forty-five minutes without reaching a decision, at which time I felt I had better leave.'*[4]

The surface escorts for the Newfoundland-to-Londonderry run were less numerous than they had been in the fall of 1941. The new requirement for North American coastal convoys had dispersed the Allied escort forces. It was not possible to reconcentrate on the transocean run, because Dönitz now had enough submarines to continue to exploit especially vulnerable coastal-waters areas, such as the Gulf of St Lawrence, while mounting pack operations at mid-ocean.

Through much of the summer and fall of 1942 there were only 11 groups in the Mid-Ocean Escort Force, each with a sailing strength of two destroyers and four corvettes, and they were a hybrid lot. By this time, only one of these was an 'A' (i.e., American) group, A 3. Its USN component was normally two ships, big modern 'Treasury'-class Coast Guard cutters that filled the role of destroyers even though their slower speed of 20 knots was not fully adequate. The whole corvette component of A 3 was from the Royal Canadian Navy (RCN).

Among the ships of the four Canadian, or 'C,' groups, there were usually two British destroyers. The RCN was very short of this type, with a grand total of eight that had sufficient endurance for the transatlantic crossing — six remaining from the modern

ships acquired in the 1930s plus HMCS *St Croix* and HMCS *St Francis*, the only 'long leg' vessels among the ex-US 'Town'-class the RCN had taken over in 1940. Because routine lay ups for boiler cleaning and refits accounted for at least a quarter of a ship's time, no fewer than 10 destroyers were needed to keep two at sea with each of the groups. The assignment of British destroyers to short-handed Canadian groups helped to fill the gap, but not, as we shall see, adequately.

Among the British ('B') groups, fully two thirds of the destroyers were old — either ex-US 'Town'-class or British ships of the same vintage. Nevertheless, they were at the leading edge of anti-submarine technology. In the mid-ocean battles of 1942, the latest devices, and the techniques based upon them, proved to be of critical importance in overcoming the German advantage. The Canadian escort force created in 1940–41 was rapidly becoming outdated, and the RCN found itself scrambling to catch up with what at the time were esoteric technologies and concepts. These developments took place, moreover, while the basic difficulties of getting more ships to sea continued. New vessels arrived from the builders at an unabated rate, and all had to be equipped and manned as quickly as possible, to meet increased operational demands.

The RCN had got off to a promising start with one of the new devices, radar. When in the summer and fall of 1940 the Royal Navy (RN) first encountered the problem of having to detect surfaced U-boats at night, the service had adapted the Air to Surface Vessel (ASV) Mark II equipment of the Royal Air Force (RAF). The great virtue of the set, the naval version of which was known as type 286, was its compactness. This allowed fitting in the cramped spaces of destroyers and corvettes. The British installed type 286 in the Canadian destroyers that served in UK waters. Only belatedly, early in 1941, did Naval Service Headquarters (NSHQ) in Ottawa find out that it was also policy to fit corvettes. This slow notice was typical of problems in technical liaison between the Canadian and British navies since the outbreak of war. As in the case of the initial corvette- and Bangor-building programmes, the difficulties were partly the result of the RCN's paucity of officers qualified for technical liaison postings in Britain, and partly because developments were so rapid that the Admiralty itself had difficulty maintaining a grip. Given these problems, and given the government policy of maximum industrial development at home, the RCN accepted the offer of the National Research Council of Canada (NRC) to develop an equivalent of the type 286. The prototype of what would become SW1C (surface warning number one Canadian) was ready for sea trials in May 1941, and general fitting of the corvette fleet was well in hand by the beginning of 1942. These achievements are all the more impressive in light of the fact that production of the established ASV Mark II design in Canada for both the Canadian and US air forces encountered delays that could be overcome only with American assistance. General fitting of Eastern Air Command aircraft was not completed until the fall of 1942.

Among the ship and aircraft crews such fancy new gizmos did not always win ready acceptance. John Roué, an engineering officer at St John's who was responsible for installing SW1C, found that one officer in HMCS *Battleford* was anything but pleased.

They had taken the officers heads [washroom] and installed the RDF in that ... there was one of the officers in the ship ... who was a south coast Newfoundlander, and when he had left [the ship for a few hours] we had not been on board with our marvellous new gadget ... he came [back to the ship] storming into what was normally the heads to use it for its assigned purpose ... here was this bloody radar set sitting there and me working on it ... there was a motor generator in the bathtub, there were nuts and bolts in the wash basin, there was a control panel across the can ... he was heard saying, 'Its a fine f—ing thing when a man can't have a f—ing shit in his own f—ing ship in peace.'[5]

More seriously, both British and Canadian air crews had little confidence in ASV because of problems with antenna design and equipment maintenance that initially hindered its performance. In the fall of 1942 Eastern Air Command had to order crews to use the equipment. The staff officers soon received an unwelcome suggestion from Squadron Leader N. E. Small, the star squadron commander — he wanted to move the radar console to the front of the aircraft, just behind the windscreen, so that the radar operator could do something useful by assisting the pilots with visual searches!

Small had a point. ASV, type 286 and SW1C all operated on a long wavelength of approximately 1.5 metres, which gave weak returns from small objects like a surfaced submarine. In clear weather, 'eyeball mark 1' was more effective in spotting a submarine than airborne ASV radar. The performance of type 286 and SW1C in naval escorts was poorer. It was impossible in the little ships to mount the antennae high enough to achieve results comparable to those in aircraft. A considerable portion of the vertically deep

beam produced at the long wavelength projected into the surface of the water, which created interference. In anything but moderate seas, the swell entirely masked a U-boat's hull.

The 1.5-metre radar proved itself for navigation at night and in foggy weather, however. It was particularly useful for naval escorts in keeping station while in convoy, and for avoiding every crew's nightmare of being run down by a large merchant ship. HMCS *Sackville* and HMCS *Brandon* were among the early recipients of SW1C, in 1941, and their seasoned merchant-marine captains, Alan Easton and John Littler, instantly appreciated the new device:

It had been an extraordinary trip in a way. Since it was foggy we came round Cape Breton instead of taking the shorter route through the Gut of Canso. We used radar, which was the curiosity that made the voyage extraordinary. It had actually picked out the coast! It was hard to believe but the operator said he was sure it was the coast. Then he reported a vessel ahead and eventually we overtook her. The radar was right! In my ignorance of modern science I had not believed it possible, but who in the summer of 1941 knew much or anything about radar? I became for the first time aware of its possibilities and saw all the dangers of fog magically disappearing. Life in the Atlantic, I misguidedly thought, was going to be almost rosy.[6]

Very soon we were headed through the cleft in the cliffs which is the entrance to St John's Harbour, and then feeling our way in dense fog towards a convoy steaming at six knots towards Britain. We were now fortunate to have a radar. It was the most primitive of its kind, and subject to the weirdest pulse variations as we slid into the troughs between waves. Nevertheless, a good operator could pick up a 10,000-ton merchantman at about 3 miles.[7]

Although Canada had done well to produce SW1C — and improved SW2C and SW3C versions — most RCN corvettes did not have radar until a year after their British counterparts. By that time the 1.5-metre equipment had been surpassed by one of the great scientific and engineering revolutions of the Second World War. British university scientists had in 1940 developed the cavity magnetron, the basis for a whole new class of miniaturized electronic tubes and components that could produce powerful emissions on a wavelength of only 10 centimetres. During 1941 the Admiralty rushed the application of this experimental technology to produce the type 271 radar within a few short months. The narrow centimetric beams could locate small targets more surely and accurately than metric radars. The effective range was only a few kilometres, and masking of U-boats

by the ocean swell remained a problem, but here, finally, was an instrument that would allow escorts to throw a continuous electronic fence around a convoy, making it far more difficult for U-boats to swarm undetected into the midst of the merchant ships for multiple, lethal, close-range shots.

Most mid-ocean RCN escorts would not receive the invaluable centimetric equipment until early 1943. Neither British nor American production could promptly meet Canadian needs. The NRC's attempt at an independent design, the RX/C 10-centimetre radar, moved much more slowly than the SW1C project because of the quantum leap to centimetric engineering.

The rapid pace of unprecedented technical change was overwhelming the Canadian navy, and not surprisingly so. Submarine warfare posed challenges that stretched the resources of the British and American navies, with their vast array of specialists, their integral scientific services, and their well-developed relationships with industry and universities. Lacking almost all of these assets, senior Canadian officers found it increasingly difficult to grasp the torrent of new developments and their complex, interrelated implications. At the same time, the expert specialists required to establish close, effective ties with the British and American equipment programmes, and to provide essential, detailed guidance to the NRC and industry, did not exist.

For these same reasons, the RCN was also slow to acquire the compact high-frequency radio direction-finding sets (H/F D/F) that were fitted in British escorts from the beginning of 1942. Modelled on the shore stations that gave bearings on U-boats' radio signals to their headquarters, the small ship-borne version was even more useful for escort commanders. Experienced operators could readily distinguish between distant transmissions and transmissions that were within 50 or 60 kilometres of the convoy. That information was sufficient for one of the destroyers of the escort to make a fast run 'down the bearing' of the transmission, forcing the U-boat to submerge and lose contact with the convoy. If two or more sets were available in the convoy, they could give fuller information by triangulating the approximate position of the U-boats. Ship-borne H/F D/F was a complement to centimetric radar, and was in some ways more effective. High seas did not affect its performance, and it could detect U-boats at greater ranges than radar, enabling escorts to respond before the submarines were in a position to attack.

* * *

(DHH, E-50834)

(Courtesy of R. L. Hennessy)

I closed U-boat to ram at full speed ... He opened fire with all his guns ... A second degree fire ... spread almost to the bridge ... : HMCS *Assiniboine* in action against *U-210,* August 1942.

Shell hits on the forward gunshield. (DHH, NF-778)

Despite the shortcomings of the Canadian escorts' equipment, the experience and energy of their crews produced what historian Marc Milner has termed 'an acceptable rate of exchange' during the early battles of the renewed German mid-ocean offensive in July, August and the first part of September 1942. Losses were moderate — four ships or fewer in three of the four main battles involving RCN groups — and Canadian warships had confirmed sinkings of three submarines. We now know that the corvette HMCS *Morden* destroyed a fourth submarine with a well-executed depth-charge attack, the method by which *St Croix* — and HMCS *Skeena* and the corvette HMCS *Wetaskiwin* in a team effort — sank two other U-boats.

The action in which HMCS *Assiniboine* destroyed *U-210* on 2 August 1942, however, was a wild surface chase. In the opening phase of a U-boat concentration against SC 94, south of Greenland, the destroyer and the submarine stumbled into one another in a clear spot amid banks of fog. There was only a moderate sea running, and *Assiniboine's* 1.5-metre radar was able to regain contact as *U-210* tried to escape at top speed into the mist. In the words of *Assiniboine's* commanding officer, Lieutenant-Commander J. H. Stubbs, RCN:

14. I closed U-boat to ram at full speed ... He opened fire with all his guns and for about 35 minutes the action continued at a point blank range of about 100 to 300 yards. A second degree fire broke out on the starboard side at the break of the forecastle and spread almost to the bridge and through the sick bay flat. The enemy took constant evading action and I was forced to go full astern on the inside engine to prevent him getting inside our turning circle, which he was obviously trying to do.

15. It was impossible to depress the 4.7" guns sufficiently at this range, but I ordered them to continue firing, more to keep the guns' crews busy while under fire than from any hope of hitting. One hit was gained on the conning tower however.

16. During most of the action we were so close that I could make out the Commanding Officer on the conning tower bending down occasionally to pass wheel orders. A gun's crew appeared on the deck and attempted to reach the forward gun but our multiple .5's [machine guns] successfully prevented this.

17. Three or four times we just missed him. The officers left the conning tower in order to dive, and in the few seconds during which he was on a steady course we rammed him just abaft the conning tower. He was actually in the process of diving at the time.

18. I turned as quickly as possible to find him surfacing again but slightly down by the stern, still firing

and making about 10 knots. After a little manoeuvring, we rammed him again well abaft the conning tower and fired a shallow pattern of depth charges as we passed. Also one 4.7" shell from 'Y' Gun scored a direct hit on his bows. He sank by the head in about two minutes.[8]

Although the bridge was in the midst of a swarm of rounds from the U-boat's automatic weapons and the billowing flames from the onboard fire, Stubbs was icy calm. Recalled R. L. Hennessy, the first lieutenant, *'I think they counted up later the number of engine orders and helm orders he had given during this process, and it was in three figures ...'[9]* Stubbs insisted the praise should go to the coxswain (helmsman), Chief Petty Officer Max Bernays, RCN, who, though entirely isolated in the wheelhouse by flames and smoke, *'carried out every command as if it were a normal Sunday.'[10]* Bernays received the Conspicuous Gallantry Medal. One witness recalled that the ship's pets also performed coolly. *'The ... puppy, who was accustomed to lie down, looking like a poached egg ... lay at its moorings throughout the tumult with every hair in place. The captain's cat, being a cat, found a comfortable hide-out within the vitals of the ship.'[11]*

The destroyer had suffered serious damage in the action. The superstructure had been charred and battered by the fire and the submarine's automatic cannon; the stem had been buckled and several compartments flooded in the ramming. One seaman had been killed in the action, and 13 others wounded. *Assiniboine* returned to port, carrying 38 survivors from the U-boat. The destroyer would be under repair until January 1943. It was a loss the under-strength RCN mid-ocean groups could ill afford.

Soon the C groups would lose another destroyer, but under tragic circumstances. Convoy ON 127 was nearing Newfoundland on the night of 13 September 1942, after a four-day struggle with a pack of some 13 U-boats. At the moment reinforcements were arriving from the Western Local Escort Force (WLEF), *U-91* made two surface torpedo attacks that crippled and then finished off HMCS *Ottawa*. Over a hundred of the destroyer's crew were lost, including its young commanding officer, Acting Lieutenant-Commander C. A. Rutherford, RCN. Although he got away from the ship, he had been so exhausted by constant action during the preceding days that he quickly succumbed in the water. T. C. Pullen, the first lieutenant, was still haunted 50 years later by one 'ineradicable memory' from the ship's last minutes:

The pitiable entreaties emanating from the voice pipe to the bridge from ... two young hands trapped in the asdic hut far below became unbearable to those on the bridge, who were totally helpless to do anything for

... the stem had been buckled; also note the wooden stakes driven through the shellfire holes in the hull as an emergency repair. (Courtesy of R. L. Hennessy)

Rear-Admiral L. W. Murray congratulates *Assiniboine*'s people. (Courtesy of R. L. Hennessy)

Assiniboine's officers: Lieutenant-Commander J. H. Stubbs is holding the ship's dog; Lieutenant R. L. Hennessy is to his left. (Courtesy of R. L. Hennessy)

them. What could, what should, one do other than offer words of encouragement that help was coming when such was manifestly out of the question? What happened at the end is hard to contemplate for the imprisoned pair, as that pitch black, watertight, sound-proofed box rolled first 90 degrees to starboard and then 90 degrees onto its back before sliding into the depths and oblivion.[12]

The board of inquiry into the sinking concluded that if *Ottawa* had been fitted with type 271 radar the crew almost certainly would have detected the submarine in the darkness before it was able to fire.

The fall of 1942 was a particularly unfortunate time for the RCN to lose one quarter of its precious long-range destroyers. The escort fleets of all the Allied powers were more thinly stretched than ever because of the redeployment of ships to prepare for the operation Torch landings in North Africa. The Canadian mid-ocean force was the hardest pressed among the Allied fleets, and partly for this reason its ships were often less well maintained and more prone to breakdowns. Repair facilities at St John's were limited, those at Halifax overburdened. The British base at Londonderry, and the base that the USN had also established there in early 1941, when it had seemed US warships might concentrate in British waters, gave excellent service to the Canadians. Still, the inability of the RCN to establish effective technical liaison in the United Kingdom created difficulties in coordinating work, setting priorities and procuring equipment. In September 1942, Rear-Admiral R. M. Brainard, USN, Bristol's successor as commander Task Force 24 at Argentia, tactfully pointed out another part of the problem. RCN ships were too dependent on protracted refits, because the crews had insufficient technical training and, equally important, lacked the necessary focus on technical matters. In particular, officers responsible for ensuring that the ship and all its component systems were fit for service were not organizing preventive maintenance routines, or working closely with dockyard personnel in anticipating and rooting out problems. Rear-Admiral Murray, who had recently been transferred to the Halifax command, not only agreed, but stated the problems were more fundamental than Brainard realized. Indeed Murray implied that Brainard's comments were pitched at a level that reflected the immense professional and industrial resources of the USN. The American admiral did not seem to understand the full extent to which the RCN had had to build from virtually a dead start, beginning only in 1940.

It is fully realized that the Canadian Naval executive personnel on the whole lack knowledge of ship mainte-nance, but they also, to some extent, lack knowledge of the tactical handling of ships employed as escorts.

With the pleas from all sides for more and more escorts, ships have been sent to sea as soon as officers could be trained to handle them, and maintenance has taken second place in the training programme of Executive Officers.[13]

So limited was the technical knowledge of many of the officers, Murray warned, that to compel them to administer maintenance programmes would be to throw unhelpful red tape in the way of the qualified engine-room personnel. Interestingly, Murray was optimistic about the *'new type of Corvette commanding Officer [who] is slowly coming to the fore — the Naval trained R.C.N.V.R. Officer.'* This was undoubtedly a reference to the many talented people, with little or no marine background, who had joined the volunteer reserve in the late 1930s or after that and who demonstrated an impressive ability rapidly to absorb and apply complex material that was entirely new to them. Murray also noted that, as Canadian shipbuilders gained experience, new vessels were proving to be better constructed, and he listed the initiatives the RCN was taking. Additional technical training programmes were in hand, as was the expansion of existing dockyard facilities and the construction of large new refit and repair bases at Sydney and Shelburne, Nova Scotia. Many of these were long-term solutions, however.

Murray did not write his reply to Brainard until 10 November, and he may have been particularly sensitive at that time, as the effectiveness of the Canadian forces was coming under much closer scrutiny. The building weight of the German offensive, the diversions of escorts to Torch and the over-commitment of the RCN produced another convoy disaster that uncannily echoed SC 42. SC 107, another convoy in that same ill-fated slow series, sailed from New York on 24 October 1942.

As the convoy passed south of Cape Race and headed northeast on 30 October, a total of 16 U-boats were gathering in its path. On that day things seemed to bode well for the defence. The direction-finding service had triangulated positions on signals from some of the submarines, and Hudsons from Eastern Air Command's 145 Squadron at the new air base at Torbay flew high-altitude search missions in these areas. One of the aircraft, close to its maximum range nearly 600 kilometres from base, destroyed *U-658*. Later in the day, a high-flying Digby from 10 Squadron at Gander, while returning from escort for another convoy threatened by the pack, sighted *U-520* and made a lethal depth-charge

attack. The destruction of two submarines in a single day was an outstanding feat and Eastern Air Command continued to produce good results. On the following day, 31 October, one of four Hudsons from 145 Squadron, providing direct support to the convoy, made an attack on *U-521* that was just a moment too late — the submarine had dived quickly enough to escape destruction by the accurate attack. Nevertheless, *U-521*, which had been shadowing SC 107 at a distance of 20 kilometres, lost contact with the convoy. The Hudson had picked up the submarine on ASV Mark II radar at a range of nearly 12 kilometres in thickening weather — an impressive performance with 1.5-metre equipment. On 1 November two Catalina flying boats from 116 Squadron, Royal Canadian Air Force (RCAF), provided support, but the weather then closed in at their Botwood base. The convoy was thus moving into the air gap when it was only 800 kilometres from Newfoundland, and just as it was arriving in the midst of the main concentration of submarines.

Unfortunately its mid-ocean escort group, C 4, had been depleted by breakdowns. There was only one destroyer, HMCS *Restigouche*. The second destroyer, *St Croix*, could not be repaired in time for the trip, and there was no replacement destroyer available. Also, HMCS *Sherbrooke*, one the group's corvettes, could not sail because of defects. Flag Officer Newfoundland, now Commodore H. E. Reid, RCN, therefore attached two of the corvettes scheduled to go overseas for Torch to strengthen the group, but one of these broke down and had to return to St John's; its replacement would not reach the convoy until attacks had already begun. That left an initial strength of *Restigouche* and four corvettes, scarcely better than the utterly inadequate escort of SC 42. Although three of the corvettes were long-time members of C 4, two had received new commanding officers less than six weeks earlier. C 4 had been the group that had gone through the ON 127 battle. After that nightmare one commanding officer had to be hospitalized for exhaustion, and it became apparent that another had collapsed into alcoholism. Their replacements were Lieutenants L. C. Audette (HMCS *Amherst*) and D. G. King (HMCS *Arvida*). Both were members of the Royal Canadian Naval Volunteer Reserve (RCNVR) who had joined only shortly before the war, and progressed brilliantly. Rear-Admiral Murray may well have been thinking of them when he spoke of his optimism for the new breed of VR officer rising to command. Still, Audette later reflected:

The transition from young lawyer and lowly new entry naval officer to the lonely and responsible office of Captain of a ship is a very drastic one [all within the space of exactly three years]. I was to become responsible for immensely valuable public property, one of 'Her [sic] Majesty's Canadian Ships,' and, more importantly, for the lives and safety of officers and men trained at great expense for the art of war as well as for the safety of convoyed ships and the lives of those sailing in them and of the urgently needed cargoes they carried. Once at sea, between God and the Captain there are no longer the many intermediaries found elsewhere in life. The Captain is the man to whom all turn in moments of crisis at sea and the man who has no one to whom to turn.[14]

The group had the advantage of high-frequency direction-finding equipment. *Restigouche* was the first Canadian warship to be fitted, and there was a second set in the rescue ship *Stockport*. Only one ship in the group, the British corvette HMS *Celadine,* had type 271 radar, however, and that set was out of action through much of the trip.

Soon after the convoy left air cover on 1 November, the pack re-established contact, and closed in that night for the first of seven attacks over the next 72 hours. The high-frequency direction-finding equipment gave warning of the large number of U-boats nearby and *Restigouche* raced out repeatedly to put down the submarines. The one destroyer, the sole warship of the escort with the necessary speed for such searches, could not be everywhere at once. Acting Lieutenant-Commander D. W. Piers, RCN, commanding officer of *Restigouche* and senior officer of the group, found himself facing the dilemma that Lieutenant-Commander Hibbard had a year before, with SC 42. Every time the destroyer pursued a promising U-boat contact, Piers had to gamble that other members of the pack would not overwhelm the inadequate corvette screen around the convoy. Despite the arrival of the fifth, replacement, corvette on 2 November and a British destroyer on the 3rd, the convoy had lost 15 of 42 merchant ships by the time it passed south of Greenland and reached the limits of air cover from Iceland on 5 November.

* * *

SC 107 was the fourth, and worst, instance of heavy losses by ocean convoys to wolf-packs since mid-October. The combined effects of the huge losses in US coastal waters earlier in the year, and American requirements for shipping to deploy and supply its forces overseas, had caused British imports to plummet by 25 percent, as compared to figures for 1941. Understandably, the British government was doubly concerned at the evidence that the Germans were regaining the initiative at mid-ocean. On

31 October, Prime Minister Winston Churchill had warned President Roosevelt that all Allied plans, not just Britain's war effort, were in jeopardy:

> *First of all, I put the U-boat menace. This, I am sure, is our worst danger ... the spectacle of all these splendid ships being built, sent to sea crammed with priceless food and munitions, and being sunk — three or four every day — torments me day and night. Not only does this attack cripple our war energies and threaten our life, but it arbitrarily limits the might of the United States coming into the struggle. The Oceans which were your shields, threaten to become your cage.*
>
> *Next year, there will be many more U-boats, and they will range far more widely. No ocean passage will be safe.[15]*

Even as the U-boats were pressing home attack after attack on SC 107, in early November Churchill established the Cabinet Anti-U-Boat Warfare Committee, under his personal direction, to focus Britain's best brains and resources on the convoy defence problem.

As it happened, the RN's Western Approaches command was just then, in November 1942, receiving a new commander-in-chief, Admiral Sir Max Horton. Horton, a submarine officer, had a near obsession with thorough training not uncommon to people who have served in that supremely dangerous and demanding environment: quick, precise teamwork can mean the difference between life and death in even the most routine operations. It was this perspective he brought to his new command:

> *The Escort Group System has proved itself to be beyond all doubt the basic principle of successful anti-submarine operations. There are many examples of well trained and equipped groups, resolutely led, beating off determined U-boat attacks. There are also examples of convoys suffering disastrous losses when escorted by a collection of ships strange to one another, untrained as a team and led by an officer inexperienced in convoy protection. Until each group is led and manned by competent officers, and until it has attained a high degree of group efficiency and is completely equipped with the latest devices, heavy losses will continue. The immediate object must therefore be: to raise the standard of the less efficient groups to the level of the most efficient ones.[16]*

There is no doubt about which groups the Western Approaches staff considered to be the least efficient. When Captain H. C. Fitz, USN, who knew the RCN well, visited Western Approaches in the summer of 1942 he had been taken aback at the attitude towards the Canadian service: 'British naval officers as a class think the Canadians very ineffective. In all the time I was there I did not hear one single word

in their favor.'[17] Any inclination Horton might have had to question this prevailing wisdom was instantly erased by reports on the SC 107 losses, which were among the first items to cross his desk as he took over his new command.

With the near panic in the British government over losses in convoy and the import crisis, it was not long before Horton's views reached the highest levels. On 17 December, Churchill sent a personal telegram to Mackenzie King, broaching a proposal that radically affected Canada's naval participation in the Battle of the Atlantic. It was nothing less than a full-scale withdrawal of the RCN from the crucial mid-ocean run. All four C groups were to switch to the United Kingdom-to-Gibraltar route for a period of four months, escorting the convoys that were supplying the Torch offensive in North Africa. British groups thereby released would allow the reinforcement of the RN component of the transatlantic forces. The main object of the change was to give relief to the C groups from the brutal north Atlantic run. Commodore J. M. Mansfield, Horton's chief of staff, rushed to Washington and Ottawa to win support with a tactful explanation:

> *It is really the first step in this concentrated training drive ... which we feel is absolutely essential, because we are not going to get more escorts; and if anything, we have got to prepare for less. It is vital that all our groups on the North Atlantic run should be as highly trained as possible, and work in teams. It is not merely a question of training the Canadian groups, but it is a question of raising the standards of all the groups, because it is quite natural that their personnel are more inexperienced than ours, and as such they, in our opinion, require additional training, and our intention always has been in this scheme that this was a temporary business to put the groups in turn on the Gibraltar run, which gives a much longer lay-over in UK than the transAtlantic run does, and we are going to develop this training drive at LONDONDERRY [which would be the C groups' main base while they were on the Gibraltar run]. When that is done the groups that are trained will be swapped with 'B' groups, which go into the same training drive ...*
>
> *... take ... a football team. If you have got two sets of persons, eleven on a side, and one side played together for a season and the other side have met for the first time — who are you going to put your money on? ... you get the answer with the trained team.[18]*

The diplomatic language did not soften the impact of the message in Ottawa. The C groups were being asked to leave the main theatre. Captain E. S. Brand, the British officer who ran the convoy

The transition from young lawyer … to the lonely and responsible office of Captain of a ship is a very drastic one: Lieutenant-Commander L. C. Audette, RCNVR. (Courtesy of P. C. Connolly)

(NAC, PL-16165)

(NAC, PL-36213)

RCAF ground crew pull a trolley of 113-kilogram aerial depth charges and hoist the weapons into the high wing of a Consolidated Canso.

organization at NSHQ, recalled the 'frightful flap' the news caused. He saw Admiral Nelles, a friend who was the godfather of Brand's baby son, and offered to try to help through his own network in the RN. Nelles turned on the British officer, saying something *nasty like "You keep the hell out of it."* [19]

Wisely, the naval staff sent Captain H. G. DeWolf, RCN, now director of plans at NSHQ, to Washington for the detailed negotiations with Mansfield and other senior British and American officers. DeWolf was one of the few senior Canadian officers who took a balanced view of the reorganization. In an easy, highly professional manner that evidently impressed the British and American officers, DeWolf explained Canada's special stake in the mid-ocean run: *'To transfer the Canadian groups to other spheres would require government decision … The government's view is that we have sort of grown up with this North Atlantic problem and feel we have a permanent interest in it.'* DeWolf freely admitted the RCN needed all the help it could get. However, calling to mind Murray's response to Admiral Brainard, he made it clear that the real source of the service's difficulties was its overextension as a result of relentless British and American requests to provide escorts at all costs. *'We are convinced that any ship is better than none. We have done that for two years.'* He pointed out that the C groups were running with no reserve, each having to keep six escorts regularly at sea from a total strength of only six. Everyone knew one result: ships had constantly to be shifted between groups to allow for refits and unforeseen breakdowns, meaning that it was extremely difficult for the ships of any one group to become a cohesive fighting unit. Because of the especially frequent switching about of British and Canadian destroyers, no one senior officer had a chance firmly to establish his leadership in a group. DeWolf went on to explain a further difficulty. Although much was being done to improve facilities for training at the Canadian bases, ships — let alone full groups — could not be released from operations to take advantage of them: *'When you have only 6 untrained [escorts in a group], then you hesitate to take one away, because any lower than that is getting scanty. It has been the six all along. We have even kept them at sea against our better judgement. Any ships are better than none.'* British groups], by contrast, each had eight or nine ships. This allowed each group dependably to run six ships, with an ample margin for the scheduling of maintenance, training and rest. Under questioning from the US officers about the details of British practice, however, Mansfield admitted that in the winter conditions now roaring down upon the

Atlantic, even eight or nine ships was not sufficient to keep six at sea: *'At the height of last winter we found ourselves down to 50 percent in the North Atlantic.'* [20]

Despite the anger at NSHQ, no one fundamentally disagreed with DeWolf's view that the C groups needed help, even if in the unpalatable form of withdrawal. A year before, senior RCN officers had raised the training problem in almost the same terms used by Horton and Mansfield, but the pressure of enemy action had allowed no slackening in the pace of RCN expansion to permit more thorough training. Any grounds for strongly questioning the transfer disappeared on 25–29 December, when ONS 154 lost 14 ships to a large wolf-pack while under the escort of C 1. As in the case of C 4 with SC 107, the experienced Canadian warships performed well, but the group, as a fighting team, had been weakened by last-minute changes. Most important, there was, once again, only one destroyer, HMCS *St Laurent* (which destroyed a submarine during the battle). The second, British, destroyer could not sail, which added fuel to resentment in Ottawa that the senior Allies gave every assistance to the C groups, except what was really needed, when it was urgently required! That sentiment was captured in the note a frustrated RCN staff officer scribbled at the bottom of Admiral Horton's critical review of C 4's performance in the SC 107 battle: *'How about giving us a few decent destroyers in the C Groups, Maxie? Instead of the discarded sweepings you've given us now!'* [21]

In fact, the withdrawal was neither complete nor as long as had been intended. The Canadian government had once again strongly supported the RCN's Atlantic commitment by agreeing to the withdrawal only if it were for no more than four months. This strict condition did not prove necessary. Only three of the four groups went to the Gibraltar run, and then only for eight to 10 weeks in February to March 1943. The Canadian ships could not be spared for longer, as it turned out. The continued expansion of the U-boat force to a peak strength of 230 operational submarines at the beginning of March 1943, and weather damage to escorts during the especially severe winter, compelled Western Approaches command to search for reinforcements. Good luck, and more effective evasive routeing as British code-breakers began to crack the four-rotor 'enigma,' saved the C groups from the most intense battles of the first part of 1943.

The one sustained north Atlantic action in which Canadian warships played a prominent part gave some weight to both British and Canadian perspectives on efficiency. ONS 166 was besieged by a large

pack on 21–25 February 1943 and lost 11 ships. The escort group, A 3, included the US Coast Guard cutters *Spencer* and *Campbell*, the British corvette HMS *Dianthus* and four Canadian corvettes. The group had a stable membership, so the ships were used to working together, and it had excellent leadership over a period of months by Commander Paul R. Heineman, USN, an experienced, superbly qualified officer. Undoubtedly, as senior British and American authorities appreciated, the losses would have been more devastating but for the superior organization of the group.

Still, problems the Canadians knew so well had made the convoy vulnerable. This slow convoy had been slowed even more by a nine-day gale. There were no destroyers, aside from the Free Polish *Burza*, which provided support during one attack, for swift offensive sweeps to keep the pack at bay. Heineman echoed the cries of Lieutenant-Commander Hibbard and Acting Lieutenant-Commander Piers for larger escort groups. The *'lack of sufficient escorts to properly screen a large convoy,'* he concluded, *'was further aggravated by casualties and damages to escorts, searches for U-boats and screening and rescue work. This at times required the release of more than half of the unit and so reduced protection around the convoy to only two or three ships …'* So far as the quality of individual ships went, Heineman had special praise for two of his Canadian corvettes:

At least three of the escorts performed in a very outstanding manner, the [USS] SPENCER, [HMCS] ROSTHERN, and [HMCS] TRILLIUM, who by their aggressive actions prevented at least five additional attacks on convoy and did yeoman duty in screening and rescue work … They were a tower of strength to the Escort Commander.[22]

ONS 166 benefited, all too briefly, from Eastern Air Command's best effort yet to push into the air gap. The command had only one squadron of long-range aircraft that could operate from Newfoundland in winter. This was 5 Squadron, the command's oldest unit, which had been equipped with the amphibious version of the Canso, fitted with landing gear so that it could work from airstrips as well as from water. The installation of the retractable wheels was a tricky modification of the original Catalina/Canso design, so deliveries of amphibians from the RCAF order placed in 1940 were later and slower than those of the straight flying-boat versions. The command's two squadrons of long-range flying boats had been obliged to head to southern bases with the freeze-up of northern waters in December.

The ubiquitous Squadron Leader Small, a very experienced Catalina/Canso pilot, worked with

5 Squadron in extending the range of the amphibians by stripping out equipment that could be spared and by carrying extra fuel. He was killed at Gander in January 1943, when the Canso amphibian he was flying suffered a mechanical failure on take-off and crashed. Nevertheless, Small's efforts paid dividends on 24 February, when four Canso amphibians reached ON 166 at 40 degrees west, some 1200 kilometres from Gander, 50 percent beyond the normal safe limits of the Cansos. Depth-charge attacks by the aircraft severely damaged one submarine and forced another to break contact with the convoy. The pity was that the command did not have four-engine Liberators, which Coastal Command on the other side of the Atlantic was now receiving in increased numbers as a result of the British government's alarm about convoy defence. With Liberators, Eastern Air Command could have reached ON 166 a day or two earlier, when the U-boats achieved their greatest success by overwhelming the depleted and exhausted naval escorts. The RCAF had long been pleading with Allied aircraft allocation authorities for Liberators. Until only shortly before that time, of course, even the most senior air forces in the Atlantic theatre had been sent to the end of a long line to await what little could be spared from the bombing offensive in Europe, or from US requirements for long-range aircraft to cover the vast distances in the Pacific.

Support for Eastern Air Command's case came from a somewhat surprising but convincing source. Shortly before the ONS 166 action, Squadron Leader T. M. Bulloch and Flying Officer M. S. Layton, the pilot and navigator of the most successful air crew in Coastal Command's very successful Liberator squadron, No 120, made a liaison visit to the Canadian command. Layton was a Canadian and a member of the RCAF, one of the tens of thousands of air crew recruited and trained for service in the RAF under the British Commonwealth Air Training Plan. These junior officers saw the rough edges and problems that worried more senior visitors, but, as members of a front-line unit, they also recognized fundamental strengths:

We were deeply impressed with the keenness and enterprise of all personnel on the Squadrons we visited. This keenness was manifest in a genuine desire to learn and find out everything possible from us. Many of the aircrew have completed more than 1,000 operational hours. They fly often more than 100 hours in a month and we found elaborate training programmes drawn up for all Squadrons. They unquestionably have a thorough knowledge of operational tactics although some of the more recent operational orders of Coastal Command

have not yet been issued to them. On every station we visited there was a universal demand for more suitable aircraft, in particular, no-one can understand why a Squadron of Liberators has not been formed on this coast. We do not hesitate to venture the opinion that with first class aircraft and equipment these Squadrons are capable of doing everything expected of them on the Western Atlantic.[23]

There was further evidence of the basic soundness of Canada's maritime forces in the record of the 16 corvettes that had gone to the Mediterranean and the three C groups that escorted Gibraltar convoys in the eastern Atlantic during the early months of 1943. After brief periods of refresher training at London-derry, and, perhaps more important, fitting with type 271 radar and improved asdic, the ships gave a good account of themselves in defending convoys that came under both submarine and air attack. In addition to the better weather in the southern waters, they had the advantage of a less demanding schedule and employment in large escort forces that combined two or more groups. As a result, the ships were able to stay together to develop teamwork, while both the crews and the vessels had more opportunity for rest and recuperation. Merchant vessels as slow as those in the Atlantic SC and ONS series were not deployed in this theatre, so speed gave a further advantage.

The Canadian vessels showed considerable offensive power. The corvettes in the Mediterranean destroyed two Italian and one German submarine in January and early February. In early March, *St Croix* and HMCS *Shediac* of C 1 destroyed another U-boat while escorting a Gibraltar convoy. This was the second victory for *St Croix*, a formidable record for such an old warship. Soon after, the Mediterranean corvette HMCS *Prescott*, which had joined a Gibraltar convoy when returning to the United Kingdom, destroyed a further U-boat in the eastern Atlantic. That brought the RCN's total while operating in southern waters to five enemy submarines within less than 10 weeks. The success came with a price. HMCS *Weyburn* and HMCS *Louisburg*, two of the corvettes assigned to the Mediterranean, were lost, the first to mines and the second, with heavy loss of life, to air attack.

CHAPTER VIII

A PECULIARLY CANADIAN CRISIS, APRIL 1943 – JANUARY 1944

When the three C groups and the operation Torch corvettes came back to the north Atlantic in late March and early April 1943, the battle against the U-boats was in the midst of great changes. The attack on ONS 166 at the end of February was the first in a string of major U-boat successes. Some easing of the ferocious winter storms, and fresh Allied difficulties in penetrating the 'enigma' cypher, enabled the Germans to intercept convoys with packs of 20 and more submarines. The early return of the Canadian ships was part of an all-out reinforcement that included temporary cessation of convoys to northern Russia and the transfer of destroyers normally assigned to screen the main Royal Navy (RN)

battle fleet. By these means, Western Approaches was able to assemble some of the best anti-submarine ships into five 'support groups.' It had become evident that even the strongest close escort could not hold the perimeter around a convoy against the scale of massed attack the U-boats were now mounting. Support groups, aided by Allied repenetration of 'enigma' in April, rushed to the assistance of threatened convoys in much the way that Commander Prentice of the Royal Canadian Navy (RCN) had brought HMCS *Chambly* and HMCS *Moose Jaw* out to support SC 42 in September 1941.

The turning point came with the battle for ONS 5 on 4–6 May 1943. Once again gales had

further slowed a slow convoy, and a temporary lapse in decryption of 'enigma' enabled a large pack to close in the air gap to the east of Newfoundland. The main Canadian participation was another outstanding effort by Royal Canadian Air Force (RCAF) 5 Squadron's Cansos, which, at a range of over 1100 kilometres, destroyed one submarine and damaged another as the battle opened. Heavy fog then rolled in, preventing further air support. Although the submarines sank 12 merchant ships, they paid heavily. In the dense mist, the U-boats were almost blind on the surface as they attempted to push home attacks. The calm seas allowed the escort, B 7, reinforced by support group EG 1 (EG was the British and Canadian designator for support groups), to use their centimetric radar to devastating effect. The warships destroyed five more U-boats and damaged others, several severely. In other words, a submarine had been lost for every two merchant vessels sunk, and virtually every surviving U-boat that attempted to close had suffered from effective fire.

Although RCN warships were committed to close escort of convoys that, as it turned out, were routed safely and protected by support groups, Canadian forces did have another chance to strike during the intense actions of May 1943. The circumstances demonstrated the great extent to which the Canadian presence in the battle had grown. Under the British Commonwealth Air Training Plan, individual RCAF air crew were not simply to be scattered as individuals throughout the Royal Air Force (RAF). The Canadian government always insisted that a portion of the personnel were to be organized into RCAF squadrons. Under this policy, a total of six RCAF squadrons were formed in the RAF's Coastal Command. The early history of these units was chequered: new squadrons suffered in the allocation of equipment at a time when Coastal Command was short of good aircraft, and they were shifted about from base to base and role to role. By early 1943, however, 422 and 423 squadrons, RCAF, had settled into long-range convoy support with the enormous Short Sunderland flying boat, an adaptation of a four-engine passenger aircraft with a performance comparable to the Catalina/Canso. The squadrons had been located at a good base, Castle Archdale in Northern Ireland, and, at Canadian insistence, RCAF officers were being posted to senior administrative positions at the station. On 13 May 1943, a 423 Squadron Sunderland, while escorting convoy HX 237, made a depth-charge attack on *U-753* that was wide of the mark. Unwisely, the U-boat stayed on the surface, using its anti-aircraft guns to try to bring down the circling aircraft.

The aircraft called for help from the naval escort, the RCN group C 2. First on the scene was the corvette HMCS *Drumheller*, which attacked the diving submarine with accurate gunfire and then obtained an asdic contact. HMS *Lagan*, a new British frigate that Western Approaches had assigned to reinforce C 2, arrived soon thereafter. Directed onto the contact by *Drumheller*, the frigate delivered a lethal attack.

Two aspects of the sinking highlight the new face of the battle. Available to support the HX 237 escort had been EG 1, which now included an escort aircraft carrier, HMS *Biter*, whose aircraft rushed to help in response to the U-boat reports. The idea of deploying small aircraft carriers with convoy escorts was a well-established one, and it had been tried by the RN in November 1941. That carrier, however, had been lost in the midst of the otherwise successful defence of a Gibraltar convoy in which the aircraft had played a prominent part. The emergency ship-building programmes the US had launched with its entry into the war were beginning to produce results in early 1943, including escort aircraft carriers. These were primitive. Large merchant-ship hulls were covered over with lightly built landing decks, and only basic aircraft operating facilities were installed. Nevertheless, the little carriers, together with the increased numbers of very-long-range shore-based aircraft, did much to close the air gap, not least because they could often sail clear of weather fronts that did not permit flying from coastal air stations.

The other notable feature of the action is that *Lagan* achieved the kill with a new anti-submarine weapon, the 'hedgehog' mortar. This equipment fired a broad circular pattern of 24 30-kilogram anti-submarine bombs ahead of the ship. The improved asdic fitted as part of the hedgehog system could thus maintain constant contact with the submarine and supply corrections to the last instant before firing. This was a marked change from depth-charge attacks in which the time of release had to be estimated by stopwatch or closely coordinated with the asdic watch of a second ship when the submarine passed under the asdic beam of the attacking vessel. Hedgehog had had teething problems but was now beginning to realize its potential. This was another important innovation that was being quickly fitted in all British ocean escorts, but it had yet to appear in any Canadian ship.

Command arrangements were also being revised in the Atlantic theatre. The change-over for control of each convoy from the British to the Americans at mid-ocean had become a needless complication, because most of the United States Navy (USN) escorts

Canadian Prime Minister William Lyon Mackenzie King and US President Franklin Delano Roosevelt at Quebec City, August 1943. (NAC, PA-195408)

had been withdrawn in the early months of 1942. Similarly, the US admiral in Newfoundland, commander Task Force 24 (CTF 24), was in the anomalous position of directing forces made up almost entirely of British and Canadian warships. That aside, the German concentration in the western part of the air gap off Newfoundland had revealed inefficiencies resulting from the patchwork of commands in the region: the RCN's Atlantic Coast and Newfoundland commands, the RCAF's Eastern Air Command and the nearly separate 1 Group RCAF in Newfoundland, and the US Army's Newfoundland Base Command, whose important force of maritime bombers operated independently of CTF 24.

Since the fall of 1942, Naval Service Headquarters (NSHQ) in Ottawa had been pressing Admiral King in Washington to have the RCN's east-coast commands take over the control of escort operations from CTF 24. The staff officers focused on questions of efficiency, such as the needless and confusing duplication by the USN of submarine warning signals to warships in the northwestern Atlantic, already produced by NSHQ's Foreign Intelligence Section. At heart, though, the campaign for a larger Canadian role in command was moralistic. Despite the fact that under the basic Anglo-American-Canadian strategic agreements Canada was responsible only for the defence of its immediate coastal waters, the nation had selflessly made a much larger naval contribution to the Allied cause. In the words of Captain H. N. Lay, the director of operations at NSHQ: *'This has been done quite often at the expense of Coastal Escort as a result of requests … from the Admiralty and Cominch [Commander-in-Chief US Fleet — i.e., Admiral King]. At the present time we have 48% of the escorts in North Atlantic Trade Convoys, and two Commands on the Atlantic with staffs capable of dealing with all escort matters.'*[1]

It was not any sense of fair play that won the RCN a command role, but Allied military politics, and the hard fact of Canada's demonstrated ability to provide substantial maritime forces. The Atlantic crisis was a lead item in Churchill and Roosevelt's summit at Casablanca in January 1943, with the need to rationalize the command structure figuring prominently. The Anglo-American combined chiefs of staff planning organization then set to work on proposals for integration of all forces in the Atlantic under a single Allied super-command. That approach was fraught with difficulties, given competing British and American interests. Admiral King preferred a solution founded on his conviction that the forces of different nations should not be mixed up together. His fervour on this point (early in 1941 he had formally protested plans to send USN forces to join British commands in the northeastern Atlantic) could only have been reinforced by long-winded Canadian complaints that the US was violating the basic agreements of 1941 by meddling in the organization and operation of the RCN groups. King seized on the Canadian claims to call a large Anglo-Canadian-American 'Allied Convoy Conference' in Washington during the first two weeks of March to settle the command question by delineating national zones. King agreed that CTF 24 in Newfoundland (and the Navy Department in Washington) should now withdraw from control of transocean convoys in the north Atlantic. This area would become exclusively a British Commonwealth preserve. Western Approaches command got what the British wanted: control over north Atlantic convoys right across to the waters immediately east of Newfoundland. The Canadians got what they wanted: control over convoy and anti-submarine operations in their own coastal waters and the adjacent ocean areas, from US waters south of Nova Scotia out to the limit of Western Approaches control east of Newfoundland. The USN, which late in 1942 had begun to help alleviate the Atlantic crisis by running convoys direct from American ports to the Mediterranean and the United Kingdom, would assume control over the full breadth of these southern routes.

On 30 April 1943 Rear-Admiral Murray was elevated to the new title Commander-in-Chief Canadian Northwest Atlantic, with authority over all Allied and Canadian air and naval forces committed to convoy operations in the area. He was the only Canadian to command an Allied theatre during the Second World War.

In fact, some weeks before the Washington conference the Canadians had begun to pull together the east-coast commands under Murray, to strengthen their case for national control. In January and February 1943 the air was buzzing with talk from the Casablanca conference and from American and British staffs about projects to integrate Atlantic commands. The Canadian forces did not want to be in the position of having outsiders impose solutions. In January the politically astute staff of the RCAF quickly and voluntarily placed the anti-submarine bomber squadrons of Eastern Air Command under naval control. Both services agreed to put behind them their previous policy of arm's-length cooperation, designed for mutual protection of their status within the Canadian defence establishment as fully independent armed forces. In February the RCN made the hitherto separate Flag Officer Newfoundland subordinate to Admiral Murray.

* * *

Soon after the inauguration of the new Canadian theatre, but not directly related to that development, the Allies achieved a sudden and unexpected victory. The combination of support groups, strengthened air cover and timely Ultra intelligence swung the balance decisively against the U-boats after the battle for ONS 5. During the first three and a half weeks of May 1943, more than 30 submarines were destroyed in exchange for the sinking of only 50 merchant vessels. The hardest actions were fought by British groups. This achievement was a tribute to their high quality, and to the magnificent orchestration of intellectual and industrial resources by the British government and fighting services. On 24 May, Admiral Karl Dönitz ordered his fleet away from the north Atlantic convoy routes.

During the late spring and summer, with better weather and the near absence of U-boat attacks, the north Atlantic crossing soon came to be known as the 'milk run.'[2] Passages were also faster. There was no need for evasive routes, and the flood of new merchant ships now coming out of US — and Canadian — shipyards allowed replacement of the slowest vessels.

The C groups of the close escort force now numbered five. The new C 5 had replaced the Canadian-American A 3 when the USN withdrew from escort on the northern route earlier in the spring. Since the crisis in the late fall of 1942, Western Approaches had assigned more and better British ships, like the frigate Lagan, to reinforce the C groups. The solution the RCN preferred was fully to transfer adequate numbers of British destroyers to the Canadian service. It made perfect sense, especially in light of a growing British manpower shortage. During the spring of 1943 four British destroyers were commissioned in the RCN. These ships were sisters or near sisters of the destroyers Canada had acquired in the 1930s and, therefore, were also renamed for Canadian rivers: HMCS Gatineau, Kootenay, Ottawa II and Saskatchewan. An additional pair, recommissioned as HMCS Chaudière and HMCS Qu'Appelle, joined the RCN in November 1943 and February 1944.

Beginning in April 1943 the Canadian mid-ocean force took on an increasing share of close escort for the north Atlantic convoys and thereby freed British warships from this duty to strengthen the support groups. The British support groups, American support groups (known as 'hunter-killer' groups) and mass of Allied shore-based maritime air power in the eastern part of the Atlantic destroyed nearly 80 U-boats in June through August 1943. Ultra intelligence contributed to the slaughter, revealing in advance when and where U-boats would be meeting on the surface for resupply or other mutual assistance.

Nevertheless, the U-boat arm was by no means a spent force. Because of Dönitz's policy of holding back new boats for extended training in the Baltic in company with experienced submarines, there were substantial reserves. German industry, moreover, was rapidly replacing losses, while researchers worked to develop equipment to help the submarines meet the Allied advantage. Among the innovations was an acoustic torpedo, later dubbed 'Gnat' by the Allies, which homed on the noise made by the propellers of a ship. During the first part of September, Dönitz sailed U-boats armed with the new torpedo. The crews had been trained to use the weapon to blast through the escort screen of convoys. Many of the submarines also carried increased anti-aircraft armament, including four-barrelled 20-millimetre automatic cannon. Ultra intelligence provided warning that a fresh attempt at pack tactics was underway, but too late to route two westbound convoys, ON 202 and the slow ONS 18, clear of danger. The first was escorted by C 2, with HMCS Gatineau, the British destroyer HMS Icarus, two RCN corvettes and the British corvette HMS Polyanthus, a long-time member of the Canadian mid-ocean force. Commander P. W. Burnett, RN, one of the senior officers lent by the British to help strengthen the C groups, was in command. The close escort for ONS 18 was B 3. Coming out in support was EG 9, one of two RCN support groups recently created with help from the RN. Under the command of Commander C. E. Bridgman, Royal Naval Reserve (RNR), in the frigate HMS Itchen, the group included the veteran ex-US 'Town'-class destroyer HMCS St Croix and the experienced corvettes Chambly (now commanded by Lieutenant A. F. Pickard, RCNR, whose skilled navigation had brought the ship to the aid of SC 42 almost exactly two years before), HMCS Sackville and HMCS Morden.

In addition to dispatching EG 9 to the scene, Western Approaches called for air support. This brought further Canadian participation. Eastern Air Command had finally received Consolidated Liberators during the spring of 1943. No 10 Squadron at Gander, Newfoundland, re-equipped with the aircraft and began to operate them in June. As it happened, several of the RCAF machines were in Iceland after completing a transatlantic escort when the orders arrived to support ONS 18, then about 1000 kilometres to the south of Iceland. On 19 September one of

the 10 Squadron Liberators assigned to the task destroyed *U-341*. That night *U-270* made contact with ON 202, to the north of ONS 18, and, in a long-range acoustic torpedo shot, blew off the stern of the frigate *Lagan*. As historians Jürgen Rohwer and W. A. B. Douglas comment, *'It was a spectacular start for Dönitz's new offensive.'*[3]

On 20 September the two convoys came together for better protection by all three groups of escorts. Despite effective coverage by British Liberators from Iceland, which destroyed another submarine, the pack remained in contact. That night the submarines had more success with the new torpedoes, sinking *St Croix*, with heavy loss of life, and *Polyanthus*, leaving only one survivor. Fog descended on 21 September, and persisted until the afternoon of the 22nd, when the convoy was still over 1300 kilometres from Newfoundland. In the words of the senior officer of the combined escort, Commander M. B. Evans, RN, of B 3:

At times I wondered if … aircraft were serving any really useful purpose in risking their lives to come so far, only to find nil visibility on arrival. I think this doubt was well answered when the instant the fog lifted three Liberators were not 'on the way' or 'expected in two hours,' but actually flying around the convoy and giving it valuable protection …

On reaching St John's I learnt that aircraft had been taking off in dense fog at very great risk … I can only say 'Thank you' …[4]

The Liberators, from 10 Squadron at Gander, engaged three of the submarines. The hail of anti-aircraft fire from the boats knocked out an engine in one of the aircraft and narrowly missed the pilot. Nevertheless, the air attacks so severely damaged *U-270* that it had to head for home immediately. Machine-gun fire from the Liberators injured the commanding officer of *U-377*, compelling the submarine to leave the battle to rendezvous with another boat for medical assistance.

Despite these good results, at least seven submarines remained in contact. That night *U-666*, cruising on the surface, achieved another kill just at the instant it was coming under gunfire from *Itchen*. The submarine let fly two acoustic torpedoes, one of which caused the attacking frigate to explode and sink almost instantly. This was the saddest of the losses as *Itchen* was carrying the survivors of *St Croix* and *Polyanthus*. Only three men were rescued, *'all that remained of nearly 400 men from three ships' companies,'* historian Marc Milner observed.[5]

* * *

The battle had amply demonstrated the capacity of the new Canadian theatre command to provide effective very-long-range air coverage under difficult circumstances. Moreover, the predominantly Canadian naval escort did reasonably well, despite the devastating effect of a powerful surprise weapon, in maintaining the protective cordon around the merchant ships: only six were lost in the intense four-day action. Nor was the rate of exchange entirely unfavourable to the defenders, as three U-boats had been destroyed, one each by the RCAF and RAF and one by the British destroyer HMS *Keppel*. Still, it was evil luck that both of the principal ships of one of Canada's two support groups had been sunk. Soon after the battle the group was disbanded so that the corvettes could be used to bring other groups up to strength. Once again, the RCN had provided a creditable defence of merchant shipping in the face of extraordinary challenges, but it had yet to join the offensive against the U-boats.

No one was more acutely aware of that fact than the officers and men of the mid-ocean groups. Since the establishment of the Newfoundland force in 1941, of course, Murray had complained bitterly that his was a forgotten fleet, a creature of the mid-Atlantic with adequate support at neither end. The difference in 1943 was that the sea-going officers themselves began to make themselves heard at the highest levels. As the veteran personnel began their third year on the north Atlantic, and saw the enormous progress in Allied fleets, they began to despair that things would never get better in the RCN.

Lieutenant-Commander D. W. Piers, the regular-force commanding officer of HMCS *Restigouche*, believed that one fundamental problem was the extreme dilution of the RCN's tiny professional cadre by an expansion that had gone far beyond that in any other navy. In a long, detailed report that he forwarded to senior authorities on 1 June 1943,[6] Piers observed:

Most Commanding Officers of the M.O.E.F. these days are 'damn good chaps', but they have very little idea of what is required of them besides actually fighting their ships. The method of running H.M.C. Ships and the customs observed are usually the individual ideas of the Commanding Officer and Executive Officer concerned, and are more than often anything but 'service' …

Any permanent force Officer cannot help but notice with regret that the R.C.N. is losing its 'service backbone', that is to say there has been a disappearance of naval customs and traditions in every day service life … The young seaman today feels he is being picked on if a Leading Hand asserts authority over him. It is not dis-

... I know what men in Corvettes at sea have to face from the elements: ministerial aide J. J. Connolly crosses the Atlantic in HMCS *Orillia*, October 1943. (Courtesy of J. M. Connolly)

(NAC, PL-25733)

New weapons: an RCAF Consolidated Liberator very-long-range bomber at Gander, Newfoundland, and the naval Hedgehog, which threw its 24 charges ahead of the warship for more accurate attacks on submarines.

(NAC, R-634)

obedience, but the wrong attitude towards discipline ...[7]

Crusty as that might sound, it reflected an intense pride in the personnel of the wartime RCN:

It is a generally accepted fact that the Officers and Ratings serving in the Royal Canadian Navy are the best 'manpower material' of all the fighting services of the Empire. This reputation which we enjoy seems justified when one considers the education, physical fitness and comparatively high standard of living of the personnel of the R.C.N. before they join up.

The Canadian sailor is very popular the world over. He suffers from no class distinction, nor is his social status immediately exposed by his speech as in England. The Canuck gets along well with the Limey and the Yank ...[8]

His concern was that Canada's excellent personnel were not being given a chance. Much of his worry about the lack of conventional naval discipline in some ships was that it adversely affected the men, whose welfare was not being properly attended to by senior ratings, petty officers and officers. In that same vein the report criticized senior authorities for shortages of warm clothing, the erratic, slow delivery of mail, and the failure to provide travel allowances to help men on leave visit their families.

Lieutenant-Commander W. E. S. Briggs, Royal Canadian Naval Reserve (RCNR), also reported on the state of the mid-ocean force in the spring of 1943. He was one of the too few Canadian officers posted to the Western Approaches command in 1943 when the Canadian ships began regularly to make long layovers at Londonderry to take advantage of the improved facilities the British were then developing. Briggs's perspective, as a reserve officer, was markedly different from Piers's:

The average R.C.N. Officer usually gets along quite well with R.N. Officers. This is understandable as an R.C.N. Officer has, as a rule, spent a considerable period in peace time living and working with the R.N. ... There are about ten R.C.N. Officers in command of ships. The rest of our C.O's are V.R's or N.R's who have had little or no prior experience of the R.N. The average V.R. and N.R. Officer's mind think along lines more akin to the American way of thinking ... Rightly or wrongly the average Canadian officer resents the reaction which he gathers when dealing with the R.N. The feeling that he is being looked upon [a]s a 'ruddy colonial' ...

There seems to be a complete lack of knowledge by the average R.N. officer of the following: —

1. Canada — her size, her population, her war production, her Navy, what it has done, what it is doing.

2. The size of the Canadian Navy in 1939.

3. The size of the Canadian Navy in 1943 ...

The general attitude is that we are completely inexperienced and a Canadian ship in port is often assumed to be making her initial appearance on this side of the water ...[9]

Yet Briggs came to many of the same conclusions as Piers:

With Canadian ships there is not much of a happy medium — our ships are either good or bad ... Our good ones are, I think, every bit as good as R.N. ships. Our inefficient ones are very bad ...

I feel sure it would pay us dividends if newly appointed C.O's could be given a talk — emphasizing ... to them the very great responsibility which is being vested in them. Responsibility not only for the ship and her fighting efficiency, but responsibility for the whole tone of the ship. The value of setting a really fine example to all his officers and men. The point is, that there is a tendency to consider us as somewhat inefficient and to view us as a rather slap happy casual bunch. There is in effect a 'strike one' upon us, and it therefore behoves every C.O to guard very jealously the good name and reputation of his ship ... Small things count for so much ...

Veterans still revel in what the RN endured from some of the 'characters' of the wartime RCN. Much of the grief had to be borne by Commodore G. W. G. Simpson, RN, who, as Commodore (D[estroyers]) at Londonderry, was responsible for the efficiency and well-being of the escorts. '*Five foot three in his bare feet,*' the commodore was inevitably known as 'Shrimp.'

Remember big Smithy [Lieutenant-Commander E. C. Smith, RCNVR, commanding officer of HMCS Morden]? *'Three-finger' Smith, he had his two fingers blown off. He used to drink, he would say, 'Two fingers!' [of whisky]*

... we had had a bad crossing and Morden was in our group, we arrived in Derry on a Saturday afternoon and we thought we had better go up to the mess, and we did ... Smithy came in, he was shot as a goat before he left the ship, but, here was our Commodore [Simpson] ... trying to attract the attention of the bartender, his nose about eight inches over the counter. Smithy looks at this ... and smacks his ass, lifted him about two feet in the air and says, 'You silly little bugger, how are you tonight?' ... He didn't get court-martialled but Shrimp had a few words with him.[10]

Such slips brightened a bleak social landscape (except, perhaps, for the commodore), but the larger matter of efficiency raised serious questions about management and leadership that led straight to Ottawa. NSHQ had the ultimate responsibility for setting standards and policies and making sure the necessary resources were available to carry them out.

According to Piers, *'the first thought concerning N.S.H.Q. that enters the head of a seagoing officer ... is "How is the R.C.N. run?"* '[11] At that time it was a very good question.

The accelerating tactical and technological change in the Battle of the Atlantic had intensified the already great pressures, on the headquarters, of expansion. The fact was well recognized. Aside from complaints from the commands on the coasts and the seagoing officers, a panel of expert senior British and US naval and air officers, the Allied Anti-Submarine Survey Board, visited the principal Canadian headquarters and bases in May–June 1943. The board had been established as an alternative to the politically unacceptable project of a supreme Allied Atlantic commander, and had a roving commission to advise all forces and commands on the most effective practices. The members were sometimes scathing about what they found in Canada. NSHQ had to become an efficient machine for gathering and analysing information, issuing directives, allocating resources and continually monitoring the results, across a broad range of disciplines and a vast expanse of geography. A fundamental reorganization of the headquarters had begun before the visit of the survey board, and the changes were modified to meet some of the board's criticisms. Among the important undertakings early in 1943 was expansion of the Foreign Intelligence Section into a full-fledged operational intelligence centre. It featured the greatly increased communications and security facilities needed to process Ultra intelligence from London and Washington and combine it with the direction-finding and other lower-grade sources the Canadian intelligence officers had previously used. These were requirements that the naval staff had not fully understood when pressing for the creation of the Canadian command, and were just one aspect of the battle that had become more complex. A large new directorate of warfare and tactics was also established, to evaluate new equipment and procedures, assess current performance by the fleet and recommend changes. Closely related were expansion of the small existing scientific research programme and creation of a new organization to carry out operational research.

In some areas, notably operational intelligence, the advice of the Allied board that Canada should closely follow the British model, by centralizing key functions at the national headquarters, was helpful. There was no other way to meet the stringent security requirements for handling of material based on decryptions of the enemy's most highly protected signals and making sure it was properly integrated with the full range of other sources. In other instances centralization was not practical, such as with the exceedingly difficult problem of achieving greater efficiency in the refit and repair of the fleet. Sufficient numbers of qualified personnel were not available to establish a new branch in Ottawa, and the great distance of the capital from the east coast made detailed administration of the dockyards from headquarters a dubious enterprise. The RCN instead created a new appointment at Halifax, Commodore Superintendent Atlantic Coast, to administer the navy's expanding network of dockyards and to oversee civilian yards that were carrying out navy work.

Important problems were being addressed, as Piers admitted in his report. The escort groups were achieving stability in their membership, and large numbers of experienced personnel were no longer being regularly transferred from ships. Training programmes were improving, and these included a special command course for promising officers. Headquarters officers, moreover, took Piers's criticisms extremely seriously. His report was circulated for detailed comments to the east-coast commands and to directorates in Ottawa. By mid-July, only six weeks after Piers had forwarded the paper, his suggestions had been thoroughly analysed and action was being taken on many of them.

There were, however, no quick solutions for the fundamental question of ship modernization. In Piers's words:

It is a blunt statement of fact that R.C.N. Ships are outdated in the matter of A/S Equipment by 12 to 18 months, compared to R.N. Ships doing the same job of convoy escort. Unfortunately this gross disparity is not taken into consideration when comparisons of U-boat sinkings and merchant shipping losses are made between British and Canadian Groups.[12]

The most serious problem was with the original corvettes of the 1940 programme, still a major part of the escort fleet, which required extensive modifications. When it became apparent that the original design was not well suited to prolonged open-ocean work, the British revised it. The high structure of the bows (the forecastle, or foc's'le), which had originally come back about a third of the length of the hull, was greatly extended to some two thirds of the length of the hull. This not only better deflected the seas away from the decks, but provided space needed to accommodate the larger crews required for long ocean voyages and to operate new equipment and additional armament. Canada had not incorporated these changes in the first 64 corvettes, in the interests of getting them to sea quickly (and luckily so in view of

the urgent need for them in Newfoundland from May 1941). Difficulties already encountered in extracting complete drawings for the original design from the Admiralty and modifying them for North American practices left little choice. Other changes, such as the installation of hedgehog and the latest models of asdic, entailed extensive internal work in the vessels. The magnetic compasses had to be replaced by an electronic gyro compass, which, together with the hedgehog outfit, necessitated the installation of a whole additional electric power system. The overburden on Canadian shipyards imposed by construction of warships, for both the Canadian and British fleets, and merchant vessels meant that only small yards were available for corvette modernization. These could do such complicated work only slowly, and with a great deal of technical help that the RCN was hard-pressed to provide. Although some space was available in British and US yards, in August 1943 the British had to close off access because of their own increasing needs.

The naval staff had also expected that the corvettes might soon be replaced by better ships. Early in 1942 Canadian yards had begun construction of frigates, the true ocean escort that the Admiralty had developed to succeed the corvette. At nearly 1300 tonnes displacement, and with a length of nearly 100 metres, the vessels were as large as destroyers but built to the simple standards of corvettes and, like them, equipped with reciprocating engines. The longer hull, and the installation of two engines rather than a single one, gave a speed of 19 knots, a small but critically important margin over that of the corvette. However, many of the same problems that had troubled the corvette programme, increased by the strains on Canada's fully mobilized industry, caused months of delay in the frigate programme. The first frigate, HMCS *Waskesiu*, did not commission until June 1943, and most of the remaining 32 of the 1942 programme were not delivered until the end of the year or the first part of 1944.

The minister of the navy, Angus L. Macdonald, received a somewhat sensationalized version of the modernization problems in August 1943 from a well-connected public relations officer, Lieutenant-Commander W. Strange, Royal Canadian Naval Volunteer Reserve (RCNVR), who had recently been to Londonderry. Macdonald had been present at most of the meetings during which senior staff had made the hard choices necessary to get large numbers of ships to sea quickly and had wrestled with the mounting challenges of changing technology. These issues, however, were highly technical and had come up piece-

meal among myriad other matters of business. Lieutenant-Commander Strange's account of the complaints from ship commanders and the British staff in Londonderry about the backwardness of Canadian ships had much more impact. Moreover, as a member of government whose leadership of the war effort was coming under sharp criticism, Macdonald was looking for good news after the troubles of 1942. He wanted to know why the RCN was not sharing in the slaughter of the U-boats.

The minister was evidently already beginning to lose confidence in the naval staff, for he demanded detailed information about the state of the fleet without revealing the specific complaints he had in hand or their source. He took the incomplete replies, which reflected the difficulty the staff was having in coming to grips with the many-faceted problems, as signs of a cover up. In October 1943 he dispatched his executive assistant, J. J. Connolly, to sea on a fact-finding mission. Connolly, a brilliant scholar and lawyer then in his mid-30s, went from Newfoundland to Londonderry in the unmodernized corvette HMCS *Orillia*. He was overwhelmed by the experience, in no small part because the commanding officer, Lieutenant J. E. Mitchell, RCNVR, was a lawyer and his own contemporary; this drove home to the minister's assistant how much the volunteers had sacrificed and accomplished. During the eight-day crossing, Connolly scribbled disjointed phrases in a pocket diary — he was seasick much of the time. They capture the north Atlantic experience with surprising force:

Beautiful — but eerie. Watch standing around in their hoods. — Always looking It is monotonous. Zig zagging. No time these men for great policy thinking. They live from watch to watch and carry on regardless weather or subs …

No school boy enthusiasm here. Just a job to be done. Maybe leave to London.

Mitchell is a reliable quiet hardworking fellow. Commands respect of his men …

I just don't think about Subs. But carry lifebelt always and wear it on deck. Not much point worrying about Subs. I wouldn't be much at a job like this — even in command. The monotony would get me down. But I am lost in admiration at these young Canadians — giving up so much at home to do this.

Times rough — others smooth. This ship rides everything. It doesn't cut into the waves so its up and down hill all the time — and pitching.

A few of the men were sick — No officers.

What a war effort! No home comforts. Rolling and pitching — keeping station Thinking out Navigation

Guarding the convoy Threatened by torpedoes every minute.

Heavy food — No exercise. Dependent on weather — engines — other ships …

Flat at home with Peter and Mummy is heaven all right …

How brave these young men are — [Lieutenant] Gerry O'Brien and [Sub-Lieutenant] Bob Lawrence — running a ship with complete confidence Joking, laughing. They are the stuff.

Captn shows his confidence by visiting the bridge only.

I am so lonesome for my wife and baby and parents. One can't go through this thing without a deep emotional reaction. The sea at night — the slender ship the clouds, the moon … the foam the roar, the whistling winds — What a power of the elements — and the God that made them

Oct 13 … We now are in the gap 30° W and 50° N. Saw the last of Newfy planes this a.m. Lots of talk of subs. Two said to be on our path moving south some officers pessimistic about ability to deal and take a dim view because of St. Croix.

When you see the waves and the rain and the pitching of the ship you realize that only fair equipment is not good enough. They need the best.

The company seems to be satisfied to get what they can at refit …

Unwarned — Action stations bells I was not happy. I shook. Out of bed fast — into Life Belt, coat and hat and up. Drama and Death — I tho[ugh]t I was sent for. Silent hooded figures on the oerlikons. Gun crew active on the 4" Officers at post. Gunnery Officer calling the routine. Bearing of ship — Bearing of enemy — range enemy in sight Fire — the half black, half blue sky, the moon …

Oct 14 Partly cloudy. Rather rough — heavy swell — not sickly but nearly so. Planes in A.M. from Iceland. Support group now with us …

Captn at supper says to-nights the night. The X-O [executive officer] says before midnight. Well its midnight now, but I don't feel any more secure. It doesn't worry these young lads …

Stood on bridge tonight for an hour — in rain. There is brilliant moonlight — Heavy clouds — danger is close. God help us. Queen of the Sea protect us …

[16 Oct] Rounds [inspection] all over the ship. My God — but these ratings know what war is. It is something to see their quarters in harbour. But at sea — with the roll — its indescribable Small spaces — piles of baggage. Twice too many men [for the capacity of the quarters as originally designed]. Slinging hammocks everywhere — sleeping on the floor (because they'd roll off

the benches). But they say — the job is all right for the war! 'Bring on the Subs.'[13]

In the United Kingdom Connolly had meetings with Admiral Horton, Commodore Simpson and RCN officers serving in Londonderry, all of whom confirmed their frustration in trying to obtain technical decisions and information from NSHQ. He also brought back detailed data: '*… 100% of the R.N. Flower class corvettes are up to date … not more than 20% of the R.C.N. Flower class ships are modernized … 42 out of 71 R.C.N. corvettes were without extended foc'sles, 53 out of 71 are without hedge hog.'*[14] With this ammunition, Macdonald directly challenged Admiral Nelles over the failures of NSHQ to manage the escort fleet, and charged that the situation had been hidden from the minister's office. Nelles was taken aback, given the minister's regular participation in senior staff meetings. The correspondence quickly became an acrimonious exchange about who knew, or should have known, what — and when. In January 1944 Nelles was transferred to London as the Canadian Naval Member Overseas, and was replaced as chief of the naval staff by the vice chief, Rear-Admiral G. C. Jones. Nelles's exit was gracefully staged, the explanation to Parliament and the press being that a strong representative was needed to preside over the growing naval effort overseas.

Connolly had recommended precisely this course of action in a long memorandum he prepared for the minister on 30 November 1943. Whether his advice was decisive is not clear. Connolly warned Macdonald at the very beginning of the paper to treat it with great caution:

My personal views cannot count in this whole business. I must admit that they are prejudiced — because I know what men in Corvettes at sea have to face from the elements — because I have been told what they must face at the hands of a desperate, scientifically armed enemy — because I doubt the ability of some of our ships to deal with submarines.

A war is not won by valour alone, or by the keenness of the individual fighter. Dieppe [the Canadian Army's disastrous raid on the French coast in August 1942] proved that, if it proved nothing else. So far, with our losses we have been lucky. If this luck does not continue neither we nor the relatives of men lost in our ships will be very comfortable about the matter.[15]

These passages reverberate with Connolly's admiration for the men with whom he sailed in *Orillia*, leaving open the possibility, admittedly speculative, that the chief of the naval staff was removed as a tribute to them and the other crews in the Atlantic. One wonders whether Macdonald remembered that

the most searing accusation against the navy during and after the First World War was that the senior officers were incompetents who had protected their own privileges at the expense of the men in the fleet. Be that as it may, the navy handled the potential political scandal over fleet equipment in 1943 immeasurably more deftly than it had responded to similar charges 25 years earlier. Nelles's departure from Ottawa elicited little comment.

CHAPTER IX

YET ANOTHER TRANSFORMATION OF THE ATLANTIC BATTLE, 1944–1945

Ironically, the Royal Canadian Navy (RCN) embarked on a fresh run of U-boat sinkings just as the crisis over escort efficiency unfolded at Naval Service Headquarters (NSHQ). Grim as the overall state of the fleet appeared in the spring and summer of 1943, and difficult as the battle for ONS 18/ON 202 had been, things were improving. The first Canadian-built frigates, priority modernization of the 'River'-class destroyers, the first modernized corvettes and the well-equipped destroyers taken over from the Royal Navy (RN) all were strengthening the mid-ocean groups. At the same time there was better training available in Canada, and the Canadian ships and personnel were now regularly joining intense, advanced exercises and courses at Londonderry and Liverpool.

On 20 November 1943 the RCN support group EG 5 destroyed *U-536* while screening a Gibraltar-to-United Kingdom convoy. The new asdic in the modernized 1940-programme corvette HMCS *Snowberry* played a critical role, making the initial contact on the submerged U-boat. This was a particularly satisfying victory, for the U-boat was return-

ing from a long, failed mission to pick up escaped German prisoners of war in Chaleur Bay, within the Gulf of St Lawrence. Though Canadian intelligence had got wind of the scheme, and a large hunting group had been waiting off the bay, the submarine heard the warships attacking a false contact in the distance, abandoned its efforts to contact the escapees on shore and made good its escape.

EG 6, the new designation for EG 5, was supporting a Gibraltar-bound convoy on 8 January 1944 when the modernized corvette HMCS *Camrose* and the British frigate HMS *Bayntyn* sank *U-757*. Another member of EG 6, HMCS *Waskesiu*, sank *U-257* on 24 February 1944, while the group was supporting the UK-bound convoy SC 153 in the eastern Atlantic. The victory was another achievement for an excellent Canadian asdic team, and it was an impressive debut for the RCN's first frigate. More impressive still was the combined effort of C 1 while providing the close escort for HX 280 in the eastern Atlantic, and C 2, which was then serving as a support group. After a 32-hour hunt to exhaustion, the second longest of the war, the groups forced the

highly experienced *U-744* to the surface and smothered it in gunfire. The U-boat had executed expert evasive measures, including prolonged dives to depths of nearly 200 metres. Admiral Horton, who as a submariner admired the fight put up by the U-boat, commented: *'The hunt and destruction of U-744 is a classic example of anti-U-boat warfare in which the operations of the opponents were conducted by experts of their profession.'*[1] It was something of a vindication, for C 2 had participated in the battle for ONS 18/ON 202; Commander P. W. Burnett, RN, was still senior officer and he directed the long hunt for *U-744*. Within days, on 10 March, C 1 and EG 9, the latter having been recently re-established with new Canadian frigates, sank *U-845*. This boat, as will be seen, was also returning from a mission in Canadian waters. On 13 March the frigate HMCS *Prince Rupert*, of C 3, assisted a US escort-carrier group in the destruction of *U-575*. In April, Canadian warships sank or shared in the sinking of two more submarines, for a total of eight since late November 1943.

During a slightly longer period, early October 1943 to early May 1944, the Royal Canadian Air Force (RCAF) sank another five submarines in the eastern Atlantic. Squadrons 422 and 423 accounted for two of the victories. Another RCAF squadron in Coastal Command, No 407, which flew twin-engine Wellington medium bombers fitted with centimetric radar and aerial searchlights for night operations, also sank two submarines. The fifth fell to an Eastern Air Command Canso amphibian squadron, No 162. Formed in mid-1942, 162 Squadron would achieve a stable organization only a year later, when production of Canadian-built Canso amphibians had come on stream. By that time the withdrawal of the bulk of the U-boat force from the central and western Atlantic had resulted in under-employment of the five Canso/Catalina squadrons then in the order of battle. The RCAF had therefore offered the unit for operations in the eastern Atlantic under Coastal Command, which assigned No 162 to Iceland. The swift movement of the unit to Iceland in January 1944 was a considerable achievement, not least because the Canso was a uniquely Canadian modification of the basic Catalina design — meaning that a mass of spare parts had to be transported. The 15 Cansos, loaded to capacity with stores, staged through Goose Bay, Labrador, and the treacherous Bluie West 1 airfield, tucked in a narrow fjord on the Greenland coast. No 10 Squadron's Liberators flew over additional stores, and heavy equipment went in the Eastern Air Command marine squadron's two supply vessels *Bea-ver* and *Eskimo*. Designed only for local coastal runs between command bases, these small transports had to battle seas nearly 20 metres in height during a ferocious gale.

Churchill had warned Roosevelt in October 1942 that more was at stake in the Battle of the Atlantic than Britain's war effort: the Western Allies' plans for landing in northwest Europe and defeating Germany rode on the outcome. If merchant-shipping losses had continued at the high rate of late 1942 and early 1943 it would not have been possible to build up in Britain the hundreds of thousands of armed forces personnel and the tens of millions of tonnes of equipment and supplies needed to mount the invasion at Normandy, France, in June 1944. Global Allied construction of new merchant ships in the fall of 1942 was already providing replacement vessels faster than the Germans could sink them; however, this would have counted for little if the ships had not been able to reach the United Kingdom safely. At the same time, after May 1943 the Allied anti-submarine commands remained constantly aware that the victory over the U-boats had been at best a partial one. In the spring of 1944, despite heavy losses, the strength of the operational U-boat fleet actually increased from 170 to 190 submarines, and this was the greatest menace to the hundreds of merchant vessels needed to carry the Allied landing forces across the English Channel and sustain them in the following weeks as they attempted to break out of the small Normandy bridgeheads. At this stage in the war Britain was hard-pressed to mount a sufficiently large share of the great enterprise to sustain a true partnership with the vast US forces. At sea, as well as in the air and on the land, Canadian forces made a critical difference by fleshing out the British order of battle.

In the weeks before the landing of the army expeditionary forces, which began during the early hours of 6 June, over 50 RCN escorts were redeployed from the north Atlantic and Canadian home waters for invasion duties. Despite these reductions, the RCN also assumed all responsibility for the close escort of north Atlantic convoys to relieve British warships for service in the invasion. All 10 of the RCN's modernized 'River'-class destroyers left the mid-ocean force to form two new support groups, EG 11 and EG 12, which operated within the English Channel to provide anti-submarine defence of the invasion fleet. The existing support groups, EG 6 and EG 9, were assigned to more distant patrols on the southern flank of the invasion area, to prevent the submarine flotillas in the Channel from gaining reinforcements. In addition, 19 RCN corvettes undertook close escort of

Dr G. N. Tucker, official historian of the navy, lectures the first WRCNS officer cadet course. (DHH, McDonald Collection)

Members of the RCAF Women's Division and the WRCNS in the operations room at St John's. (NAC, PA-176130)

A member of the WRCNS operating direction-finding equipment at Coverdale, New Brunswick. (NAC, PA-142540)

invasion shipping, and 16 Bangors from Canadian home waters hurriedly retrained and re-equipped from their usual escort role to do minesweeping, the original purpose of the flat-bottomed Bangor design. These vessels had the perilous role of proceeding in darkness ahead of the leading invasion forces, to clear channels through the heavily mined waters off the Normandy beaches.

The years of experience in the Battle of the Atlantic showed in the professional performance of the Canadian ships. Particularly notable was the success of the Bangors in the unfamiliar minesweeping role, requiring as it did painstakingly precise navigation and ship handling. The RCN also played its full part in the massive anti-submarine effort that overwhelmed the U-boats. Canadian warships had sunk a total of five enemy submarines in the Channel and adjacent waters by the end of August. Of these, three had fallen to the destroyers of EG 11, one of the most successful Allied groups. This is perhaps not surprising, for the senior officer was Captain J. D. Prentice, whose zeal for training and innovative tactics had brought the RCN's first confirmed submarine sinking in 1941. Prentice had recently come back to sea after a long shore appointment as Captain (D[estroyers]) at Halifax, in which position he had done much to improve the training and readiness of the fleet in 1943 and early 1944.

More remarkable still was the achievement of 162 Squadron. The unit sent aircraft forward to an advanced base at Wick, in northern Scotland, to press patrols towards the U-boat bases in Norway and thereby prevent reinforcement of the French coast. During the month of June the Cansos sank four submarines and shared in the destruction of a fifth. The cost was considerable. Anti-aircraft fire from the submarines downed three Cansos in the course of these operations: 13 air crew died and one airman was taken prisoner. In one of the attacks, on 24 June 1944, Flight Lieutenant David E. Hornell, a quiet, modest but intensely professional pilot from Mimico, Ontario, dropped depth charges accurately, destroying *U-1225*, even though the aircraft had been severely damaged by the submarine's automatic cannon fire. The Canso then crashed, and only one of the life rafts — too small for the eight-man crew — inflated properly. Hornell took long turns in the water, and then had to be restrained by his crew mates from attempting to swim for a boat dropped by a rescue aircraft at some distance from the raft. A vessel did not reach the scene until 21 hours after the crash, by which time Hornell had so suffered from exhaustion and exposure that he could not be revived. He re-

ceived the Victoria Cross, the highest decoration for courage in the British Commonwealth: *'By pressing home a skilful and successful attack against fierce opposition, with his aircraft in a precarious condition, and by fortifying and encouraging his comrades in the subsequent ordeal, this officer displayed valour and devotion to duty of the highest order.'*[2]

Allied escort and maritime air forces destroyed some 60 U-boats in June, July and August 1944. The Canadian share of a sixth of that figure, even though the RCN and RCAF anti-submarine units constituted a much smaller proportion than that of the forces engaged, was one measure of how much the Canadian maritime services had achieved.

There was no opportunity to revel in the accomplishment. Despite the heavy losses, and the fact that the Germans were being forced by the Allied land, air and sea assaults to abandon their French bases, the U-boat arm was endeavouring mightily, and with some success, to regain the initiative. This speaks volumes for the morale of the force, and for the power of Admiral Dönitz's personal leadership. Canadian maritime forces would be fully engaged on both sides of the Atlantic until the very end of the war. During the last year of the conflict, in fact, enemy submarines would sink eight RCN warships and severely damage four others. These losses to enemy action are higher than those for the whole period September 1939 to April 1944 (eight sunk, one severely damaged).

Early in 1944 the Germans had begun to fit U-boats with schnorkels — breathing tubes on extendable masts — in a bid to counter the devastating effects of Allied air power and radar. Schnorkel allowed the boat to cruise submerged for weeks on end, if need be, using its powerful air-breathing diesel engines. Only the tip of the mast with the intake valve showed above water — too small a target for the best Allied radar to pick up under any conditions but rare, flat calm. Operations in the English Channel during the invasion showed that schnorkel gave protection from not only aircraft, but asdic searches as well. Warships had usually depended on a visual or radar contact on a still-surfaced submarine to narrow the search area for the short-ranged asdic after the enemy had dived. Schnorkel submarines eliminated that opportunity for an initial surface contact, and even searches in a position where the U-boat revealed its presence by attacking had little success. The many shipwrecks, boulders and other bottom features of shallow coastal waters masked the U-boats by throwing off a welter of confusing echoes, while the complex tides and currents in coastal waters degraded

U-625 under lethal attack by a Short Sunderland of 422
Squadron, RCAF, based in Northern Ireland, March
1944. (NAC, RE-68-585)

(CFPU, PMR 94-244)

(DHH, 0-94-1)

(Courtesy of C.P. Nixon)

The hunt and destruction of U-744 is a classic example of anti-U-boat warfare: German survivors and their Canadian
rescuers scramble aboard HMCS *St Catharines;* boats from the Canadian warships put parties aboard the shattered
submarine to gather secret documents and equipment.

asdic performance. Among the early victims of the U-boats' first return to British coastal waters since increased defences had driven them out in late 1940 and early 1941 were the RCN corvettes HMCS *Regina* and HMCS *Alberni*. Both went down quickly, in August 1944, with heavy loss of life, after submerged attacks in which the submarines achieved such complete surprise that the Canadian crews believed their ships had struck mines.

* * *

There had been a foretaste of these tactics in Canadian waters. In late 1943 and early 1944 U-boats came back to the northwest Atlantic to try to reestablish a presence on both sides of the ocean, and to find easy targets. In the latter respect they were disappointed. The defences forced them to stay beneath the surface, except at night, and soon they were seeking out hiding places from which to make very occasional submerged attacks.

In late October and early November 1943, *U-537* attempted a patrol on the sea routes east of Newfoundland, but was attacked on three separate occasions by Eastern Air Command aircraft, which also summoned naval escorts to the scene. The submarine escaped with minor damage but was unable to contact any shipping. The commanding officer, Kapitänleutnant Peter Schrewe, concluded that *for me this part of the coast has been made unhealthy*[3] and speculated that the Allies might have been using a new type of radar to find him.

The truth was more complicated. Schrewe had had a peaceful entry into the arctic reaches of Canadian waters, on a mission to place a battery-powered automatic weather station on shore near Cape Chidley, at the northern tip of Labrador. Because of the westerly prevailing winds in the northern hemisphere, weather information from the north Atlantic was essential for German meteorologists to be able to provide accurate forecasts, one of the fundamental needs in all types of military operations. So sensitive was *U-537*'s task that there was no mention of it in radio transmissions (the weather station was not in fact discovered until 1980). When Dönitz's headquarters then broadcast orders for the boat to hunt off southern Newfoundland, decryptions of the signal were immediately shared among the operational intelligence centres in London, Washington and Ottawa. The staff at the centre in Ottawa, using its knowledge of the technical properties and patrol habits of U-boats, devised search areas that were revised daily to take account of the U-boat's estimated movements and any further intelligence that came to

hand. These signals were sent to Admiral Murray's headquarters at Halifax each night to serve as the basis for operations the following day. Because the decrypt intelligence was usually at least 24 hours old, the search areas had to be quite large — 15,000 to 30,000 square kilometres — to allow for the submarine's movements in the intervening period. Such an area, however, could be swept by one or two patrol bombers during a normal 10- to 12-hour mission. It was with these methods that Eastern Air Command repeatedly found *U-537*.

The suppression of the U-boat shows the effectiveness of the expanded, more closely integrated organization for operational intelligence and command of air and sea forces that had been created in Ottawa, Halifax and St John's since the establishment of the Canadian Northwest Atlantic theatre in the spring of 1943. A notable feature of the organization was the part played by women in uniform. The Canadian Women's Army Corps and the Canadian Women's Auxiliary Air Force, which in early 1942 was redesignated the Women's Division of the RCAF, had been established during the summer of 1941. Initially, women had been restricted to a few of the more domestic trades, such as preparing food and driving motor vehicles, but, by dint of the sheer competence and frequently superior levels of education of women personnel, the army and the air force soon widened the opportunities for them. This was especially the case in the air force. Air operations bring only a tiny percentage of personnel into direct contact with the enemy; the vast majority serve to provide the large and numerous supporting services required to keep aircraft flying. The exclusion of Canadian women from combat therefore closed off only a small proportion of air force trades. Members of the Women's Division rose to prominence in information-handling trades such as communications, in which large numbers of people with the capacity for quick, precise work were required for flying-control and headquarters staffs. Thus the small detachment of 34 women among the 643 personnel at Eastern Air Command headquarters in Halifax in July 1942 grew to 287 of 929 personnel by August 1943, and to 394 women in a total of 1211 — or just under a third of all personnel — in January 1944.

Airwoman Mary Buch, who arrived at Eastern Air Command Headquarters in April 1943, was taken aback at conditions in wartime Halifax.

We are allowed to live in the City if we prefer. — That's a joke — nice work if one could get a room — not even a decent room — just a room. The accounts of this place were grossly understated, believe me. I have

not the slightest intention of walking around alone in broad daylight, much less after dark. The five wise virgins would <u>need</u> to trim their lamps here. — (What am I saying?) Anyway — it would be too expensive to live out, even with our subsistence allowance, and we'd miss all the fun of the Station, so we are resigned to travelling in by bus or truck — a matter of five minutes' ride.

The Recreation Centre here is the best equipped in Canada, they say. — Bowling, tennis, billiards — all the rest — right on the Station. Movies every night, dances twice a week, and three million lonely men — rather a grim prospect in some ways.[4]

The Women's Royal Canadian Naval Service was not established until July 1942. The delay can be at least partly explained by the fact that the RCN had not embarked on all-out expansion until the summer of 1940, nearly a year after the other armed forces had done so. The requirement for a substantial infrastructure ashore, in which women personnel would be needed in large numbers, moreover, had not become fully evident until after the German offensive in the western Atlantic, in January 1942; then it became clear that much of the RCN fleet would be serving in home waters and require support from Canadian bases.

From the first, the RCN, drawing on the model of the British Women's Royal Naval Service, recognized the special capacity of women personnel for communications and intelligence work. Senior authorities were not disappointed. In the words of the quarterly report on the development of the RCN covering the period January to March 1943, '*WRCNS officers are proving especially successful in Communications and Operational duties, and in some cases outshine their Naval Brethren in courses: So far the brethren have taken this in good part.*'[5] At NSHQ, WRCNS (or 'Wren') officers and ratings soon took up positions in Captain E. S. Brand's shipping-control organization (now known as the trade division), the operational intelligence centre, the naval intelligence division (which was responsible for all information other than operational intelligence) and the signals division (in which Wrens took on much of the work of organizing and distributing the thousands of incoming and outgoing messages).

An early and successful experiment was to staff a new wireless interception and direction-finding station entirely with Wrens, excepting a few men for heavy physical work. Among the first personnel at the station, located at Gloucester, Ontario, just outside Ottawa, was Lavinia Crane, who had learned morse code from her father, a veteran of the army's Royal Canadian Corps of Signals. Crane was one of the many Canadian women who had been eagerly awaiting the formation of the WRCNS, and she joined as soon as the recruiting party arrived in her native Vancouver. At Gloucester, she recalled:

We had the central station [building] and ... about three or four shacks which were each about half-a-mile out, in different directions and out at those shacks they had the direction-finding equipment. Inside [the central building] were the wireless operators who did the receiving ... usually we could hear [a U-boat] coming up before they even sent anything ... There'd be a sort of whine on the wireless set when they were coming up and you'd pick up this. And as soon as you heard that you could recognize that it was a sub coming up to give a signal. We'd immediately push our button and alert the Wrens out in the [direction-finding] shacks and they would start getting a bearing on it. Sometimes they got a good bearing before they even gave a message.

... It was very, very fast. And of course, speed was the important thing because they were very short messages, usually. We always sort of competed with other naval [wireless intercept] stations, like Harbour Grace in Newfoundland, and in the other ones where the men were, to get our signals in before they did. We had a very good record. [The interception and bearings information] was then sent in to Ottawa by teletype ... And we had a very good record of getting there first.[6]

Deployment of Wrens to the east coast was delayed some months by the grievous shortage of accommodation at the bases there, and the abysmal quality of what was available. A revealing comment on the over-crowded, uncomfortable conditions personnel endured at Halifax and other naval ports is contained in the official history of the RCN's 'Activities on Shore': '*The formulating of standards for Wren housing ... was the first instance of such an approach to naval accommodation ashore; and this concern with greater comfort and more amenities may well have influenced the adopting of a similar policy for the entire navy.*'[7]

The first group of Wrens to report to Halifax, in March 1943, arrived at night in the midst of a black-out exercise. It must have provided the women with '*some of their grimmest memories,*' reported Lieutenant Eleanor McCallum, who was responsible for organizing WRCNS accommodation at the east-coast bases. '*They arrive at almost pitch black quarters, to be greeted by a dark figure who reads out their names with the help of a flash light. Then, under a pile of bed linen they stagger down unlighted "gangways" [halls] to equally dark cabins and attempt to unpack and make their beds.*'[8] Among the Wrens was a school friend of Air-woman Mary Buch, who reported how tradition-

bound the navy was, as compared to the air force: '*I [Buch] asked her if the WRENS get their tot of rum, and she said "No, — but apart from that everything is just the way Nelson left it."*'[9]

By July 1943 over a thousand Wrens had arrived in Halifax. In the following months, as barrack buildings were completed, hundreds reported to other bases, including HMCS *Avalon* at St John's. In 1944 Wrens provided the staff for the large new wireless interception and direction-finding station at Coverdale, near Moncton, New Brunswick, and also smaller long-range radio navigation (LORAN) stations, one of them at Lower Whitehead,

about thirty-five miles down the coast from Canso [Nova Scotia] and two hundred miles up the coast from Halifax. There were a dozen fishermen's houses in the village, and the place was an island when the tide was in. It was very isolated.

[The station] had been run by sailors before we got there, and some of them stayed on as technicians. They ran the diesel which generated our electricity. There was a Petty Officer too. Our Wren officer was in command, and that was a bit unusual.

We were armed in the early days, in case we were attacked by an enemy submarine. There was a rack of .303 rifles in the Quonset hut where we did the transmitting, and there was a Bren [machine] gun on a tripod. We worked in pairs, in a kind of cage, and there were .45 colt revolvers inside, in case of trouble. But we had very little training in how to use them. The Petty Officer took us out and fired a few practice rounds.[10]

From late January to June 1944, Admiral Dönitz kept one or two U-boats in Canadian waters almost continuously. The long, six-week patrols by a total of six submarines achieved only one significant victory, the destruction of the frigate HMCS *Valleyfield*, on the night of 6 May 1944. Otherwise, the score included only the sinking of a small freighter and damage to a large merchant ship. The situation was not unlike that in the Gulf of St Lawrence from late September through November 1942, except that, with the benefit of Ultra, better communications and increased air resources, Admiral Murray's command achieved these results over a much larger area. Significantly, with the exception of two fleeting encounters the Canadian forces did not make firm contact with the enemy after mid-February 1944, when *U-845* attempted to operate on the surface off Newfoundland and was rewarded by damage and casualties inflicted by a 10 Squadron Liberator. So low did the U-boats lie thereafter that many of the large-scale Canadian air and sea hunts were in fact directed against convincing but false radar and asdic returns

produced by the cluttered, complex coastal waters. The price of the U-boats' caution was that they were seldom able to pursue shipping. On the few occasions the U-boats attacked, the prompt appearance of aircraft and surface escorts dissuaded them from hanging about to try again.

The intense game of cat and mouse is well illustrated by the circumstances in which *Valleyfield* went down to a surprise submerged attack, not unlike the ones that schnorkel-equipped U-boats would begin to make in British waters several months later. Alerted by Ultra intelligence, Eastern Air Command had been searching for *U-548*, on its track towards St John's, Newfoundland, for 10 days. On 1 May 1944 a Liberator caught a fleeting glimpse of the diving submarine in the distance, off Conception Bay. The U-boat did not realize it had been seen, but the arrival of additional aircraft and surface escorts and the absence of merchant-shipping traffic persuaded it to move south. On the night of 2 May the submarine surfaced, about halfway between St John's and Cape Race, and was startled to see the newly commissioned British frigate HMS *Hargood* only 2500 metres away. The submarine fired a torpedo that missed. Moments later, as the U-boat closed to take a second shot, the destroyer, still unaware of the danger, was suddenly illuminated by the brilliant searchlight of a 10 Squadron Liberator that was searching for the U-boat (the strong return from the destroyer on the aircraft's radar obliterated any trace of the small profile of the nearby submarine, however). *U-548*, although still seen by neither the aircraft nor the warship, abandoned the attack, fired a burst of anti-aircraft fire and dived. Unwittingly, the Liberator had saved the British warship, but the air crew returned to base incensed, believing they had come under anti-aircraft fire from a friendly vessel. Shore authorities evidently pieced together what had actually happened, for they soon shifted the search areas for *U-548* south, to the vicinity of Cape Race. On the evening of 6 May, group C 1, having just completed an escort run with a convoy from the United Kingdom, made its way towards Cape Race en route to St John's. The warships encountered a group from the Western Escort Force (as the Western Local Escort Force had been redesignated in 1943) and a Canso still searching for *U-548*, although the trail was getting cold. The submarine was in fact in the near vicinity, hiding at periscope-depth even during the early hours of darkness. Fragmented ice floes cluttered the surface, giving the submarine nearly perfect protection against asdic or radar detection.

... schnorkel gave protection from not only aircraft, but asdic searches as well: *U-889* after its surrender to Canadian forces in May 1945, showing the breathing tube that allowed U-boats to operate without surfacing to replenish air. (DHH, HS-1377-13)

(NAC, PA-150442)

(NAC, PA-134330)

... new asdic ... played a critical role: control equipment for the improved sound detection equipment installed in Canadian ships as of 1943.

Less than three hours after passing the search group, C 1 crossed *U-548*'s lair. The U-boat let fly a homing torpedo that broke the *Valleyfield* in half. The escorts were proceeding in a widely dispersed formation, separated by a distance of over three kilometres. It took some minutes for the nearest member of the group, HMCS *Giffard*, to realize *Valleyfield* had disappeared and close the scene; the rescue was then interrupted when *Giffard* made an asdic contact. Many of *Valleyfield*'s scantily clad people died of hypothermia in the 1°C water. Only 38 of the 168 aboard the frigate survived. *U-548* escaped the ensuing hunt by dropping to the bottom of the shallow Grand Banks.

The submarine waited for three days, until it was well clear of shore some 360 kilometres south of Cape Race, before it signalled news of its victory to U-boat headquarters. Accurate direction-finder bearings on the signal immediately brought a search by US warships and aircraft that were escorting a convoy in the vicinity, and Canadian aircraft and warships then continued the hunt until 12 May. The U-boat in fact had headed further south, to US waters. It subsequently came to the Halifax approaches, where it lingered from 17 to 27 May, paralysed by the constant sight of aircraft and escorts.

Although aircraft could harass and deter submarines, it was becoming obvious, as the U-boats remained submerged through much of their patrols in Canadian waters, that aircraft had little chance of making attacks. This situation increased the burden on naval patrols and highlighted the deficiencies of the thinly stretched forces available at Halifax and St John's. Admiral Murray had no choice but to conduct hunts for submarines with convoy escort groups that happened to be free for a few days, or by ad hoc groups that included new ships, or ships just out of long refits, that needed training. As Rear-Admiral Reid at St John's put it:

Recent unsuccessful hunts off Halifax and Newfoundland, where a U-boat was known to be present, by motley assortments of ships in various states of efficiency and training, lend emphasis to the fact that none but a highly trained, thoroughly coordinated and ably led team can hope to destroy U-boats at this stage of the campaign.[11]

The truth of this was demonstrated by the fact that *U-845*, after escaping hunting forces in Canadian waters, was destroyed in the eastern Atlantic by the well-equipped and trained RCN groups operating there. It was also true that in the eastern Atlantic the U-boats were still trying to shadow convoys, thus putting themselves in close proximity to escort groups. This was not the case in Canadian waters, where the rule was extremely evasive tactics. The weakness of Murray's naval forces, moreover, was a matter of policy. Only enough ships to provide basic close escort to convoys were retained in Canadian waters, so that the maximum effort could be made in British and European waters, where the war would be decided.

That policy did not change very much even in the late summer and fall of 1944, when Dönitz employed the schnorkel U-boats to strengthen the campaign in Canadian waters as he also began to press into British waters. Given that the Canadian and US air forces had been largely responsible for shutting down the coastal U-boat campaign of 1942, Dönitz hoped that he could again achieve a large number of sinkings with the schnorkel submarines, impervious as they were to air attack. In late August and September 1944, five schnorkel boats arrived in Canadian waters, three assigned to the Gulf of St Lawrence and two to the Halifax approaches. They were relieved in late November and December by five more boats with the same initial assignments, but allowing the St Lawrence submarines to shift to Halifax when the freeze-up came.

The Canadians had important early help from two highly experienced US escort carrier groups that had been pursuing the submarines across the Atlantic. Aircraft from one of the groups, which included USS *Bogue*, the most successful escort carrier of the war, destroyed *U-1229* when that submarine carelessly ran on the surface in daylight. The other boats all reached their patrol areas while the carrier group pursued a string of radar contacts — all of which proved to be false — off southern Newfoundland. It says much about operating conditions in the Canadian area that this was *'probably the most frustrating time of the war for … the* Bogue *group.'[12]*

Admiral Murray carried on with the procedures that had been developed since late 1943, dispatching aircraft for intense sweeps of probability areas derived from Ultra intelligence. For naval searches of these areas he had one and then two newly formed support groups of frigates (EG 16 and EG 25). The second of these went overseas in the fall in response to appeals from the Admiralty for help in meeting the schnorkel submarine offensive in British waters, and was replaced by another new group, EG 27. At that same time, frigates were withdrawn from the RCN's mid-ocean close-escort groups for yet another Canadian frigate group for British waters (EG 26), making a total commitment of four RCN frigate groups around the shores of the United Kingdom. (The

additional frigate groups compensated for the departure of the worn and battered destroyers of EG 11 and 12 for refit in Canada.)

Apart from their inexperience, Murray's support groups were also worked to the point of exhaustion and had no chance to improve their training or refine their tactics. The simultaneous threats to the widely separated St Lawrence and Halifax areas kept the two groups almost constantly at sea. Because of the thinness of the close-escort forces, moreover, support-group ships were repeatedly pulled away from hunting duties to reinforce the escorts of convoys passing through danger zones. For weeks at a time, the frigates had to dash from one task to another, from one locality to another, at intervals of only a few days. When, as often happened, additional groups were needed to saturate the area of a recent attack, or to pursue a submarine arriving or departing on the ocean routes, there was no choice but to persist in the practice of pulling together ad hoc formations from whatever ships happened to be handy.

Nevertheless, the Canadian forces held the schnorkel submarines in check. The air and naval sweeps persuaded the submariners it was too dangerous to surface, even at night, so they could not pursue shipping. Thus they were able to strike only at the few unfortunate vessels that passed close by. In most cases, the quick response by air- and sea-hunting groups to an attack discouraged the U-boat from making a second attempt. The eight submarines that made patrols from August to the end of December got modest results: two escorts sunk, one damaged; two merchant vessels sunk (one of them in US waters, off the coast of Maine), one damaged. Only half of these losses occurred in the Gulf of St Lawrence, where four of the U-boats made extended patrols, with a fifth hunting in the Cabot Strait. The very few attacks by the submarines in the Gulf reflected well on the defences. Under heavy pressure from British supply departments, which needed quickly to move bulk cargoes from the Gulf ports in the fall of 1944, the RCN had reluctantly allowed large numbers of ocean-going merchant vessels to enter the St Lawrence at the very time the schnorkel submarines were operating there.

Most of the successes of the schnorkel U-boats occurred in areas where the submarines had been freed of harassment for days because false contacts or other ambiguities in intelligence had led the air and naval patrols astray. Ultra intelligence was less useful in coastal waters than for mid-ocean convoy operations. German messages indicated only the general coastal area for which a U-boat was headed. Direction-finding bearings on radio reports from the U-boats had always been essential to determine if and when the submarine reached the target area, and to identify its hunting zone within that area. By the summer of 1944 virtually no such bearings were available, for the submarines had learned not to radio after they began to approach North American waters from mid-ocean (although bearings by Canadian and other Allied stations on submarine signals from mid-ocean continued to be a critically valuable complement to Ultra intelligence in verifying the position of U-boats and providing accurate estimates of the courses they would follow in their approach to the coast). Even signals from Dönitz begging for reports from coastal waters could not persuade the schnorkel boats to break silence and risk the sudden descent of aircraft.

The two worst losses close to Canada's shores in the latter part of 1944 occurred during periods when Allied intelligence was completely in the dark. The orders for *U-1228*, one of the November group of submarines, to go into the Gulf of St Lawrence were decrypted in good time. Canadian patrols to follow the submarine's track into the Gulf were based on very sound estimates of its progress. What no one could know was that *U-1228*'s schnorkel was not functioning, and that the commanding officer was so fearful of entering the Gulf without this protection that he hung back along isolated stretches of the south coast of Newfoundland for several days trying to make repairs. The boat made a final attempt to enter on the night of 24 November, but the poor performance of the schnorkel persuaded the captain to abandon the mission. At virtually the moment the submarine began to turn back, the corvette HMCS *Shawinigan*, making a routine patrol off Port-aux-Basques, Newfoundland, passed nearby. The chilling words of the submarine's log say it all: '*Torpedo and screw noises merge. A hit after 4 min 0 secs. High, 50m, large explosion column with heavy shower of sparks ... destroyer [sic] disappeared.*'[13] There were no survivors among the 91 men aboard the warship.

In the case of *U-1230*, one of the November wave of submarines assigned to Halifax, no orders had been broadcast, for it was first to carry out a special mission to put agents ashore on the coast of Maine. The Canadian steamship *Cornwallis* had meanwhile proceeded without escort through the apparently safe Gulf of Maine. The ship went down so quickly when torpedoed on the morning of 3 December that all but six of the 48 crew members were lost.

* * *

In British waters the availability, by November 1944, of 22 support groups — four of which were RCN — allowed a more systematic response to the schnorkel submarines, including regular training exercises. Initially, while new techniques were being developed, there were meagre results. Canadian forces, however, achieved three notable sinkings, two of them after making asdic contacts in deep water — a rare event now that submarines no longer attempted to close with convoys at sea. On 16 October, EG 6 destroyed *U-1006* north of Scotland while participating in a sweep to catch U-boats as they transited from their Norwegian bases to British waters. *U-877* was north of the Azores, on its way to North American waters, when on 27 December it had the bad luck to stumble into the mid-ocean group C 3, escorting convoy HX 327. On 30 December a Wellington of 407 Squadron achieved one of the maritime air forces' very few kills during the last year of the war after detecting the schnorkel of *U-772* in the English Channel.

By this time, the failure to prevent increasing numbers of schnorkel boats from slipping into British waters had brought Western Approaches to pull the support groups closer inshore for intense patrols of the focal areas of shipping. One of the greatest problems was the enormous number of wrecks on the seabed produced by centuries of commerce and combat, including the remnants of U-boats destroyed during both world wars. New precision radio navigation systems, in which equipment in the ships oriented on beacons from shore stations to give a position accurate within metres, allowed the ships to make meticulous asdic and depth-sounder searches of the seabed in the patrol area to locate and map

wrecks. Anything showing a submarine-like profile that did not correlate with a known wreck at that exact position received a rain of underwater weapons. As well, the frigates now reinforced the close escort of convoys passing through the patrol area, ready — with detailed knowledge of the local seabed and hydrographic conditions — to pounce quickly on an attacking U-boat.

These operations were an endless grind that wore out ships and their crews. Even with the help of radio navigation, there had to be a relentless concentration on fine detail to counteract wind and tide that, in coastal waters, could so readily and imperceptibly shift a group out of position. The constant detonation of underwater weapons, moreover, increased wear on hulls; the frigates, like the corvettes, had been hastily built to standards lower than those of normal naval specifications. Nevertheless the new methods worked. The RCN groups destroyed a total of three U-boats during February and March 1945, part of increased success by Western Approaches — some 17 boats in the two months — that brought Dönitz to withdraw most of the submarines from inshore waters by the end of the latter month. The enemy had continued to show striking power, however. Among the losses to Allied warships in British waters in February were HMCS *Trentonian*, one of the corvettes brought over before D-Day for close-escort duties and still employed in that work, and the Bangor minesweeper HMCS *Guysborough*. On 29 March *U-246* scored a hit on HMCS *Teme* that blew off 20 metres of the frigate's stern. Fortunately, the vessel survived the tow to port, and suffered only light casualties.

EPILOGUE

In Canadian waters, the new year brought more frustration. During the first part of January 1945, Kapitänleutnant Kurt Dobratz, in *U-1232*, the last of the group of submarines sent at the end of 1944, finally demonstrated what a boldly handled schnorkel U-boat could accomplish. On two occasions, just outside the entrance to Halifax harbour, he pressed into the screen of convoys, firing repeatedly and hitting a total of five merchant ships. During the second attack, frigates of EG 27 were reinforcing the close escort of the convoy. Dobratz came in so close he was sent spinning when one of the frigates, HMCS *Ettrick*, collided with the attack periscope in the bad visibility. In both convoy attacks the submarine escaped five-day-long air and sea hunts in which highly trained US Navy (USN) hunter-killer groups assisted. Asdic was almost blind; the chill winter air created a cold surface layer over warmer water below, conditions in which only weak echoes (or none at all) can be detected in a hull-mounted asdic within the cold surface layer.

In late February and March a new wave of seven U-boats proceeded to North American waters. As Ultra revealed, at least two were making for Halifax, the rest for northern US ports. The US Atlantic Fleet continued to turn hunter-killer groups over to Admiral Murray for operations in the Canadian area, as they had done in January and on a number of previous occasions. Task Group 22.14, a new formation manned by US Coast Guard personnel, destroyed one of the Halifax-bound submarines, *U-866*, near Sable Island on 18 March after an eight-day hunt. The second submarine, *U-190,* arrived about 30 March but gave no sign of its presence for over two weeks. Then, at daybreak on 16 April, the U-boat fired an acoustic torpedo at the Bangor HMCS *Esquimalt* as it made a routine lone patrol off the broad mouth of Halifax harbour. The ship went down quickly. No distress signal could be dispatched and the ship was not missed until it failed to turn up for a rendezvous some hours later. By the time rescuers reached the scene, six hours after the sinking, dozens of the crew had succumbed to exposure. T. C. Manuel, the ship's writer (a rating who carried out administration), recalled the ordeal some 40 years later:

After what seemed an eternity and with bursting lungs I surfaced to the oil slick swell of the Atlantic above, having exited Esquimalt under water, the last one out of her, my feet coming to rest on the submerged and rolled over bulkhead of Esquimalt. I was at nose level to the sea, gasping for air and drinking in sea water and fuel oil, flapping my arms to keep my head above it for I was not a swimmer. A quick look to the left of me revealed approximately ten feet of Esquimalt's overturned bow out of the water beyond, rising five-six feet in the air — she began to roll again under my touching feet and suddenly the support was no longer there — a voice carried across the rolling water 'Swim damn it — swim, she's going.'

Rousing myself to that call I endeavoured to do just that but my efforts were impeded by a desperate sailor floundering in the water clutching at me and pushing me under. We struggled and I managed to break his hold just as my eyes caught the movement of an object in the water, it was a sailor's sea-bag. I grabbed my companion's disappearing head by the hair and attacked the water to get a hand hold on it. We held on to it until it became waterlogged and began to settle under water. An anxious shout from me to a float drifting away from us brought the response 'Hang on Scribe' and Carl Jacques, a P.O. Motor Mechanic from Truro, Nova Scotia, swam out to us and pulled us to the float where we grasped the hand-hold ropes along its rounded sides.

Jacques claimed his perch on the float, after a short interval of time he slumped over and was thought to be sleeping from his extra exertion in the water, however, investigation by his immediate companion revealed he was dead as all efforts to rouse him failed. Another died in a similar manner and two others drowned in the 'hole of the donut' the bottom of the float covered with rope netting. Such was the cold rolling water and the slipperiness of the float's rounded sides that grip was near impossible to hold and in addition to this the clamour of other sailors seeking a purchase too. Shock as well with its terrible body shaking and shivering in tightly clenched self-embrace, or just sheer exhaustion from the struggle and enormity of it all took their toll that morning. Coiled in a foetal position I too had a difficult time of controlling my own shaking and shivering once a place opened up for me on the carley-float. I was clad only in undershorts and the First Lieutenant's life jacket, identified in white stencil markings, which I obtained from the floating debris in the water. My companion of the water preceded me onto the float and happily to say he survived the ordeal of those hours adrift, returning to Regina after the war, his home town.[1]

These events, the last loss of a Canadian warship to enemy action, occurred nearly within sight of the Halifax headlands, only three weeks before the end of the war with Germany.

The final successful strike against the U-boats that included Canadian maritime forces took place on 2 May, close to Germany's shores. DeHavilland Mosquito fighter-bombers of 404 Squadron, Royal Canadian Air Force (RCAF) of the British Coastal Command, participated in a raid that destroyed *U-2359* in the Kattegat, the channel between Denmark and Sweden. The victim was a type XXI U-boat, a new model built for fast underwater running so that it could chase shipping while submerged and speed away from escorts that attempted to approach. Even now, Allied anti-submarine commands worried that if the Germans managed to get a large number of these craft to sea they could again mount an offensive against convoys. The best Allied underwater weapons and detectors would be very hard-pressed to counter these supremely elusive and deadly U-boats. Allied bombing of manufacturing facilities and the difficulties of the new design had in fact set back the programme by months, but completion of several of the superb new submarines demonstrated the tenacity and skill with which the Germans pursued the war against Allied shipping to the bitter end.

It seemed likely that the type XXIs would be used to revive attacks on convoys in the central and eastern ocean while the older submarines continued to press into areas that were less heavily defended, including Canadian waters. A new German offensive off Halifax and in the Gulf of St Lawrence during the spring and summer of 1945 might well be more intense than the campaign in the fall and early winter of 1944 had been. In April, therefore, Naval Service Headquarters (NSHQ) had called back EG 6 from British waters so that the east coast would have the three support groups that were needed for effective defence. Admiral Murray's command was occupied bringing the St Lawrence route into full operation for the summer season and making preparations to meet the enemy's third incursion into these waters when Germany accepted unconditional surrender on 7 May. The next day, U-boat headquarters began to broadcast instructions for the submarines in all theatres to run on the surface and report their positions to Allied commands.

The unpleasant surprise of May 1945 did not come from the U-boats, which complied with the surrender orders, but from the Royal Canadian Navy's (RCN's) own people. On the afternoon of 7 May, following the announcement of Germany's surrender,

riots broke out in Halifax, with naval personnel prominently in the lead, and continued late into the night. There was further rioting on the 8th. It ended only in the evening, after Admiral Murray himself went through the streets in a truck equipped with a public address system ordering personnel to return to their units and urging civilians to go back to their homes. Troops had to be brought in from the large army training camp at Debert, 120 kilometres from the city, to ensure the restoration of order. Some $5 million in damage was done to businesses as the rampaging military personnel and civilians smashed plate-glass windows and looted stores.

For a second time within a single generation the city seemed to be cursed by the navy's presence. However unfairly, Haligonians had never fully absolved the navy of responsibility for the horrific explosion of December 1917, and now once again sailors had a large hand in trashing the town. The Royal Commission that investigated the riots pointed the finger firmly at a *failure on the part of the Naval Command,*[2] and it is hard to disagree. The civic authorities had previously warned Admiral Murray's staff that restaurants, cinemas and liquor stores would be shut down to celebrate the victory in Europe. Little had been done to arrange for recreation and refreshments within the sprawling naval organization to keep men off the streets even as thousands of personnel were granted leave. They joined disgruntled civilians in breaking into liquor stores and Keith's Brewery for *'the biggest collective drunk this city ever has seen.'*

Men and women by the scores reeled through the streets, carrying cases of beer, cases of whiskey or rum …

The parks were turned into virtual beer gardens … as couples and groups sprawled on the grass with a case of whiskey …[3]

Conditions at Halifax had in fact long been a source of concern for both civic officials and the navy. Since early in the war the city had been the central pressure point for all of the myriad difficulties created by the unheralded expansion of the maritime forces. Accommodation had always been two or three steps behind the influxes of personnel, leading to poor living conditions and the necessity to board people in rented rooms in the already over-crowded city, all of which ran directly counter to the inculcation of discipline. The problem was exacerbated by a shortage of experienced officers and non-commissioned personnel: ships had priority over shore establishments for the best-qualified people. Nearly half of the 17,000 naval personnel in Halifax, moreover, were assigned to HMCS *Stadacona,* the 'barracks' in

which seamen awaiting postings were held temporarily; the provision of proper supervision and support for these people in transit was an especially difficult task.

Significantly there were no serious incidents at other bases on VE Day. The other bases were not nearly so large as the Halifax establishment and did not feature the many units performing diverse functions. For that reason officers were able to maintain closer touch with all ranks.

One of the first things the navy did after the Halifax riots was to rush in Captain K. F. Adams, a seasoned professional officer with a deserved reputation for down-to-earth common sense and a good rapport with the 'troops,' to take over command of *Stadacona.* Adams must have had a sense of déjà vu, for he had previously commanded the barracks in 1942, and warned at that time of the kind of problems that would help foment the riots two and a half years later: *'My Officers and myself are looking forward to the day when the majority of HMCS "STADACONA" ratings will be housed and amused in this Establishment without recourse to the dubious recreation which the Port of Halifax provides.'*[4]

Admiral Murray accepted responsibility for the riots. He was relieved of his command on 12 May 1945 and soon thereafter left both the RCN and Canada. It was a sad finish to a brilliant career in which Murray had led both of Canada's foremost maritime commands and become the country's only commander-in-chief of an Allied theatre during the Second World War.

The German surrender — and the wild party at Halifax — did not mark the conclusion of full-scale trade defence operations in the Atlantic. To guard against the danger that some of the many U-boats still at sea might not receive, or might choose to ignore, the orders to turn themselves over to Allied forces, shipping continued to sail in convoy until the end of May, while aircraft and support groups constantly swept the focal areas where the schnorkel-equipped submarines had been hunting. Even then the training bases and shipyards in eastern Canada continued to work at full pressure to refit ships, including those returning from British waters, and to prepare personnel for service in the Pacific for the final offensive against Japan. Similarly, the RCAF at home and in Britain began to reorganize, re-equip and train for the war in the Pacific.

The end really came only after Japan's sudden surrender following the explosion of the atomic bombs over Hiroshima and Nagasaki in August 1945. Thereafter, the Canadian maritime forces melted away with

astonishing speed. Within a few short months the bustling, over-worked naval bases became quiet graveyards for row upon row of silent escorts, rocking at their moorings, awaiting the scrapyard cutting torch. Aircraft disappeared to central depots for disposal as many of the air bases were turned over to the Department of Transport for development as civilian airports.

* * *

Canada's part in the Atlantic war was large and significant by any standard. What makes it an outstanding achievement, however, is the fact that in 1939 the country was a maritime power by right of little more than geography. It possessed only a few dozen Canadian-registered merchant ships, a single flotilla of destroyers and a single squadron of modern military flying boats. The infrastructure available, moreover, was barely adequate under almost every heading to support even this minor maritime presence. Yet by 1942 Canada was one of the foremost Allied powers in the Battle of the Atlantic, able to carry a major share of the defence of North American waters against heavy attack while also serving as Britain's principal partner in the defence of the trans-ocean convoys. By 1944 Canada's Atlantic forces had developed the flexibility, professionalism and strength to play a significant part in most maritime phases of the Normandy invasion while also protecting British home waters and fully maintaining the mid-ocean and North American commitments. By that time, as well, a substantial Canadian merchant marine was carrying cargoes to most corners of the globe.

The RCN reached a peak wartime strength of 95,705 personnel, of which 6027 were members of the Women's Royal Canadian Naval Service, at the end of November 1944. The navy's responsibilities and operations had grown well beyond the battle with the U-boats to include major warships for surface combat in European waters and the Pacific. The majority of the navy's people, however, were committed to the Atlantic war: ships' crews for the Atlantic fleet and personnel at the east-coast bases included more than 65,000 men and women. The principal Canadian anti-submarine forces at that time included 261 sea-going escorts (Bangors, corvettes, frigates and escort destroyers). Hundreds of other craft — Fairmile launches, tugboats, coastal tankers and other kinds of transports — protected Canadian waters, serviced the fleet and kept the bases running. All but a handful of the RCN's ships, moreover, were built in Canada, an accomplishment of critical importance to the Allied cause. During the dark years of 1941 and 1942 when

Canadian production came on stream, the larger Allies simply had no other source of escorts.

Warship construction was only one part of the shipbuilding achievement. In addition to some 500 combat craft (including small vessels such as the Fairmile launches and wooden coastal minesweepers), Canadian yards produced 410 ocean-going merchant vessels. Early in the war only some 3600 people had worked in Canadian shipyards; that figure swelled to 126,000.

The RCAF's Eastern Air Command reached a peak strength of 21,233 personnel, including 1735 members of the Women's Division, at the end of January 1944. Of this total, something over 1200 were air crew. The rest were the many personnel needed to operate bases, communications, navigation systems and the wide range of other services without which it would have been impossible to operate multi-engine aircraft over the unfriendly expanse of the northwest Atlantic. At this same time, nearly 2000 RCAF air crew were serving in both Canadian and British squadrons of the Royal Air Force Coastal Command. Taken together, the Canadian air crew flying maritime patrols from Canada, Newfoundland, Iceland and the British Isles made up a third of all the British Commonwealth air crew in the north Atlantic in early 1944.

The main object of Canada's Atlantic forces was always the protection of shipping. Indeed one of their great contributions to the Allied cause was to relieve pressure on British and US forces so they could assign adequate numbers of aircraft and warships to develop and apply techniques for hunting U-boats. Canadian forces held the ring around the convoys — in fact made possible the expansion of the convoy system that was the single most important measure in defeating the U-boats — while the larger Allies prepared to search out and destroy the enemy. Admiral Sir Percy Noble, commander-in-chief of the British Western Approaches command in 1941–42, spoke a profound truth when he said the Canadians *'solved the problem of the Atlantic convoys.'* [5] The most important achievement was the 25,343 merchant-ship voyages made from North American to British ports under the escort of Canadian forces. These vessels delivered 164,783,921 tonnes of cargo to sustain the United Kingdom and make possible the liberation of Europe. In the process Canadian warships and aircraft sank, or shared in the destruction of, 50 U-boats.

The Atlantic war was a bloody one. Of the 1170 U-boats commissioned during the war, over 750 were lost to Allied action or marine accidents, and of the

ICI REPOSENT
50 MARINS CANADIENS
9.5.44

(DHH, 0-600-2)

41,000 personnel in the U-boat arm more than 27,000 were killed. British merchant shipping, which was the main target of the U-boats, lost over 1300 vessels and nearly 23,000 seamen. By these standards Canadian losses, although tragic, were mercifully modest. The RCN's casualties included 2024 personnel killed by all causes in all theatres, the vast majority in the Battle of the Atlantic; 752 members of the RCAF died in maritime operations as a result of enemy action and flying accidents in the unforgiving environment. The Canadian Merchant Navy suffered more heavily, losing fully one man in 10 of the 12,000 who served in the crews of Canadian and Allied merchant vessels.

NOTES

PROLOGUE

1 A knot is the measure of the speed of a ship in nautical miles per hour. A nautical mile equals 1.852 kilometres.
2 William R. Acheson diary, biographical files, Directorate of History and Heritage [DHH].
3 Mainguy to Captain (D) 12, Greenock, 'Report of Proceedings — 1st November, 1940 including convoy W.S.4.,' 15 November 1940, Naval Historical Section [NHS] file 8000 'Ottawa I,' pt 2, DHH.
4 Quoted in Michael L. Hadley and Roger Sarty, *Tin-Pots and Pirate Ships: Canadian Naval Forces and German Sea Raiders 1880–1918* (Montreal and Kingston: McGill-Queen's University Press, 1991), 212.
5 Quoted in ibid., 289.
6 'Finding,' 5 October 1918, file NS 47-23-L.64, National Personnel Records Centre.

CHAPTER I

1 5 February 1918.
2 House of Commons, *Debates* (unrevised edition), 7 May 1919, 2265.
3 Arthur Hezlet, *The Submarine and Sea Power* (London: Peter Davies, 1967), 94–95.
4 Borden to Ballantyne, 31 August 1918, R.L. Borden papers, National Archives of Canada [NAC], MG 26H, reel C-4416, 136282-3.
5 Ballantyne to Borden, telegram [late November 1918], DHH 77/58 pt 20.
6 Quoted in James Eayrs, *In Defence of Canada: From the Great War to the Great Depression* (Toronto: University of Toronto Press, 1964), 163–64.
7 G. J. Desbarats to Under Secretary of State for External Affairs, 30 December 1922, file NS 26-2-3, NAC, RG 24, vol. 5597.
8 House of Commons, *Debates*, 30 March 1939, 2429.
9 F. L. Houghton, 'A Sailor's Life for Me,' 91, biographical files, DHH.
10 Houghton, 13.
11 [K. F. Adams memoir,] 37, biographical files, DHH.
12 C. E. Richardson interview with Roger Sarty, 12 November 1982, biographical files, DHH.
13 W. H. Willson interview with Hal Lawrence, nd, p. 3, biographical files, DHH.
14 F. C. Frewer interview, Salty Dips project, nd, biographical files, DHH.
15 Houghton, 123–24.
16 Houghton, 138.
17 E. S. Brand journals, 1939, pp. 179–80, DHH.

CHAPTER II

1 Frewer interview.
2 America and West Indies Station war diary, Great Britain, Public Records Office [PRO], Admiralty [ADM] 199/367.
3 Frewer interview.
4 NSHQ to Captain (D) Skeena, Fraser, C Halifax, C Esquimalt, repeated Commander-in-Chief America and West Indies, Admiralty, 1151/1 September 1939, NHS 1650 (Operations General) pt 2, DHH.
5 Sir Kenelm Creighton, *Convoy Commodore* (London: William Kimber, 1956; Futura Publications, 1976), 48.
6 Quoted in ibid., 49.
7 Nelles to deputy minister, 30 September 1938, file X-51, I. A. Mackenzie papers, NAC, MG 27 IIIB5, vol. 32.
8 Goolden to Commanding Officer Atlantic Coast, 8 September 1939, file 36-1-8 pt 1, NAC, RG 24, vol. 11063.
9 Randell to Schwerdt, 11 July 1940, file 5-0-7, NAC, RG 24, vol. 11987.
10 Chiefs of Staff Committee to minister, 17 September 1939, Appendix A, file HQS 5199 pt 6, NAC, RG 24, vol. 2685.
11 William Lyon Mackenzie King diary, 29 January 1940, NAC, William Lyon Mackenzie King papers, MG 26 J13.
12 'History of the British Admiralty Technical Mission,' 30 April 1946, pp. 42–43, DHH.
13 Ibid., p. 43.
14 Sheridan to Heward, 16 February 1940, file NS 29-25-1 pt 3, NAC, RG 24, vol. 5608.
15 Nelles to deputy minister, 16 November 1939, file NSS 1017-10-22 pt 1, NAC, RG 24, vol. 3841.

CHAPTER III

1 David R. Murray, ed., *Documents on Canadian External Relations, Vol. 7: 1939–1941, Part 1* (Ottawa: Department of External Affairs, 1974), 845–46.
2 Mackenzie King diary, NAC, MG 26 J13.
3 [Lay], 'The Wanderings of the "RESTIGOUCHE" as told by her commanding officer,' NHS 8000 'Fraser I,' pt 1, DHH.
4 G. Bisson, Mirror Landing, Alberta, father of Stoker 1st Class G. P. Bisson, to Creery, nd, DHH 87/200.
5 Grace Call, Victoria, BC, wife of Stoker Petty Officer George Call, to Creery, 5 August 1940, DHH 87/200.
6 FOIC Greenock to Admiralty, signal 0144/4 July 1940, NHS 8000 'St Laurent I (1937–43),' DHH.
7 R. P. Welland interview with Hal Lawrence, 25 May 1983, biographical files, DHH.
8 'The Arandora Star Rescue,' *The Crowsnest* (July 1958).
9 Mackenzie King diary, 23 May 1940, NAC, MG 26 J 13.
10 Ibid.
11 Quoted in C. P. Stacey, *Arms, Men and Governments: The War Policies of Canada 1939–1945* (Ottawa: Department of National Defence, 1970), 341.
12 Ibid.
13 Croil to the minister of National Defence, 'An Appreciation of Air Force defence of Canada Atlantic Coast,' 9 June 1940, DHH 181.003(D107).
14 David R. Murray, ed., *Documents on Canadian External Relations, Vol. 8: 1939–1941, Part II* (Ottawa: Department of External Affairs, 1976), 166.
15 Nelles to First Sea Lord, signal 1735/14 June 1940, file 30-1-15 pt 1, NAC, RG 24, vol. 11056.

16 Read, 7 February 1941, file 0-6-b, US, National Archives and Records Administration [NARA], RG 38, Office of Naval Intelligence Attaché Reports 1940-1946, Register 2358-C.

17 Palmer, commanding officer USS *Utah*, to Chief of Naval Operations, 22 March 41, ibid.

18 Welland interview, pp. 39–40.

CHAPTER IV

1 J. A. M. Lynch, ed., *Salty Dips*, vol. 2: *"...And All Our Joints Were Limber"* (Ottawa: Ottawa Branch, Naval Officers' Association of Canada, 1985), 31.

2 P. E. Parker, Commodore, RNR, Convoy Form D [for SC 36], 19 July 41, PRO, ADM 199/56.

3 Stevens to Commodore Commanding Newfoundland, 1 October 1941, DHH 81/520/8280-SC 42.

4 Hibbard to Commander-in-Chief Western Approaches, 'Report of Proceedings S.C. 42,' 18 September 1941, ibid.

5 Grubb [to Captain (D) Newfoundland], 6 November 1941, file 8280-SC 42, NAC, RG 24, vol. 11334.

6 Stevens to Commodore Commanding Newfoundland, 1 October 1941, DHH 81/520/8280-SC 42.

7 Willson interview, p. 23.

8 Grubb to [Captain (D) Newfoundland], 6 November 1941, file 8280-SC 42, NAC, RG 24, vol. 11334.

9 Naval Control Service Officer, Lockewe to Commander-in-Chief, Western Approaches, 19 September 1941, DHH 81/520/8280-SC 42.

10 Stark to Commander-in-Chief Atlantic Fleet [Cinclant], 'Availability of British and Canadian Vessels for employment under future war plans,' 17 July 1941, file A16-3, NARA, RG 313, Cinclant, Red, 1941 Secret, box 156.

11 Commodore H. E. Reid for Chief of the Naval Staff , 'Memorandum to Ass't Naval Attache, Washington,' 25 August 1941, file 'Joint Defence Plan,' NAC, RG 24, vol. 11129.

12 O. M. Read [then in the office of the Chief of Naval Operations, Washington] to Low, 22 August 1941, file A14-1 Jacket No 2, NARA, RG 313, Cinclant, Red, 1941 Secret, box 154.

13 See, e.g., Cinclant to Senior Officer Present Afloat Argentia, signal 1830 6 September 1941, Atlantic Fleet secret messages, NARA, RG 313, entry 69, box 1.

14 'Personal from First Sea Lord to CNS Canada,' signal 2141A/ 18 September 1941, file NSS 1048-48-1 pt 7, NAC, RG 24, vol. 3972.

15 *U-553* log, 15 October 1941, DHH. Translation by Jan Drent.

16 John Caldecott Littler, *Sea Fever* (Victoria, BC: Kiwi Publications, 1995), 179–80. Commanding officer HMCS *Hecla* to Captain (D) St John's, 'HMCS BRANDON — Main Inlet Valve,' 18 October 1941, file CS 384-2, NAC, RG 24, vol. 11745, explains that the problem was the result of improper installation during construction, indicates that the same problem was discovered in *Shediac*, produced by the same builder, and warns that other corvettes built by the firm must be checked.

17 Ibid., 172–73.

18 Michael L. Hadley, *U-Boats against Canada: German Submarines in Canadian Waters* (Montreal and Kingston: McGill-Queen's University Press, 1985), 25.

19 Quoted in W. A. B. Douglas, *The Official History of the Royal Canadian Air Force*. Vol. II: *The Creation of a National Air Force* (Toronto: Department of National Defence and University of Toronto Press, 1986), 482.

CHAPTER V

1 Stevens to Commodore Commanding, Newfoundland, 'Strain on personnel in ships of the Newfoundland Escort Force,' 16 October 1941, file 00-220-3-6, NAC, RG 24, vol. 11929.

2 Murray to Naval Secretary, Naval Service Headquarters, 'Strain on personnel in ships of the Newfoundland Escort Force,' 16 October, 1941, ibid.

3 Prentice to Captain (D), Newfoundland, 4 November 1941, ibid.

4 Murray to Naval Secretary, Naval Service Headquarters, 'Relief of trained officers and men from H.M.C. Ships of the N.E.F.,' 6 November 1941, ibid.

5 James B. Lamb, *The Corvette Navy: True Stories from Canada's Atlantic War* (Toronto: Macmillan of Canada, nd), 116.

6 D. W. Piers interview with Hal Lawrence, 7 January 1982, pp. 96–99, biographical files, DHH. The factual content is very close to Piers's report of proceedings drafted immediately after the incident and reproduced in Naval Historical Section, 'History of HMCS Restigouche,' 11 July 1957, pp. 53–54, DHH, which has been used to edit the later account.

7 Director of Naval Personnel to Deputy Chief of the Naval Staff and Chief of the Naval Staff, 19 November 1941, file NSS 1033-7-2, copy in NHS 8440-70, DHH.

8 Deputy Chief of the Naval Staff to Chief of the Naval Staff, 14 [?] November 1941, ibid.

9 Director of Naval Personnel to Deputy Chief of the Naval Staff and Chief of the Naval Staff, 19 November 1941, ibid.

10 George Young, *The Short Triangle: A Story of the Sea and Men Who Go Down to It in Ships* (Lunenburg, NS: Lunenburg County Press, 1975), 58.

11 George Anderson Wells, *The Fighting Bishop* (Toronto: Cardwell House, 1971), 531–32.

12 Ibid., 534.

13 Flag Officer Newfoundland war diary, January 1942, file NSS 1000-5-20 pt 1, DHH.

14 Lay to Chief of the Naval Staff and Deputy Chief of the Naval Staff, 25 January 1942, file NSS 1048-48 pt 7, NAC, RG 24, vol. 3972.

15 Frank Curry, *War at Sea: A Canadian Seaman on the North Atlantic* (Toronto: Lugus Productions, 1990), 69–71.

16 Jean Williams, 'RCNVR: The War Years 1939–1945 [Memoirs of Howard J. Williams],' 131, DHH.

17 Ibid., 184.

18 Ibid., 190–91.

19 Willson interview, pp. 27–31.

CHAPTER VI

1 Pierre Camu, *Le Saint-Laurent et les Grands Lacs au temps de la voile 1608–1850* (Ville LaSalle, QC: Éditions Hurtubise HMH, 1996), 27–28. Translation by the author.

2 William Lyon Mackenzie King, *Canada and the Fight for Freedom* (New York: Duell, Sloan and Pearce, 1944; Freeport, NY: Books for Libraries Press, 1972), 124.

3 *Globe and Mail* (Toronto), 13 May 1942.

4 Lacasse, Matane Detachment, RCMP, 'S.S. NICOYA —Torpedoed in the St. Lawrence River,' 13 May 1942, file NSS 8871-5502, NAC, RG 24, vol. 6893.

5 *U-553* log, 21 May 1942, DHH. Translation by Jan Drent.

6 130 Squadron Operations Record book, 6 July 1942, DHH.

7 'E.A.C. Anti-Submarine Report,' July 1942, DHH 181.003 (D25).

8 *U-165* to BdU, signal, 18 September 1942, DHH 85/77 pt 23. Translation by David Wiens.

9 Fraser McKee, *The Armed Yachts of Canada* (Erin, ON: Boston Mills Press, 1983), 142–43.

10 Russell, 'Torpedoing of S.S. Sagana and S.S. Lord Strathcona by enemy submarine while laying at anchor near Little Bell Island loaded with iron ore,' 6 September 1942, file 310-24-1, NAC, RG 24, vol. 11954.

11 *U-517* log, 25 September 1942, DHH. Translation by David Wiens.

12 Anderson, 'Summary of RCAF Attack on U-boat,' 29 March 1943, DHH 181.003 (D1326).

13 Michael Hadley, *U-Boats against Canada: German Submarines in Canadian Waters* (Montreal and Kingston: McGill-Queen's University Press, 1985), 115–16.

14 *Globe and Mail* (Toronto), 16 October 1942.

15 Hadley, *U-Boats against Canada*, 135–37.

16 Douglas How, *Night of the Caribou* (Hantsport, NS: Lancelot Press, 1988), 146–47.

17 Godbout to King, 21 October 1942, NAC, MG 26 J1, reel C-6806, p. 276171.

14 L. C. Audette, 'Naval Recollections,' 40, DHH.

15 Warren F. Kimball, ed., *Churchill and Roosevelt: The Complete Correspondence*. Vol. I: *Alliance Emerging, October 1933–November 1942* (Princeton, NJ: Princeton University Press, 1984), 648–49.

16 W. S. Chalmers, *Max Horton and the Western Approaches* (London: Hodder and Stoughton, 1954), 162–63.

17 Captain H. C. Fitz to Commander Task Force 24, 'Report of visit to Commander in Chief Western Approaches,' 12 October 1942, unnamed files, NARA, RG 313, CTF 24, Red, box 8701.

18 [Minutes of conference], Navy Department, Washington, 30 December 1942, file 222-1, NAC, RG 24, vol. 11968.

19 Brand journals, 1943, p. 64, DHH.

20 [Minutes of conference], Navy Department, Washington, 30 December 1942, file 222-1, NAC, RG 24, vol. 11968.

21 [Captain R. E. S. Bidwell, RCN], undated minute on Horton to Admiralty, 8 December 1942, file 8280-SC 107, NAC, RG 24, vol. 11335.

22 Heineman to Commander Task Force Twenty-Four, 'Report of Escort of Convoy ON-166,' 28 February 1943, file A14-1(2), pt 3, NARA, RG 313, CTF 24, Red, 1943 Confidential, box 8745.

23 Bulloch and Layton, 'Report of trip made ... to the operational stations and general reconnaissance schools of Eastern Air Command,' 1 March 1943, file HQS 15-1-350 pt 3, NAC, RG 24, vol. 5177.

CHAPTER VII

1 Williams, 'RCNVR: The War Years,' 193.

2 Alan Easton, *50 North: An Atlantic Battleground* (Toronto: Ryerson Press, 1963), 165–66.

3 Admiralty, *Monthly Anti-Submarine Report* (October 1942), 5.

4 Captain H. C. Fitz to Commander Task Force 24, 'Report of visit to Commander in Chief Western Approaches,' 12 October 1942, unnamed files, NARA, RG 313, CTF 24, Red, box 8701.

5 John Roué interview, Salty Dips project, nd, biographical files, DHH.

6 Easton, *50 North*, 11.

7 John Caldecott Littler, *Sea Fever* (Victoria, BC: Kiwi Productions, 1995), 175.

8 Stubbs, 'S.C. 94 — Reports of Proceedings of H.M.C.S. "Assiniboine",' 10 August 1942, NHS 1650-'U-210,' DHH.

9 R. L. Hennessy interview with Hal Lawrence, 26 May 1983, biographical files, DHH.

10 'Royal Canadian Navy Press release,' 19 September 1942, NHS 8000 'Assiniboine I,' DHH.

11 Naval Historical Section, 'A Brief History of HMCS Assiniboine,' 16 November 1961, NHS 8000, 'Assiniboine I,' DHH. This account is from the naval historian Dr G. N. Tucker, who happened to be taking passage in the ship.

12 T. C. Pullen [with W. A. B. Douglas], 'Convoy O.N. 127 and the loss of HMCS *Ottawa*, 13 September, 1942: A personal reminiscence,' *Northern Mariner*, vol. 2 (April 1992), 15.

13 Murray to Secretary, Naval Board, 10 November 1942, file A3-1, NARA, RG 313, CTF 24, Red, 1942 Confidential, box 8810.

CHAPTER VIII

1 Lay to Chief of the Naval Staff, 'Conference at Washington ...,' 26 December 1942, file NSS 1057-5-1, NAC, RG 24, vol. 3998.

2 Hodgson, 'The first year of Canadian operational control in the Northwest Atlantic,' 18 August 1944, DHH 81/520/8280A pt 1.

3 Jürgen Rohwer and W. A. B. Douglas, 'Canada and the Wolf Packs, September 1943,' in W. A. B. Douglas, ed., *The RCN in Transition 1910–1985* (Vancouver: University of British Columbia Press, 1988), 169.

4 W. A. B. Douglas, *The Official History of the Royal Canadian Air Force*. Vol. II: *The Creation of a National Air Force* (Toronto: Department of National Defence and University of Toronto Press, 1986), 565–66.

5 Marc Milner, *The U-Boat Hunters: The Royal Canadian Navy and the Offensive against Germany's Submarines* (Toronto: University of Toronto Press, 1994), 70.

6 Piers, 'Comments on the Operation and Performance of H.M.C. Ships ... in the Battle of the Atlantic,' 1 June 1943, file NSS 1057-3-24 pt 1, NAC, RG 24, vol. 3997.

7 Appendix V, 'Efficiency of H.M.C. Ships,' ibid.

8 Appendix II, 'Personnel of H.M.C. Ships,' ibid.

9 Briggs, 'Personal appreciation of situation for R.C.N. ships in United Kingdom,' 23 April 1943, file NSS 1057-3-24 pt 1, NAC, RG 24, vol. 3997.

10 Angus H. Rankin interview, Salty Dips project, nd, biographical files, DHH.

11 Piers, 'Comments,' 1 June 1943, Appendix XIII, 'Naval Service Headquarters,' file NSS 1057-3-24 pt 1, NAC, RG 24, vol. 3997.

12 Appendix IV, 'Equipment of H.M.C. Ships,' ibid.
13 Diary, 'June-December 1943,' file 2-6, J. J. Connolly papers, NAC, MG 32 C71, vol. 2.
14 Connolly to minister, 8 November 1943, file 3-12, ibid., vol. 13.
15 Unsigned memorandum for the minister in Connolly's handwriting, 30 November 1943, file 3-14, ibid., vol. 3.

CHAPTER IX

1 Quoted in Marc Milner, *The U-Boat Hunters: The Royal Canadian Navy and the Offensive against Germany's Submarines* (Toronto: University of Toronto Press, 1994), 118.
2 *London Gazette*, 28 July 1944, printed in George C. Machum, *Canada's VCs* (Toronto: McClelland and Stewart, 1956), 182–83.
3 *U-537* log, 31 October 1943, DHH. Translation by David Wiens.
4 Buch to Strang, 22 April 1943, letter no 11, Mary Buch papers, NAC, MG 30 E560.
5 'Summary of Naval War Effort,' for 1 January to 31 March 1943, p. 4, file NSS 1000-5-8 pt 4, DHH.
6 Lavinia Crane interview with Hal Lawrence, 9 August 1989, biographical files, DHH.
7 Gilbert Norman Tucker, *The Naval Service of Canada: Its Official History. Activities on Shore during the Second World War* (Ottawa: King's Printer, 1952), 320.
8 'Royal Canadian Navy Press Release ... Monday, November

1st, 1943,' file 'Wrens Canada,' NAC, RG 24, vol. 11724.
9 Buch [to Strang], 'Ye Olde Grave Yarde Shifte,' 31 May 1943, 'very early,' letter no 19, NAC, MG 30 E560.
10 Anonymous memoir in Jean Bruce, *Back the Attack! Canadian Women During the Second World War — at Home and Abroad* (Toronto: Macmillan of Canada, 1985), 104.
11 Flag Officer Newfoundland war diary, March 1944, file NSC 1926-112/3 pt 1, DHH.
12 Samuel Eliot Morison, *History of United States Naval Operations in World War II.* Vol. 10, *The Atlantic Battle Won, May 1943–May 1945* (Boston: Little, Brown, 1956), 328.
13 *U-1228* log, 25 November 1944, DHH. Translation by David Wiens.

EPILOGUE

1 Manuel to *The Trident* [Maritime Command's newspaper], nd [probably early 1980s], Salty Dips project, biographical files, DHH.
2 Quoted in Stanley R. Redman, *Open Gangway: An Account of the Halifax Riots, 1945* (Hantsport, NS: Lancelot Press, 1981), 163.
3 *Ottawa Citizen*, 9 May 1945.
4 Adams to Commanding Officer Atlantic Coast, 12 October 1942, file NSS 1000-5-13 pt 14, DHH.
5 Quoted in Joseph Schull, *The Far Distant Ships: An Official Account of Canadian Naval Operations in the Second World War* (Ottawa: Queen's Printer, 1961), 122.

BIBLIOGRAPHY

GENERAL

Admiralty, Historical Section. *Defeat of the Enemy Attack on Shipping 1939–1945: A Study of Policy and Operations.* Naval Staff History Second World War. 1 vol. in 2 parts. London: Admiralty, 1957.

Beesly, Patrick. *Very Special Intelligence: The Story of the Admiralty's Operational Intelligence Centre 1939–1945.* London: Hamish Hamilton, 1977.

Blair, Clay. *Hitler's U-Boat War: The Hunters, 1939–1942.* New York: Random House, 1996.

Chalmers, W. S. *Max Horton and the Western Approaches.* London: Hodder and Stoughton, 1954.

Creighton, Sir Kenelm. *Convoy Commodore.* London: William Kimber, 1956; Futura Publications, 1976.

Hessler, Gunther. *The U-Boat War in the Atlantic, 1939–May 1945.* German Naval History Series. 3 vols. London: Admiralty, 1950–77; Her Majesty's Stationery Office, 1989.

Hezlet, Arthur. *The Submarine and Sea Power.* London: Peter Davies, 1967.

Hinsley, F. H., et al. *British Intelligence in the Second World War: Its Influence on Strategy and Operations.* 3 vols. in 4 parts. London: Her Majesty's Stationery Office, 1979–88.

Howarth, Stephen, and Derek Law, eds. *The Battle of the Atlantic 1939–1945: The 50th Anniversary International Naval Conference.* London and Annapolis, MD: Naval Institute Press, 1994.

Howse, Derek. *Radar at Sea: The Royal Navy in World War 2.* Annapolis, MD: Naval Institute Press, 1993.

Kahn, David. *Seizing the Enigma: The Race to Break the German U-boat Codes, 1939–1943.* Boston: Houghton-Mifflin, 1991.

Kimball, Warren F., ed. *Churchill and Roosevelt: The Complete Correspondence.* Vol. I: *Alliance Emerging, October 1933–November 1942.* Princeton, NJ: Princeton University Press, 1984.

Morison, Samuel Eliot. *History of United States Naval Operations in World War II.* Vol. 1: *The Battle of the Atlantic September 1939–May 1943.* Boston: Little, Brown, 1947.

_____. *History of United States Naval Operations in World War II.* Vol. 10: *The Atlantic Battle Won, May 1943–May 1945.* Boston: Little, Brown, 1956.

Rohwer, Jürgen. *The Critical Convoy Battles of March 1943: The Battle for HX.229/SC. 122.* London: Ian Allan, 1977.

_____. *Axis Submarine Successes 1939–1945.* Annapolis, MD: Naval Institute Press, 1983.

Roskill, S. W. *The War at Sea 1939–1945.* History of the Second World War: United Kingdom Military Series. 3 vols. in 4 parts. London: Her Majesty's Stationery Office, 1954–61.

Runyan, Timothy J., and Jan M. Copes, eds. *To Die Gallantly: The Battle of the Atlantic.* Boulder, CO: Westview Press, 1994.

Smith, Bradley F. *The Ultra-Magic Deals and the Most Secret Special Relationship, 1940–1946.* Novato, CA: Presidio, 1993.

Syrett, David. *The Defeat of the German U-Boats: The Battle of the Atlantic.* Columbia: University of South Carolina Press, 1994.

CANADA

Boutilier, James A., ed. *RCN in Retrospect, 1910–1968.* Vancouver: University of British Columbia Press, 1982.

Bruce, Jean. *Back the Attack! Canadian Women during the Second World War — at Home and Abroad.* Toronto: Macmillan of Canada, 1985.

Cafferky, Shawn. '"A useful lot, these Canadian ships": The Royal Canadian Navy and Operation Torch, 1942–1943.' *Northern Mariner* 3 (October 1993): 1–17.

Camu, Pierre. *Le Saint-Laurent et les Grands Lacs au temps de la voile 1608–1850.* Ville LaSalle, QC: Éditions Hurtubise HMH, 1996.

Curry, Frank. *War at Sea: A Canadian Seaman on the North Atlantic.* Toronto: Lugus Productions, 1990.

Douglas, W. A. B. 'The Nazi Weather Station in Labrador.' *Canadian Geographic,* 101 (December 1981–January 1982): 42–47.

_____. *The Official History of the Royal Canadian Air Force.* Vol. II: *Creation of a National Air Force.* Toronto: Department of National Defence and University of Toronto Press, 1986.

_____, ed. *The RCN in Transition 1910–1985.* Vancouver: University of British Columbia Press, 1988.

Easton, Alan. *50 North: An Atlantic Battleground.* Toronto: Ryerson Press, 1963.

Eayrs, James. *In Defence of Canada: From the Great War to the Great Depression.* Toronto: University of Toronto Press, 1964.

Edwards, Bernard. *Attack and Sink! The Battle for Convoy SC42.* Corfe Mullen, Dorset: New Era Writers' Guild (UK), 1995.

Fisher, Robert C. ' "We'll Get Our Own": Canada and the Oil Shipping Crisis of 1942.' *Northern Mariner* 3 (April 1993): 33–39.

_____. 'Canadian Merchant Ship Losses 1939–1945.' *Northern Mariner* 5 (July 1995): 57–73.

_____. 'Return of the Wolf Packs: The Battle for ON 113, 23–31 July 1942.' *American Neptune* 56 (Winter 1996): 45–62.

_____. 'Tactics, Training, Technology: The Royal Canadian Navy's Summer of Success, July–September 1942.' *Canadian Military History* 6 (Autumn 1997): 7–20.

_____. 'The Impact of German Technology on the Royal Canadian Navy in the Battle of the Atlantic, 1942–43.' *Northern Mariner* 7 (October 1997): 1–13.

German, Tony. *The Sea Is at Our Gates: The History of the Canadian Navy.* Toronto: McClelland and Stewart, 1990.

Greenhous, Brereton, Stephen Harris, William Johnston and William G. P. Rawling. *The Official History of the Royal Canadian Air Force.* Vol. 3: *Crucible of War.* Toronto: Department of National Defence and University of Toronto Press, 1994.

Hadley, Michael L. *U-Boats against Canada: German Submarines in Canadian Waters.* Montreal and Kingston: McGill-Queen's University Press, 1985.

_____, and Roger Sarty. *Tin-Pots and Pirate Ships: Canadian Naval Forces and German Sea Raiders 1880–1918.* Montreal and Kingston: McGill-Queen's University Press, 1991.

_____, Rob Huebert and Fred W. Crickard, eds. *A Nation's Navy: In Quest of Canadian Naval Identity.* Montreal and Kingston: McGill-Queen's University Press, 1996.

Halford, Robert G. *The Unknown Navy: Canada's World War II Merchant Navy.* St Catharines, ON: Vanwell Publishing, 1995.

How, Douglas. *Night of the Caribou.* Hantsport, NS: Lancelot Press, 1988.

Johnston, Mac. *Corvettes Canada: Convoy Veterans of WWII Tell Their True Stories.* Toronto: McGraw-Hill Ryerson, 1994.

Kennedy, J. DeN. *History of the Department of Munitions and Supply: Canada in the Second World War.* 2 vols. Ottawa: King's Printer, 1950.

King, William Lyon Mackenzie. *Canada and the Fight for Freedom.* New York: Duell, Sloan and Pearce, 1944; Freeport, NY: Books for Libraries Press, 1972.

Lamb, James B. *The Corvette Navy: True Stories from Canada's Atlantic War.* Toronto: Macmillan of Canada, nd.

Littler, John Caldecott. *Sea Fever.* Victoria, BC: Kiwi Publications, 1995.

Lynch, J. A. M., ed. *Salty Dips* (vols. 1–3). Ottawa: Ottawa Branch, Naval Officers' Association of Canada, 1983–88.

Machum, George C. *Canada's VCs.* Toronto: McClelland and Stewart, 1956.

Macpherson, Ken, and John Burgess. *The Ships of Canada's Naval Forces, 1910–1993.* 2nd rev. ed. St Catharines, ON: Vanwell Publishing, 1993.

Macpherson, Ken, and Marc Milner. *Corvettes of the Royal Canadian Navy 1939–1945.* St Catharines, ON: Vanwell Publishing, 1993.

McAndrew, William J. 'Canadian Defence Planning between the Wars: The Royal Canadian Air Force Comes of Age.' *Aerospace Historian* 29 (June 1982): 81–89.

_____, Donald E. Graves and Michael Whitby. *Normandy 1944: The Canadian Summer.* Montreal: Art Global, 1994.

_____, Bill Rawling and Michael Whitby. *Liberation: The Canadians in Europe.* Montreal: Art Global, 1995.

McKee, Fraser. *The Armed Yachts of Canada.* Erin, ON: Boston Mills Press, 1983.

_____, and Robert Darlington. *The Canadian Naval Chronicle 1939–1945: The Successes and Losses of the Canadian Navy in World War II.* St Catharines, ON: Vanwell Publishing, 1996.

Mckillop, R. 'Staying on the Sleigh: Commodore Walter Hose and a Permanent Naval Policy for Canada.' *Maritime Warfare Bulletin. Special Historical Edition: Maritime Command Historical Conference 1990. Canada's Navy: Continuity or Change* [1991?]: 67–82.

McLean, Douglas M. 'The U.S. Navy and the U-Boat Inshore Offensive.' In William B. Cogar, ed., *New Interpretations in Naval History: Selected Papers from the Twelfth Naval History Symposium* (pp. 310–24). Annapolis, MD: Naval Institute Press, 1977.

_____. 'The Battle of Convoy BX-141.' *Northern Mariner* 3 (October 1993): 19–35.

_____. 'The Loss of HMCS *Clayoquot*.' *Canadian Military History* 3 (Fall 1994): 31–44.

_____. 'Confronting Technological and Tactical Change: Allied Antisubmarine Warfare in the Last Year of the Battle of the Atlantic.' *Naval War College Review* 47 (Winter 1994): 87–104.

Milner, Marc. *North Atlantic Run: The Royal Canadian Navy and the Battle for the Convoys.* Toronto: University of Toronto Press, 1985.

_____. *The U-Boat Hunters: The Royal Canadian Navy and the Offensive against Germany's Submarines.* Toronto: University of Toronto Press, 1994.

Murray, David R., ed. *Documents on Canadian External Relations.* Vols. 7 and 8: *1939–1941,* parts I and II. Ottawa: Department of External Affairs, 1974–76.

Neary, Steve. *The Enemy on Our Doorstep.* St John's, NF: Jesperson Press, 1994.

O'Connor, Edward. *The Corvette Years: The Lower Deck Story.* Vancouver: Cordillera Publishing, 1995.

Pullen, T. C. [with W. A. B. Douglas]. 'Convoy O.N. 127 and the Loss of HMCS *Ottawa,* 13 September, 1942: A Personal Reminiscence.' *Northern Mariner* 2 (April 1992): 1–27.

Ransom, Bernard. 'Canada's "Newfyjohn" Tenancy: The Royal Canadian Navy in St John's, 1941–1945.' *Acadiensis* 23 (Spring 1994): 45–71.

Redman, Stanley R. *Open Gangway: An Account of the Halifax Riots, 1945.* Hantsport, NS: Lancelot Press, 1981.

Richards, S. T. *Operation Sick Bay: The Story of the Sick Berth and Medical Assistant Branch of the Royal Canadian Navy 1910–1965.* West Vancouver, BC: Centaur Publishing, 1994.

Sarty, Roger. *The Maritime Defence of Canada.* Toronto: Canadian Institute of Strategic Studies, 1996.

_____. 'The Limits of Ultra: The Schnorkel U-boat Offensive against North America, November 1944–January 1945.' *Intelligence and National Security* 12 (April 1997): 44–68.

Schull, Joseph. *The Far Distant Ships: An Official Account of Canadian Naval Operations in the Second World War.* Ottawa: Queen's Printer, 1961.

Stacey, C. P. *Arms, Men and Governments: The War Policies of Canada 1939–1945.* Ottawa: Department of National Defence, 1970.

Thomas, Robert Hall. 'The Absolute Necessity: The Naval Defence of Trade in the St. Lawrence 1939–45.' MA thesis, Royal Military College of Canada, Kingston, Ontario, 1983.

Tucker, Gilbert Norman. *The Naval Service of Canada: Its Official History.* 2 vols. Ottawa: King's Printer, 1952.

Watt, Frederick B. *In All Respects Ready: The Merchant Navy and the Battle of the Atlantic 1940–1945.* Toronto: Prentice Hall Canada, 1985.

Wells, George Anderson. *The Fighting Bishop.* Toronto: Cardwell House, 1971.

Whitby, Michael. 'In Defence of Home Waters: Doctrine and Training in the Canadian Navy during the 1930s.' *Mariner's Mirror* 77 (May 1991): 167–77.

_____. 'The Seaward Defence of the British Assault Area, 6–14 June 1944.' *Mariner's Mirror* 80 (May 1994): 191–207.

White, Jay. 'Conscripted City: Halifax and the Second World War.' PhD thesis, McMaster University, Hamilton, Ontario, 1994.

Winters, Barbara. 'Women Who Served in the Air Force: A Response to Ruth Roach Pierson.' MA research paper, University of Victoria, British Columbia, 1991.

Young, George. *The Short Triangle: A Story of the Sea and Men Who Go Down to It in Ships.* Lunenburg, NS: Lunenburg County Press, 1975.

Zimmerman, David. *The Great Naval Battle of Ottawa.* Toronto: University of Toronto Press, 1989.

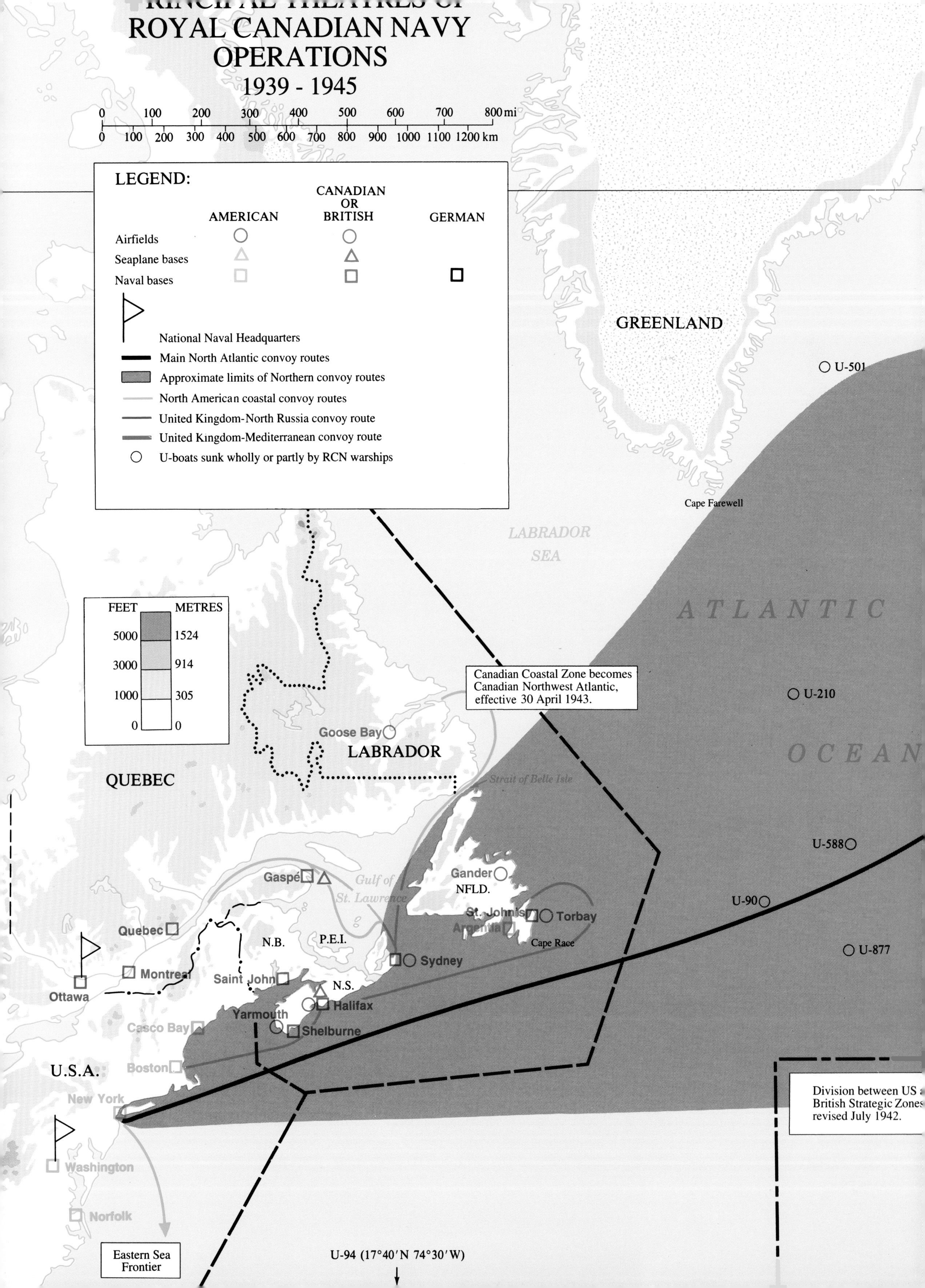

PRINCIPAL THEATRES OF ROYAL CANADIAN NAVY OPERATIONS
1939 - 1945

0   100   200   300   400   500   600   700   800 mi
0 100 200 300 400 500 600 700 800 900 1000 1100 1200 km

LEGEND:

	AMERICAN	CANADIAN OR BRITISH	GERMAN
Airfields	○	○	
Seaplane bases	△	△	
Naval bases	□	□	□

⚑ National Naval Headquarters

▬▬ Main North Atlantic convoy routes

▓ Approximate limits of Northern convoy routes

— North American coastal convoy routes

— United Kingdom-North Russia convoy route

▬ United Kingdom-Mediterranean convoy route

○ U-boats sunk wholly or partly by RCN warships

GREENLAND

○ U-501

Cape Farewell

LABRADOR SEA

ATLANTIC

Canadian Coastal Zone becomes
Canadian Northwest Atlantic,
effective 30 April 1943.

○ U-210

Goose Bay ○

LABRADOR

OCEAN

Strait of Belle Isle

QUEBEC

U-588 ○

FEET   METRES
5000   1524
3000   914
1000   305
0   0

Gaspé □ △   Gulf of St. Lawrence

Gander ○
NFLD.

U-90 ○

St. John's □ ○ Torbay
Argentia □

Quebec □   N.B.   P.E.I.

Cape Race

○ U-877

□ Montreal

Saint John □   N.S.

□ ○ Sydney

⚑
Ottawa
□

△
□ ○ Halifax
Yarmouth ○

Casco Bay □

□ Shelburne

U.S.A.

Boston □

New York □

⚑

□ Washington

Division between US a
British Strategic Zones
revised July 1942.

□ Norfolk

Eastern Sea Frontier

U-94 (17°40′N 74°30′W)
↓

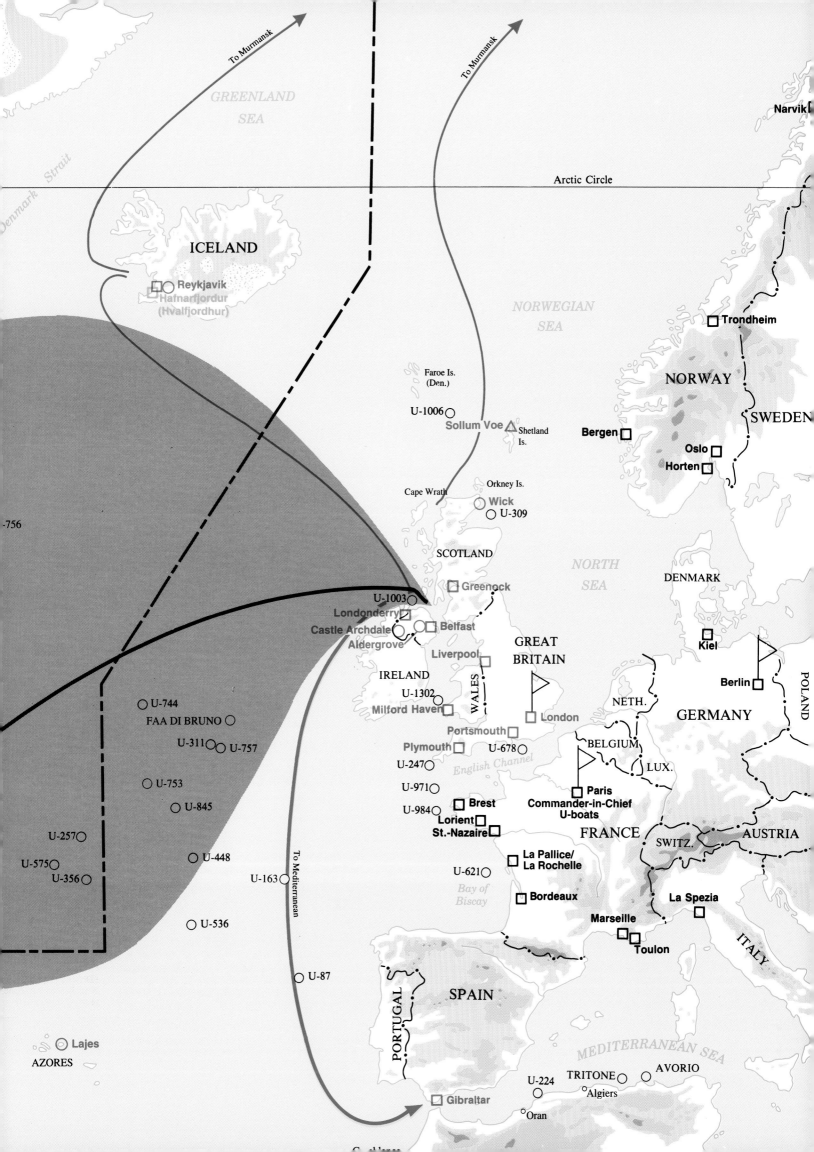

GREENLAND
SEA

Denmark Strait

To Murmansk

To Murmansk

Arctic Circle

ICELAND

□ ○ Reykjavik
Hafnarfjordur
(Hvalfjordhur)

NORWEGIAN
SEA

NORWAY

Narvik

□ Trondheim

Bergen □

SWEDEN

Oslo □
Horten □

Faroe Is.
(Den.)

U-1006 ○

Sollum Voe △ Shetland
Is.

Cape Wrath

Orkney Is.

○ Wick
○ U-309

SCOTLAND

NORTH
SEA

DENMARK

-756

U-1003 ○
Londonderry □
Castle Archdale ○ ○ □ Belfast
Aldergrove

Greenock □

Liverpool □

GREAT
BRITAIN

Kiel □

Berlin □

POLAND

IRELAND

U-1302 ○

Milford Haven □

WALES

NETH.

GERMANY

U-744 ○
FAA DI BRUNO ○

London □

U-311 ○ ○ U-757

Portsmouth □

BELGIUM

LUX.

○ U-753

Plymouth □ ○ U-678

English Channel

○ U-845

U-247 ○

U-971 ○

Paris
Commander-in-Chief
U-boats

U-257 ○

U-575 ○
U-356 ○

○ U-448

U-984 ○

□ Brest

FRANCE

SWITZ.

AUSTRIA

Lorient □
St.-Nazaire □

U-163 ○

To Mediterranean

U-621 ○

La Pallice/
La Rochelle □

La Spezia □

○ U-536

Bordeaux □

Marseille □

Bay of
Biscay

Toulon □

ITALY

○ U-87

PORTUGAL

SPAIN

○ ○ Lajes

AZORES

MEDITERRANEAN SEA

TRITONE ○ ○ AVORIO

U-224 ○
Algiers ○

□ Gibraltar

Oran ○

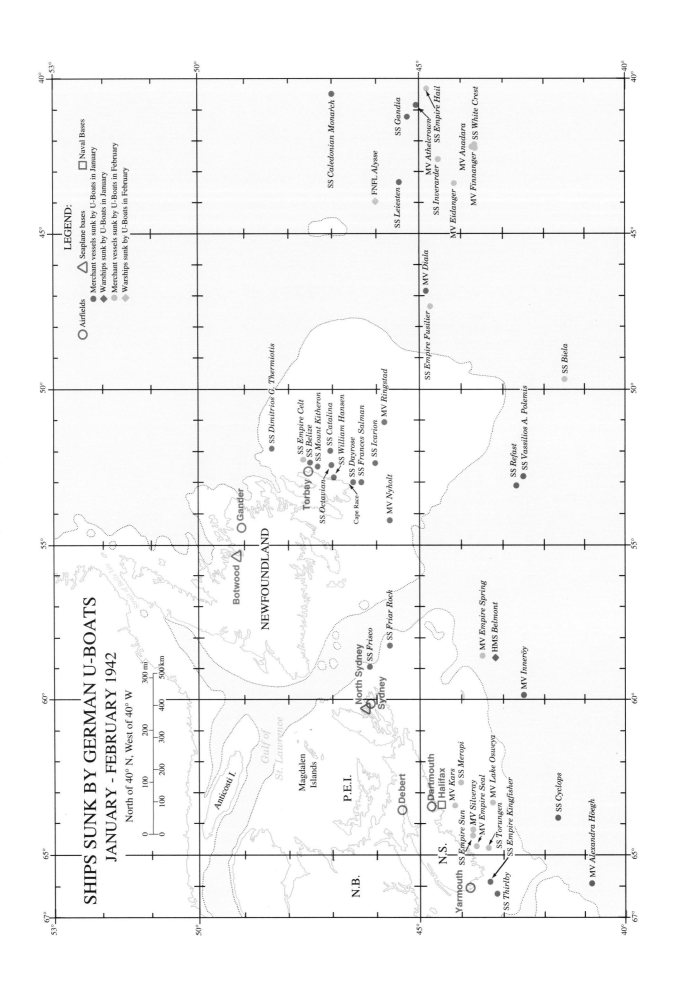

SHIPS SUNK BY GERMAN U-BOATS
JANUARY - FEBRUARY 1942

North of 40° N, West of 40° W

LEGEND:

○ Airfields   △ Seaplane bases   □ Naval Bases

● Merchant vessels sunk by U-Boats in January
◆ Warships sunk by U-Boats in January
● Merchant vessels sunk by U-Boats in February
◆ Warships sunk by U-Boats in February

NEWFOUNDLAND

Gulf of St. Lawrence

Anticosti I.

Magdalen Islands

P.E.I.

N.B.

N.S.

○ Debert

Dartmouth ○
□ Halifax

Sydney △
North Sydney ○

Botwood △

○ Gander

Torbay ○

Cape Race

Yarmouth ○

0   100   200   300 mi
0   100   200   300   400   500 km

SS Caledonian Monarch

FNFL Alysse

SS Leiesten

SS Gandia

SS Inverarder

MV Athelcrown
SS Empire Hail

MV Eidanger

MV Anadara
MV Finnanger
SS White Crest

SS Empire Fusilier

MV Diala

SS Biela

SS Dimitrios G. Thermiotis

SS Empire Celt
SS Belize
SS Mount Kitheron
SS Catalina
SS William Hansen
SS Dayrose
SS Frances Salman
SS Icarion
MV Ringstad
SS Octavian
MV Nyholt

SS Refast
SS Vassilios A. Polemis

SS Friar Rock

SS Frisco

MV Empire Spring
HMS Belmont

MV Inneröy

MV Kars
SS Meropi
MV Silveray
MV Empire Seal
MV Lake Osweya
SS Torungen
SS Empire Kingfisher
SS Empire Sun

SS Thirlby

SS Cyclops

MV Alexandra Högh

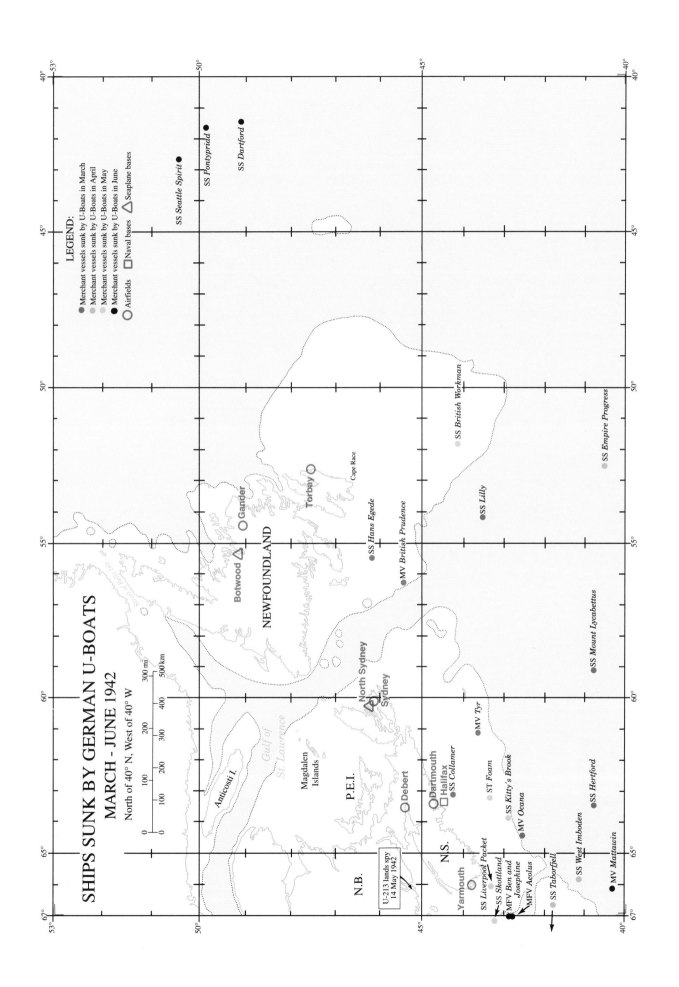

SHIPS SUNK BY GERMAN U-BOATS
MARCH - JUNE 1942
North of 40° N, West of 40° W

LEGEND:
● Merchant vessels sunk by U-Boats in March
● Merchant vessels sunk by U-Boats in April
● Merchant vessels sunk by U-Boats in May
● Merchant vessels sunk by U-Boats in June
○ Airfields ☐ Naval bases △ Seaplane bases

● SS Seattle Spirit

● SS Pontypridd

● SS Dartford

Cape Race

○ Torbay △

○ Gander

NEWFOUNDLAND

Botwood △

● SS Hans Egede

● MV British Prudence

● SS British Workman

● SS Lilly

● SS Empire Progress

● SS Mount Lycabettus

Gulf of St. Lawrence

Anticosti I.

Magdalen Islands

P.E.I.

North Sydney
Sydney △

MV Tyr ●

○ Debert

N.S.

☐ Halifax
○ Dartmouth

● SS Collamer

ST Foam ●

SS Kitty's Brook ●

MV Ocana ●

● SS Hertford

SS West Imboden ●

● MV Mattawin

Yarmouth

SS Liverpool Packet ●

SS Skottland ●
MFV Ben and Josephine ●
MFV Aeolus ●

SS Taborfjell ●

N.B.

U-213 lands spy
14 May 1942

0   100   200   300   400   500 km
0   100   200   300 mi

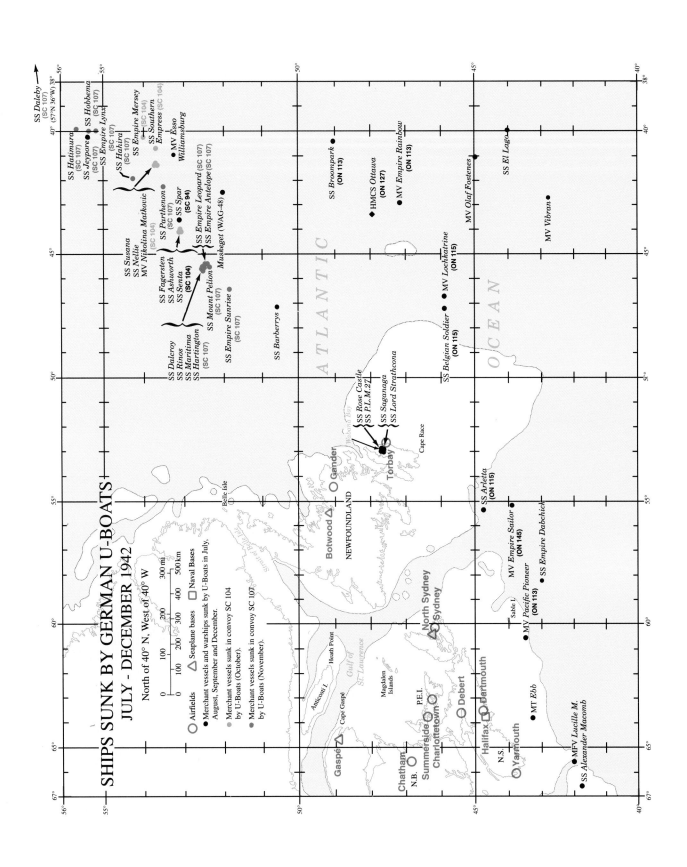

SHIPS SUNK BY GERMAN U-BOATS
JULY - DECEMBER 1942
North of 40° N, West of 40° W

0   100   200   300   500 km
0   100   200   300 mi

○ Airfields   △ Seaplane bases   □ Naval Bases

● Merchant vessels and warships sunk by U-Boats in July, August, September and December.

● Merchant vessels sunk in convoy SC 104 by U-Boats (October).

● Merchant vessels sunk in convoy SC 107 by U-Boats (November).

SS Daleby →
(SC 107)
(57°N 36°W) 38°

SS Hatimura
(SC 107)
SS Jeypore
(SC 107)
SS Hobbema
(SC 107)
SS Empire Lynx
(SC 107)
SS Hahira
(SC 107)
SS Empire Mersey
(SC 104)
SS Southern
Empress (SC 104)
MV Esso
Williamsburg

SS Broompark
(ON 113)
HMCS Ottawa
(ON 127)
MV Empire Rainbow
(ON 113)

MV Olaf Fostenes
SS El Lago

SS Parthenon
(SC 107)
SS Spar
(SC 94)
SS Empire Leopard (SC 107)
SS Empire Antelope (SC 107)
Muskeget (WAG-48)

SS Susana
SS Nellie
MV Nikolina Matkovic
(SC 104)
SS Fagersten
SS Senta
SS Ashworth
(SC 104)
SS Mount Pelion
(SC 107)

MV Vibran

MV Lochkatrine
(ON 115)

SS Empire Sunrise
(SC 107)

SS Barberrys

SS Dalcroy
SS Rinos
SS Maritima
SS Hartington
(SC 107)

SS Belgian Soldier
(ON 115)

A T L A N T I C

O C E A N

SS Rose Castle
SS P.L.M. 27
SS Saganaga
SS Lord Strathcona

Cape Race

Gander ○
Wabana Bay
Torbay ○

NEWFOUNDLAND

Botwood △

Belle Isle

Strait of Belle Isle

SS Arletta
(ON 115)

MV Empire Sailor
(ON 145)
SS Empire Dabchick

Sable I.
MV Pacific Pioneer
(ON 113)

North Sydney ○
Sydney △

Heath Point
Gulf
of
St Lawrence

Anticosti I.
Cape Gaspé

Magdalen
Islands

P.E.I.

Gaspé △
N.B.

Chatham ○

Summerside ○
Charlottetown ○

Debert ○

Dartmouth □
Halifax □
N.S.

Yarmouth ○

MT Ebb

MFV Lucille M.
SS Alexander Macomb

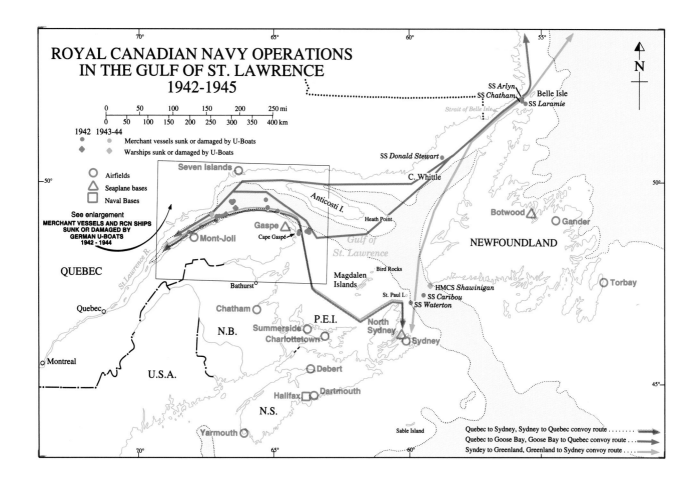

ROYAL CANADIAN NAVY OPERATIONS
IN THE GULF OF ST. LAWRENCE
1942-1945

| 0 | 50 | 100 | 150 | 200 | 250 mi |

| 0 | 50 | 100 | 150 | 200 | 250 | 300 | 350 | 400 km |

1942 1943-44

Merchant vessels sunk or damaged by U-Boats

Warships sunk or damaged by U-Boats

○ Airfields

△ Seaplane bases

□ Naval Bases

See enlargement
**MERCHANT VESSELS AND RCN SHIPS
SUNK OR DAMAGED BY
GERMAN U-BOATS
1942 - 1944**

QUEBEC

N

Seven Islands ○

Anticosti I.

Gaspe △
Cape Gaspé

○ Mont-Joli

Heath Point

*Gulf of
St. Lawrence*

SS *Arlyn*
SS *Chatham*   Belle Isle
● SS *Laramie*

Strait of Belle Isle

SS *Donald Stewart*
C. Whittle

Botwood △
○ Gander

NEWFOUNDLAND

Bird Rocks

Magdalen
Islands

St. Paul I.

○ Torbay

HMCS *Shawinigan*
● SS *Caribou*
● SS *Waterton*

Quebec ○

Chatham ○

N.B.

Summerside ○
Charlottetown ○

P.E.I.

North
Sydney

Sydney

Bathurst

Montreal ○

U.S.A.

○ Debert

Halifax □○ Dartmouth

N.S.

Yarmouth ○

Sable Island

Quebec to Sydney, Sydney to Quebec convoy route . . . .
Quebec to Goose Bay, Goose Bay to Quebec convoy route . . .
Syndey to Greenland, Greenland to Sydney convoy route . . . .

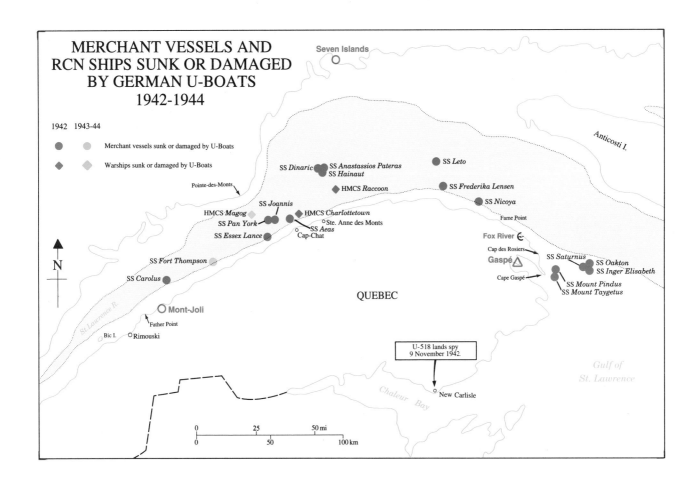

MERCHANT VESSELS AND RCN SHIPS SUNK OR DAMAGED BY GERMAN U-BOATS 1942-1944

1942   1943-44

● ● Merchant vessels sunk or damaged by U-Boats

◆ ◆ Warships sunk or damaged by U-Boats

Seven Islands

Anticosti I.

SS Leto

SS Dinaric   SS Anastassios Pateras
SS Hainaut

Pointe-des-Monts

HMCS Raccoon

SS Frederika Lensen

SS Nicoya

SS Joannis

HMCS Magog

Fame Point

HMCS Charlottetown

SS Pan York

Ste. Anne des Monts

SS Aeas

Fox River

SS Essex Lance

Cap-Chat

Cap des Rosiers

SS Saturnus

N

SS Fort Thompson

Gaspé

SS Oakton
SS Inger Elisabeth

Cape Gaspé

SS Carolus

SS Mount Pindus
SS Mount Taygetus

QUEBEC

Mont-Joli

Father Point

Bic I.   Rimouski

U-518 lands spy
9 November 1942

Gulf of
St. Lawrence

St. Lawrence R.

Chaleur Bay

New Carlisle

0   25   50 mi

0   50   100 km